Warlords and Holy Men

Scotland AD 80–1000

Warlords and Holy Men

Scotland AD 80–1000

Alfred P. Smyth

Edinburgh University Press

© Alfred P. Smyth 1984

First published 1984 in The New History of Scotland by
Edward Arnold (Publishers) Ltd
and reprinted 1989, 1992, 1995, 1998, 2003, 2005 by
Edinburgh University Press
22 George Square, Edinburgh

Printed and bound in Great Britain by
The Cromwell Press, Trowbridge,
Wiltshire

British Library cataloguing in
   Publication Data
Smyth, Alfred P.
Warlords and holy men.–(New history of Scotland; 1)
1. Scotland–History–To 1057
I. Title   II. Series
941.101   DA760

ISBN 0 7486 0100 7

Contents

Maps

Genealogical Tables

Preface

Jenny Wormald has been a very patient editor. I am in her debt for the immense care she has taken and for her encouragement during the early days of research for this book when it seemed to all parties except the editor that I should fail to persevere. Geoffrey Barrow and Patrick Wormald have read the text and saved me from many errors, not least from the worst excesses of my own prose. Arthur Keaveney has read the chapters on Roman Britain and David Kirby has given generous help with information on the Northern Britons. Graham Anderson has helped, as always, with textual problems in medieval Latin and Bruce Webster has made available his great fund of knowledge on medieval Scottish historiography. Geoffrey Linnell, Colin Gerrard, and my wife Margaret, have provided expert advice on bibliography. My student Rachel Martin St Valery has helped with the proof-reading of chapters on Columba and Adomnán, and Douglas Matthews of the London Library has helped with the Index.

The editorial staff at Edward Arnold have had to endure long lectures from an author unschooled in the practicalities of publishing in times of economic recession. Their firmness and tact have contributed to producing a book which at one stage threatened to become as unmanageable as its author. I am grateful to my colleagues at the University of Kent who have helped me to develop my ideas on early Scotland through the Medieval and Early Modern Seminar, and in particular to Patrick Collinson, who brought that seminar into being and whose enthusiasm for and knowledge of early Christianity have been a constant source of inspiration. It is impossible in a book of this scope to do justice to the works of those writers who have established early Scottish history on a sound and scholarly basis. All too often their names may appear in my text only when I choose to disagree with their ideas. It needs to be said therefore, that I could never have written this book without having constant recourse to the publications of a multitude of distinguished Scottish historians and archaeologists, living and dead, which are cited in *A Note on Further Reading* at the end of this volume.

Fifteen years ago my supervisor first advised me on the crucial nature of the role of St Wilfrid in the development of Christianity and kingship in northern Britain. Years later in writing this book I have had to think a great deal about Wilfrid and his relationship with Picts, Scots and Britons, and while I had a poor understanding of subject as a student, I do not pretend to have mastered it now. But I am grateful for what I have been taught, and so this book is dedicated to Michael Wallace-Hadrill in the year of his retirement.

Alfred P. Smyth
Canterbury,
February 1984

The author and publishers wish to thank J.M. Dent and Sons Ltd for permission to quote the poem by Bjorn Cripplehand from *Heimskringla* edited by S. Laing, revised by Jacqueline Simpson and published in Everyman's Library. Quotations from Adomnán's *Life of Columba* are taken from or based on the edition by A.O. and M.O. Anderson (Thomas Nelson and Sons Ltd., Edinburgh, 1961).

1

'Men of the North': Britons in the Shadow of the Roman Wall

The inhabitants of ancient Scotland were separated from the Roman province of *Britannia* by a series of *limites* or frontier walls combined with a network of forward defences and fallback positions, all of which were controlled by the praetorian governor at the legionary fortress of York. The notion of defending Roman territory, and later its citizens, with a physical barrier from barbarian attack was not peculiar to northern Britain. It was an obvious development in an empire whose leaders realized that it could not go on expanding forever. Frontier forts, palisades and fortified roads were a feature of the German and North African frontiers from the reign of Domitian (AD 81–96), Trajan (98–117) and Hadrian (117–138). What was peculiar to northern Britain was the fact that Roman defences boxed in the barbarian tribes of Scotland, limiting not only their opportunities for movement and contact with other barbarians but also ensuring their permanent contact with the Roman province over four centuries. While the Germanic tribes between the Rhine and Elbe, or the Sarmatians beyond the Danube were frequently moving or being moved from one homeland to another, the barbarians in what is now Scotland had no option but to defend their highland retreat from the encroachments of Rome or lose their identity within the melting pot of empire. To that extent, Tacitus was correct in recognizing the barbarians of northern Britain as 'the last of the free' even if his assessment of the northern British situation was in other respects quite false.

Given the enforced contact over so many centuries between Britons, Picts and Scots on the one hand, and the Roman province on the other, we might expect the northern barbarians to have undergone profound Romanization by the fifth century at latest. If the more numerous and more powerful Goths and Franks, and even latecomers like the Bulgars, had absorbed so much Roman influence on the fringes of the continental empire, how much more would the Romans have influenced their weaker neighbours cooped up for centuries in the furthest corner of Britain? Yet the more we examine this question, which is central to early Scottish history, the more we come to recognize the paradox it entails. For the remnants of the free tribes of Britain whom Agricola is alleged to have described as 'a pack of spiritless cowards' preserved their political identity and their Celtic culture remarkably free of Roman influence, in spite of those centuries of enforced proximity to an advanced civilization more sophisticated than their own in every way.

The question of Romanization among Scottish border tribes inevitably leads into the wider problem of how far Roman civilization had put down roots within the province of Britain to the south. This is a subject which highlights the gap between ancient and medieval historiography, and the consequent contradictory findings reached by scholars from both disciplines. Thus, despite Professor Salway's comment that 'direct evidence for Roman Britain is so thin as to be practically non-existent', estimates for the population of the province have soared from Collingwood's half a million to a present possible – but very improbable – maximum of six million. The problem has a bearing on almost every aspect of the ancient and medieval history of Britain, not least upon the degree of Romanization under the empire, and is aggravated by conflicting findings of medieval historians whose current estimates for the population of England at the time of the Domesday survey are put at two million or less.

Roman life and organization clearly did not stop dead in their tracks when the beleaguered Britons were reported by Zosimus to have expelled their Roman officials in 409 and to have organized their own defences against Saxon invaders. Archaeological evidence from Verulamium, Lincoln, London and elsewhere shows that urban life and a consequent degree of civic organization lingered on into the second half of the fifth century in lowland Britain. Nevertheless, the withdrawal of the army of Britain in the time of Constantine III (c. 407) was followed by a collapse of the monetary economy which depended on Roman government expenditure and especially on army pay. The immediate end to coinage and mass-produced factory goods, and the relatively speedy demise of the towns, in spite of valiant archaeological efforts to prolong their agony into the late fifth century, clearly indicates that Roman life was a phenomenon imposed even on lowland Britain from above, rather than something which had taken deep roots within the island. Britain had escaped the worst of the barbarian onslaught that had befallen the western continental empire, yet Roman life had been so resilient in Gaul that barbarians there continued to use Roman coin or imitations of it, and the Franks took over the Rhineland glass industry in a way which was in sharp contrast to Anglo-Saxon attitudes in Britain. If the Anglo-Saxons adopted little of Roman ways when they invaded Britain it was not because they were less civilized than the Franks. While the last word has not been said on the elusive Romano-British establishment in the decaying towns and villas, it seems clear that the Anglo-Saxons did not encounter a Roman population in Britain, but rather a Celtic people who had recently rid themselves of the veneer of Roman ways.

While arguments may rage as to the degree of Romanization of the native population in the vicinity of London, St Albans or Colchester, in the so-called southern lowland zone, we must accept the re-emergence of indigenous Celtic tribal culture and kingship, and above all the survival of Celtic language at all levels of the social scale, in highland areas *within* the Roman province itself. This revival of Celtic tribes, led by their own aristocracies, was not confined to Wales and Cornwall but extended also to kingdoms such as Rheged west of the Pennines in Cumbria and Lancashire; and to Elmet, a British kingdom in the Leeds area. The re-emergence of these tribes within the Roman province cannot be explained away as a gradual process of cultural regression whereby those Romano-British 'tyrants' as described by Gildas in the mid sixth century, left to their own devices after the withdrawal of the Roman army of Britain, eventually reverted to type and somehow mysteriously fabricated their own 'medieval' kingdoms. Given that these British tribes in Wales and northern England emerged with their tribal organization intact – and many had a significant achievement in Celtic literature and the arts still ahead of them – their survival into the fifth and sixth centuries after 400 years of conquest requires an explanation other than mere cultural regression. The crucial point at issue about the Dark Age British kingdoms is that in the medieval period they displayed so many of the characteristics of other Celtic barbarian peoples such as the Irish or even ancient continental Celts as described by Classical writers. This similarity between former Romano-British population groups and those in the remoter Celtic world shows conclusively that Celtic tribal society must have survived intact albeit underground within the highland zone of the Roman province. No invasion of Wales by lesser tribal aristocracies from southern Ireland or northern Britain in the late Roman period can account for the full-blooded Celtic nature of post-Roman British society there. Given the limitations of Roman technology and communication difficulties in highland regions it appears certain that éntire tribes and sections of their traditional aristocracies, with impoverished warbands and retainers, survived in the Cumbrian fells, the Pennines, and the mountains of Wales. Archaeology cannot always help in identifying the status of so-called 'native' settlements and their occupants, for its reliance on material evidence, so fundamental to the discipline, has severe limitations when it comes to showing the spiritual or political aspirations of a people. An impoverished Celtic aristocrat may well have lived at the subsistence level of a neolithic farmer while still retaining his social position within an embattled tribal order. A good analogy for the survival and reemergence of a Celtic society is that of fourteenth-century Ireland. There, after three centuries of oblivion, tribes who, if we were to rely on Anglo-Norman records alone, had long been obliterated then re-emerged to occupy their old homelands with their aristocracies badly mauled but with their social order intact. In spite of differences in time, the Gaelic analogy from Ireland is still valid, and Romano-British historians would do well to bear in mind that however Romanized the Celtic establishment of lowland Britain may have become, the survival of a Celtic aristocracy such as the house of Gododdin or of Urien of Rheged even in isolated pockets of the highland zone could have been sufficient to ensure a full regeneration of Celtic life as soon as the military and economic conditions which supported the veneer of Roman civilization had been removed.

The survival of Celtic life in the highlands within Roman Britain is eloquently vouched for on the Roman side not only in Wales but further north, by a chain of fortresses which held down the Pennines and ringed the Cumbrian dales. Forts on coastal Cumbria from Ravenglass through Maryport to Carlisle were designed to protect the rich farmlands of northern Cumbria from barbarian raiders crossing the Solway Firth by sea from Galloway. Such farms fed the garrisons on the frontier and the coastal forts were an integral part of a military complex whose central feature was Hadrian's Wall sealing off the British land mass north of the Tyne–Solway line. These fortifications were designed in part to protect Britannia from barbarians from without, but there were dangerous enemies of Rome *within* the province itself. The Lake District was ringed with roads and held down by forts such as Ambleside, Papcastle and Old Penrith, strategically placed to block exits from within the dales and to cut off communication with other Brigantian tribes in the northern Pennines to the east. These Cumbrian forts testify to the survival of a hostile population in these mountains, and the dearth of Roman archaeological finds in the Lake District underlines the native Celtic character of the settlers there. The intense Roman military presence by way of forts and signal towers along the road leading from Carlisle over the Stainmore pass from Brougham to Greta Bridge and Scotch Corner testifies to the insecurity of the Roman hold over the heartlands of the Brigantes.

The presence of these fortifications when taken with other fragmentary evidence confirms that the Agricolan conquest in the days of Queen Cartimandua and her rebellious consort, Venutius, (*c.* AD 74) was not by any means complete. Roman hopes of smoothly integrating the Brigantian aristocracy into the imperial system were finally dashed by the serious revolt of the Brigantes *c.* 150 when in the Reign of Antoninus, they forfeited the privilege of running their own *civitas* based on Aldborough (Isurium) in the lowlands, north-west of York. The subsequent confiscation of Brigantian territory may have meant nothing more than the seizure of fertile lowland farmland in Yorkshire, the Eden valley, and coastal Cumbria. Roman forts in Brigantian hill country were not designed to enslave or annihilate the population. They were built to keep a careful watch on intransigent natives in a relatively useless countryside, maintain communications and afford protection to mining enterprises such as the lead mines near Whitley Castle. The Brigantian revolt of the mid second century had been helped by the gradual evacuation of Roman forts in the Pennines as Antoninus Pius had the frontier pushed forward into Scotland as far as the Forth–Clyde isthmus. Rebellion in the Pennine region proved that Britain had not been sufficiently subdued within those Roman borders earlier set by Hadrian *c.* 125 to allow for further advance into Scotland.

When at the close of the second century Roman Britain was disturbed by the civil war between Septimius Severus and Clodius

Albinus, archaeological evidence shows that Pennine fortifications were singled out for destruction. In the ensuing Severan recovery of Britain it was the Pennine forts which were first to be restored in advance of those on Hadrian's Wall in AD 197. It was as though the Pennine garrisons were still considered to be an integral part of the frontier defences even if some lay over 50 miles south of the Hadrianic line. Over a century later, during the great 'barbarian conspiracy' of 367, the *areani* or Roman frontier scouts who patrolled the northern Pennines and the Scottish border connived at a major assault by the Picts and Scots which caused havoc in the Roman province. This assault, described by Ammianus Marcellinus, is connected in the archaeological record with repairs to Pennine forts. The evidence suggests that attack from the north was a signal for disgruntled Brigantian enclaves to turn against their local Roman garrisons. Continued political unrest was the reason why these forts were maintained in the first instance until the final withdrawal of garrisons from the Pennines which began as early as the reign of Magnus Maximus in the late 380s. A countryside which could not be controlled by the Antonines or Severans was not likely to be kept in check during the chaos which accompanied the run-down of Roman occupation in the fourth century. The emergence of the Dark Age Celtic kingdoms of Rheged and Elmet on either side of the Pennines can best be understood as part of a gradual recovery and expansion of Brigantian tribalism which persisted right through the Roman period in the remoter parts of Cumbria and the Pennine chain. Further north, the Cheviots and southern uplands provided an umbrella for the emerging kingdoms of Gododdin and Strathclyde. The survival of these political groupings owed nothing to Roman civic influence – virtually non-existent in northern Britain – and owed everything to their Celtic tribal past.

The monumental proportions of Hadrian's Wall which still survive, combined with cartographers' use of two heavy parallel lines to denote the Hadrianic and Antonine Walls on modern maps, give the false impression that Rome faced the barbarians of Scotland across clearly defined physical frontiers. On the contrary, these Roman defences provide eloquent testimony that Scotland has never had a clearly defined border with northern England. This is not to say that Scotland lacked its own geographical identity – on the contrary we shall see how geography endowed south-east Scotland with a natural power base in Fife and Strathmore which was virtually impregnable to Southern enemies. The problem for ambitious rulers whether in Scotland or in the south in ancient and medieval times lay in the natural frontier which separated the best lands of Fife from those in the Vale of York: a vast highland wilderness stretching from the southern uplands through the Cheviots and Pennines. Such an enormous barrier clearly had its advantages for those on the defence, but for all parties it lacked definition. While the Tyne Gap and the Liddesdale–Teviotdale valleys present natural breaks in the highland chain, they are not sufficient to break its inexorable grip on well over 100 miles of the northern British landscape. An even greater disadvantage for these two natural breaks was that they occurred in the middle of the highland zone and and were so far removed from the natural power centres in York and Fife as to be difficult to defend with a permanent military presence. Any permanent garrison in this region could easily be cut off from its supply base, whether in the Scottish lowlands or Yorkshire. Another crux of this frontier was not just its inordinate size, but the fact that it most inconveniently ran north-south in an island similarly orientated, with the result that natural breaks in the terrain such as the Tyne Gap afforded access from one side of the island to the other rather than offering any real barrier between north and south. This point is well illustrated by the Hadrianic line, for before Hadrian ever decided to build a wall through the Tyne Gap, Roman engineers had already built Stanegate, a road linking Carlisle with Corbridge on the Tyne.

These fundamental geographical facts dominate the history of Roman and medieval Scotland, and it is in studying how the Romans grappled unsuccessfully with their frontier problem that we gain new insights into the evolution of the medieval Scottish kingdom. Hadrian's Wall, built on the instructions of that emperor during the period 122–136, followed the natural break between the Cheviots and Pennines along the northern edge of the Tyne-Solway Gap through the valleys of the Tyne, Irthing and Eden. This wall, with its milecastles, intervening turrets, northern ditch to the front, and vallum to the rear, was not so much a monumental attempt to mark the precise limits of Roman territory, as an effort to carve out a gigantic fire-break preventing the spread of rebellion and conspiracy between the highland tribes to the north and south. The vallum above all else underlined this purpose. This was a continuous flat-bottomed ditch. 20 feet wide and 10 deep, flanked on either side by a bank 20 feet high. The vallum ran on the southern or so-called Roman side of the wall, and if the complex made any military sense we must accept that the vallum defended wall patrols and sealed off the military zone of the wall from enemies to the south. In other words Hadrian's Wall never marked the bounds of Roman Britain. It was rather a determined attempt by the Romans to monitor movement among barbarians throughout a frontier zone which stretched from the Peak District in the English Midlands to the Firth of Forth some 200 miles to the north. In this sense it was a monument constructed in defiance of the essential cultural unity of the highland zone of Britain. (see map 1) On the other hand, the wall and vallum were but the central part of a larger complex network of defences which included 50 miles of coastal forts south of the Solway, and a network of forward and rearward forts in the Cheviots and Pennines connected by a system of arterial roads. The forts of coastal Cumbria separated the Novantae of Galloway and their northern allies from the population penned up in Cumbria. Hadrian's Wall split Brigantian territory across the Eden valley, reminding us of that essential unity of the terrain north and south of the wall. Brigantian lands along the lower Esk and the Lyne were monitored by forward forts such as Bewcastle and Netherby in Cumberland, and Birrens and (later at least) Broomholm in Dumfries. These territories about the Solway Firth were to be reunited under the Celtic kingdom of Rheged, after the Roman withdrawal.

Most of the forward positions from Hadrian's Wall were ranged out along two major roads which joined the Forth–Clyde line to that of Hadrian and whose routes had been marked out from the time of Agricola. In the west a road ran from Carlisle through Netherby and Birrens northwards to Crawford and into the heart of Damnonian territory in the middle Clyde valley. The Damnonii were the most inaccessible of all the British tribes between the walls – from a southern or Roman point of view – and it is no coincidence that they survived longest of all the northern Britons into the early eleventh century, under their later guise as the Britons of Dumbarton or Strathclyde. For most of the way the north-western network of roads and forts served to isolate the Novantae of the extreme south-west from the Selgovae who occupied the central valleys of the southern uplands. The eastern road (Dere Street) running from Corbridge, just south of Hadrian's Wall, probably ran all the way north to Inveresk on the Forth, monitoring movement between the Selgovae and the

Votadini on the east coast. The Votadini occupied Lothian, Berwick and Northumberland, and survived the Roman occupation to re-emerge as the Goddodin in the Dark Ages. Major forts such as Risingham, High Rochester, and Newstead on the Tweed, were to act as forward positions in this eastern sector of the frontier zone.

An alternative strategy to dividing up the barbarian frontier on the Tyne–Solway Gap was to opt for a curtain wall or line of garrisons further north from the Forth to the Clyde. The later Scottish border from the Liddel to the Tweed, while offering yet another alternative, was too great a land mass to contain and garrison. The Forth–Clyde line on the other hand crossed relatively wide stretches of open country in the Scottish Lowlands. It was only some 37 miles across from Old Kirkpatrick to Bridgeness, and enjoyed the natural defences of two great sea inlets. This was the option first taken up by Agricola in AD 81 and later revived by Antoninus Pius in about 143 – in the view of some historians to outdo his predecessor, Hadrian. The idea of a new wall, however, was not quite so extravagant as might seem in spite of the colossal effort recently put into the construction and manning of Hadrian's line. The Antonine option tried to cope with the border problem at the northern end of the zone adjoining the Pictish power base in Perth and Fife. Also the Antonine line, although of modest dimensions compared to Hadrian's, and of turf construction, was very practical in its more abundant use of wall forts. The resulting fortification if properly manned could seal off northern Scotland from more southerly tribes. But it is unlikely that the Antonine Wall was intended to mark a physical limit of Roman power any more than Hadrian's. It was merely an elaboration of the Hadrianic principle of holding down a barbarian buffer zone by dividing it into monitored segments, thereby creating greater stability for the province further south.

Admittedly, the Antonine Wall initially saw Hadrian's circuit go out of commission, but equally, it was backed up with an even greater concentration of forts between the walls as well as additional forward positions in Perth. Hadrian's defences were not made irrevocably obsolete; they could always be brought back into commission, as happened twice subsequently. Indeed, part of the reason why chaos reigns in Romano-British studies as to the correct chronology and sequence of occupations of the Antonine and Hadrianic Walls in the period AD 150–207 is the insistence of historians

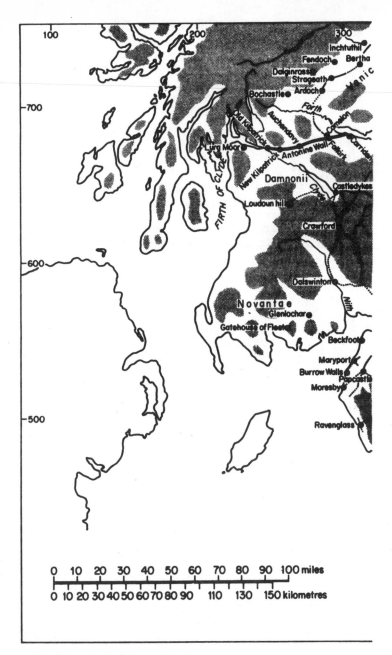

1 The Frontier in Roman Britain

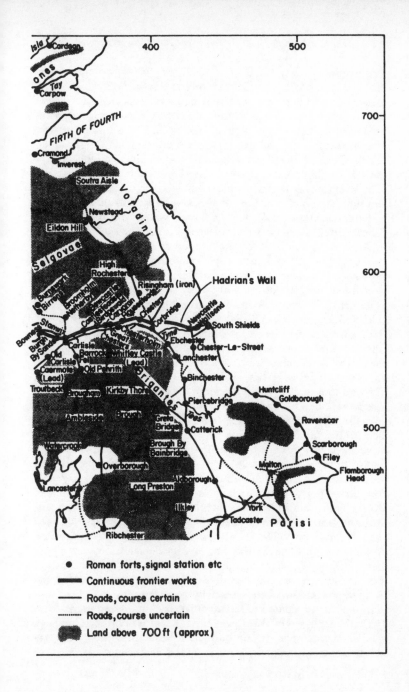

Symbol	Legend
●	Roman forts, signal station etc
▬	Continuous frontier works
—	Roads, course certain
⋯⋯	Roads, course uncertain
■	Land above 700 ft (approx)

on assuming that either one wall or the other must have marked the absolute limits of empire at any given time. The evidence such as it is, suggests that both walls formed part of two alternative but mutually interlocking strategies whose forward and rearward defences in particular formed part of a unified scheme designed to monitor barbarian tribes from the Peak District to the Forth. One or other of the walls could come in or go out of commission depending on the relative strength or weakness of Roman and barbarian in any period. It is possible that the Antonine line was not maintained after about AD 163, but its forts could always provide forward bases and could be hastily put back into commission by competent Roman engineers when the need arose.

Ancient writers believed that emperors from Hadrian to Commodus (117-192) all had to cope with unrest in Britain – trouble coming mainly from across the frontier. Whether we regard this as a cliché or not, it was certainly true, and if anything, an understatement. The confused history of the Antonine Wall is connected with political turmoil in the whole of northern Britain from *c*. 140 to 200, and whatever lands the Romans then held must have been administered under military rule. Indeed, it is difficult to see how we can view the northern half of Roman Britain as a settled province under civil government during much of the second century. Nor did the trouble end in the reign of Commodus: if anything, it got worse. Septimius Severus made a determined and personal effort in the tradition of Agricola and Hadrian to bring the Picts to heel with a military offensive beyond the Forth, but the death of Severus during this northern campaign saw his son Caracalla coming to terms with the Scottish tribes and withdrawing south to a frontier resting on the Hadrianic line. This pattern was to repeat itself in the fourth century when Constantine (AD 306) also came to power while his father was planning a campaign in northern Britain, but Constantine like Hadrian and Caracalla decided against an all-out offensive against the Picts and consolidated the frontier on the Tyne–Solway line. While Constantine's reign may have fostered a golden age for Roman civic life in the south of Britain, as long as the Pictish problem remained unsolved the Roman north remained essentially a frontier zone. After Constantine's death chaos ensued at all levels culminating in the 'barbarian conspiracy' of 367. It was either Severus or his son Caracalla who divided Roman Britain into two separate provinces. This was surely a recognition of the fundamental difference between the two regions, and it meant that northern or 'Lower Britain' (Britannia Inferior) was in fact if not in name a military zone under the control of a miltary commander at York. Any semblance of settled Roman life within this zone must have been confined to the lowlands of Yorkshire and more confined stretches of coastal lowlands elsewhere.

Britannia Inferior, then, was a buffer zone designed to protect the towns and villas of southern Britain not only from the Caledonii and Maeatae of the far north, but also from rebellious British tribes in the Pennines and Cheviots. Prosperous towns even in the deep south, such as Cirencester, had gates and walls for their defences perhaps as early as the late second century, when native hostility was compounded by unrest in the army of occupation in Britain. Civic pride undoubtedly lay behind the public buildings in Verulamium, Gloucester or London, but town defences were thrown up as a response to military threat, and it is significant that even the settled Roman south of Britain had town defences a century before they were considered necessary in Gaul. The northern frontier had its urban communities, but it would be foolish to confuse the citizens who sat in the theatre at Canterbury, in the early second century, with the Klondike conditions which prevailed in the *vici* or shanty towns which grew up around the Severan forts on the Scottish frontier. Some of the *vici* were quite large and properly planned, as at Corbridge or Carlisle, but the *vicus* housed the camp followers of the army of occupation and from first to last depended for its existence on the military presence.

Initially the *vicus* was rigidly segregated from the military zone proper by the vallum which ran south of Hadrian's Wall, but the legalization of soldiers' marriages by Septimius Severus combined with the increasing dangers of the northern frontier, sent the buildings of the *vici* sprawling over the military defences and huddling against the walls of the forts. These forts and their satellite villages admittedly housed a cosmopolitan and sometimes exotic population from all corners of the empire. In the time of Marcus Aurelius, for instance, several thousand Sarmatian cavalrymen served in northern Britain and later settled as veterans at Ribchester in Lancashire. Among the traders, we know of Barates of Palmyra who was probably an army contractor specializing in standards. He erected a tombstone (*c.* AD 200) to his wife at the maritime depot at South Shields and he himself is commemorated on a tombstone at Corbridge. Other traders may be represented by Flavius

Antigonus, a Greek whose fourth-century tombstone was found at Carlisle. The two Salmanes (probably father and son) commemorated at Auchendavy, on the Antonine Wall in Dunbartonshire, probably came from further east in the empire and may have belonged to a military family rather than to camp followers. Another father and son, from Commagene in northern Syria perhaps belonging to a trading family, are commemorated in a Greek inscription at Brough under Stainmore near that treacherous road from Carlisle to Greta Bridge.

Such inscriptions are rare, and while they vouch for the cosmopolitan nature of the Roman colony in the north and for the presence of families among traders and soldiers alike, they do not even suggest evidence for the extensive Romanization of the native population. Whatever the precise function of the *vici* their essentially alien character vis-à-vis the native population is highlighted by their disappearance after the great barbarian inroads of the 360s. Apart from Piercebridge on the Tees on the road from York to Corbridge, and from Chesterholm on the wall, most of the *vici* collapsed after the barbarian conspiracy of 367. Such recovery in the north as there was under Theodosius involved a strictly military reconstruction including a regarrisoning of wall forts, and this lack of civic settlement on the frontier persisted until the final withdrawal of the Roman army from northern Britain. Whereas before, the *vici* huddled outside the forts, now everyone connected with the Roman colonial system was accommodated within fort walls. This arrangement suggests that whatever remained of Roman civil life had been subsumed into a military system put on full alert, and it suggests also that the gulf between Roman and native was widening even further than in earlier centuries.

The speech which Tacitus put into the mouth of the Caledonian leader Calgacus, who fought Agricola in AD 83, is clearly a set piece which the first named inhabitant of Scotland is highly unlikely ever to have uttered. Yet the sentiments expressed in this speech do show us how Tacitus viewed the native attitude to Rome and the points raised fairly represent everything the British aristocracy stood to lose under the Roman conqueror. We hear not only of ruthless conquest butchery, but of subsequent exploitation of the conquered, conscription into foreign armies, forced labour on road works, and heavy taxation. All this we know to be true, and those isolated forts along the sprawling frontier of Roman Britain most certainly housed press-gangs and slave raiders who preyed on the native settlers in order to supplement the unscrupulous procurators' income and to maintain the supply of forced labour in the iron mines at Risingham in Northumberland, and in numerous other industries further south. Taking the northern British tribes as a whole, it is hard to see what incentives they had to collaborate with Rome to the degree of becoming Romanized, in view of the undisguised exploitation, not to mention the lessons that had been learnt from treatment meted out to the Iceni, the Brigantes, and many others.

Scholars have argued for Roman client status for some of the British tribes between the walls whereby their independent kings were responsible with their own warbands for the defence of the Antonine line against Picts and Scots. This may well have been true for the Votadini back in the second century when their hillfort at Traprain Law overlooking the valley of the Haddington Tyne has yielded an abundance of Roman coins and pottery including figured Samian Ware from central Gaul. The discovery of the Roman alphabet at Traprain Law also shows that here, at least, elements of the higher civilization were percolating through to the native Britons, though what use, if any, these Roman letters were put to is quite unknown. Traprain Law is in this and in other respects a special case. The evidence from Traprain Law is essentially archaeological and the material remains can be interpreted in other ways. Whereas in southern Britain the British population quickly adapted to Roman needs and was able to supply its own pottery to the Roman army, the Votadini on the other hand, while importing exotic wares, were incapable of producing an adequate pottery type of their own. Such pottery as they made was poorly executed and based on archaic Iron Age and outmoded Roman forms, incapable of satisfying contemporary Roman needs. All this suggests that while the Votadini were able to buy or loot high-quality Roman products, they were not exposed to close enough contact with Rome for a sufficient length of time to have undergone any appreciable degree of Roman influence. The hoard containing over 100 pieces of Roman silver plate discovered in Traprain Law in 1919 has been dated on its coin evidence to the end of the reign of Honorius (395–423). This haul had already been crushed for scrap or bullion before being hidden, and suggests that if the Votadini were involved with it, their close contact with Rome in Antonine days had now given way to a more violent exchange.

When Old Welsh traditions of the early ninth century preserved in the *Historia Brittonum* and in Welsh genealogical notes take up the story of the sub-Roman Votadini, we seem at first to have confirmatory evidence for the alliance of this tribe with its late Roman neighbours. These sources focus on Cuneda, a chieftain of Manaw of Gododdin, a territory in the extreme north of the lands of the Votadini (later Gododdin centred on Stirling and covering the plain at the western end of the Firth of Forth. (see map 2) Old Welsh tradition asserted that Cuneda and eight of his sons migrated from Manaw to north Wales where they drove out Irish invaders who had settled there and founded in their turn various Welsh kingdoms and sub-kingdoms in Gwynedd. Historians have been tempted to recognize in this tale evidence for the deliberate Roman policy of employing one barbarian tribe as *foederati* or auxiliaries in an effort to drive out other less desirable barbarians. H.M. Chadwick first undermined this idea by pointing out that Cuneda's migration cannot have taken place very long before *c*. 450, while Nora Chadwick later exposed several elements in the tradition which she believed relegated it to the realm of a fictitious Celtic origin tale – a conclusion reiterated by David Dumville in his iconoclastic assault on early Welsh historiography. While reluctant to dismiss the idea of a Dark Age migration from Manaw to Wales out of hand, we must nevertheless accept that these Welsh sources lend no weight whatever to an argument for an alliance between the Votadini and the Romans in the late Empire.

The argument for *foederati* status of the northern tribes has been strengthened for late Roman and sub-Roman periods by the Latin influence seen on the names of Votadinian and Damnonian leaders in the medieval Welsh genealogies of those British tribes who were known in Welsh tradition as *Gwŷr y Gogledd* ('Men of the North'). Cuneda, that northern British chieftain from Manaw had immediate ancestors and descendants bearing Latin names. Much has been made of the name of Cuneda's grandfather, *Patern Pesrut* ('Paternus of the Red Tunic'), who may have flourished in the mid fourth century. The nickname is taken to imply Roman investiture of a barbarian with the insignia of an auxiliary commander. Similarly, late fourth-century levels in the genealogy of the Damnonii yield the names *Cinhil* and *Cluim*, taken to represent the Latin forms *Quintilius* and *Clemens*. Cluim's descendant was Ceretic or Coroticus, king of the Strathclyde Britons who received a letter from St Patrick castigating him for his part in a raid on the infant Irish Christian community. Patrick regarded Coroticus and his

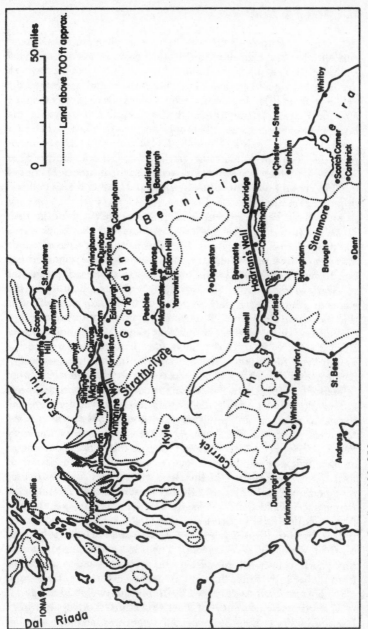

2 Southern Scotland AD 400–850

followers as Roman citizens but this may be taken as a sub-Roman conceit since the Damnonii of Strathclyde were too far removed from the Roman sphere of influence at any time after the Severan age to be considered citizens of the late empire, and besides, all the evidence from early Irish scholarship now tends to favour the date 491 for Patrick's death rather than the earlier 461. As for the borrowing of Latin names, this could easily have taken place under the influence of Christianity – and Coroticus was a Christian – or from the desire to emulate the glories of the Roman world. That was a world which was so far removed from the northern Britons of the fifth century as to constitute a heroic ideal rather than a political or physical reality.

An archaic Leinster poem speaks of Mes Delmann of the Irish *Domnainn* (distant cousins of the Damnonii on the Clyde) as a 'mighty tribune' (*trebunn*). If Mes Delmann ever existed as an ancestor of the kings of Leinster, then he would have reigned in the late Roman period. As yet no historian has advanced a claim for this warlord to have ruled Leinster as a client king of Rome with the status of tribune. What the borrowing of these Latin titles tells us is that barbarian Celts were impressed by Roman pomp and status, a conclusion which amounts to nothing more than common sense. Even if we were to agree that such titles point further to a specific military role for the northern Britons within the Roman system of defence, that in itself would not necessarily prove wholesale Roman influence on these Celtic tribes. On the contrary, the recognition of independent kings among the Britons might serve to consolidate native aristocratic and military institutions. When at last the Votadini emerge in the Dark Ages from the pages of the early Welsh poem, the *Gododdin*, we can glimpse this people not through archaeological or colonial Roman eyes but through the eyes of their own bards. This picture of the late sixth-century Votadini is far removed from the conjectural world of a sub-Roman military élite striving to uphold the *pax Romana*. On the contrary, we are confronted with a full-blooded barbarian Celtic aristocracy accoutred in Iron Age torcs and engaged in the characteristic reckless bravery of their continental ancestors. The Gododdin appear to be untouched by even the thinnest veneer of Romanization, and apart from their Christianity, they might just as well belong to the world of the ancient Celts as described by Herodotus or Poseidonius.

The complete absence of east Yorkshire pottery north of Hadrian's Wall after 367 not only confirms abandonment of

Roman forward positions, but also suggests a lack of contact between the Votadini, for instance, and their Roman neighbours to the south. A barbarian cordon was being drawn around the vulnerable northern province from the second quarter of the fourth century onwards. The barbarian conspiracy of 367 not only involved Picts and Scots but also Saxons sailing across the north sea. Seaborne Germanic invaders were capable of attacking the one-time secure Roman heartland of the Plain of York, and the exposed nature of this Roman base is underlined by the building of coastal watchtowers from Huntcliff to Filey, north of Flamborough Head. Whatever the subsequent role of these Germans in the politics of sub-Roman Britain, the threat which they posed to the rich farmlands of Yorkshire in the fourth century must have dramatically altered Roman priorities for the defence of the north. It became futile to invest too much effort in holding down the unmanageable highland frontier if the supply line from York and the whole focal point of Roman organization there could be threatened from the flank. This explains the abandonment of forward positions in the Cheviots and the economy of military investment in the defence of the Hadrianic line after the invasions of 367. It implies too, a much earlier reassertion of native British power in the north among the Votadini and Damnonii than was possible for Britons further south and in Wales.

As Roman organization collapsed north of the Humber, Germanic mercenaries, originally in the pay of the Roman commander at York, saw their ranks swelled by further Anglian invaders from across the North Sea accompanied by their women and children. This Germanic colony, centred on York and on the rich farmland of the Yorkshire Wolds, was eventually organized, by the sixth century, under aristocratic leadership into the Northumbrian kingdom of Deira. At about the same time, another Germanic people organized under a rival house of kings had established itself on coastal Northumberland and ruled from the old British fortress of *Din Guoaroy*, renamed *Bebbanburh* or Bamburgh ('the fortress of Bebba') by the invaders. This northern kingdom of Bernicia was still only a piratical colony in the later half of the sixth century sprawling along coastal Northumbria with its main strength between the Aln and the Tweed and on the lower Tyne. Charles Thomas has suggested that Anglian Bernicia may have taken its name, *Berneich*, from the first British kingdom to have fallen into the hands of the Angles at Bamburgh. This kingdom based on Greater

Tweeddale would have had its sub-Roman centre at the Celtic hill-fort on *Trimontium* where the Roman fort of Newstead guarded the Dere Street crossing of the Tweed. Later, some time after 635, Scottish missionaries under new Anglian patronage were to found the monastery of Old Melrose in this very region, but the retention of the British place-name *Mailros* for the English monastery was significant, and reminds us that the old British population of Tweeddale had already become Christian in part at least by the early sixth century, as Christian memorial stones at Peebles, Manor Water and Yarrowkirk prove. The Yarrowkirk stone commemorates two British princes, *Nudus* and *Dumnogenus*, perhaps remnants of the Selgovan aristocracy, who may well have survived into the early sixth century.

The survival of the Selgovae and Novantae into the Dark Ages may be in doubt, but other neighbouring Celtic tribes were to play a crucial role in the history of southern Scotland and northern England in the sixth and seventh centuries. The story of this British survival is best studied against the background of resistance to the common enemy encountered in the Northumbrian Angles. Ida was the founder of the Bernician dynasty at Bamburgh, according to Bede, and we may date his reign to about the middle of the sixth century. The Bernician colony must have posed a threat to the British Gododdin from the beginning since the descendants of the Votadini occupied Lothian and stretched along coastal Berwick and Northumberland as far south as the Wear if not to the Tees. The advent of the Bernicians must have pushed Gododdin power back to the Lammermuirs and driven other Celtic magnates further west into the uplands of the Selgovae in the Cheviots and the southern uplands. Meanwhile, the Angles of Deira occupying York and the East Riding hemmed in the British kingdom of Elmet (or Elfed) between the Pennines and the Ouse. But Deiran expansion proceeded up the Vale of York in the second half of the sixth century and the eventual English occupation of Catterick and its hinterland marked a crucial stage in the tightening of the Anglian hold on north-eastern Britain.

Control of Catterick secured the Yorkshire lowlands and consigned the Britons henceforth to an exclusively 'highland' role. Just as for the Romans, so now for the English, control of Catterick allowed its masters to monitor all movement along Dere Street, and to cut off British Rheged in Cumbria and the Eden Valley from the Gododdin in the north-east. The Old Welsh poems ascribed to

Taliesin describe Urien, the British king of Rheged (*fl. c.* 570–590), as prince of Catterick. The centre of Urien's kingdom was based on Carlisle, the Eden Valley, coastal Cumberland and Dumfries, but his immediate predecessors, if not Urien himself, once ruled over the Stainmore Pass down to Catterick and Scotch Corner – that crucial area which formerly marked a geographical if not a political frontier between the Brigantian highlands and Roman lowlands. The rulers of Rheged probably occupied a royal estate at Catterick in the sub-Roman period. There was a royal vill there in Anglo-Saxon times, where incidentally, Bede tells us the Roman missionary, Paulinus, baptized his converts in the nearby Swale soon after 627.

An indication of the strategic importance of Catterick and the magnitude of its loss to northern British chieftains is afforded by the Old Welsh poem, the *Gododdin* of Aneirin, composed in an oral setting at the Gododdin court in Edinburgh about 600. Aneirin tells us of a concerted British attack on the heathen English of Catterick by Christian British chiefs from the court of Mynyddog of Gododdin who ruled his people from *Din Eidyn* or Edinburgh. Mynyddog's army included warriors from Ayrshire, from Elmet in Yorkshire, from north Wales, and by implication also some Pictish leaders from 'beyond Bannog'. This British assault on Catterick, which must have involved more than the 300 chosen warriors commemorated by the poet, was a desperate attempt to contain the Anglian advance, and was repulsed with the almost complete slaughter of the assailants. This ill-fated Gododdin offensive took place around 600 early in the reign of the Northumbrian king, Ethelfrith (593–617). It was a British response not only to English control of Catterick but to the recent English destruction of a northern British coalition led by Urien of Rheged and his sons.

Another cycle of literature based on Urien's dynasty was composed by his court poets and survives in fragments in the *Historia Brittonum* and in poems ascribed to Taliesin. We learn from the *Historia Brittonum* of warfare between Urien and Theodric (572–579) and Hussa (585–592), the sons and successors of Ida, founder of the house of Bamburgh in Bernicia. Things came to a head when Urien along with Riderch, king of the Strathclyde Britons, and two other leaders, besieged Hussa in Lindisfarne (Old Welsh, *Medcaut*). Urien was betrayed by Morcant, an unidentified northern British leader, and was slain probably at the mouth of the river Low opposite Lindisfarne. The death of Urien may not have

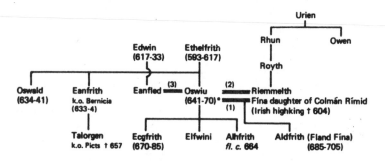

NORTHUMBRIAN KINGS   British House of Rheged

* Oswiu ruled as king of Bernicia only
  until 655 and as king of Northumbria
  thereafter

(1) Various marriages of Oswiu
    (chronological sequence uncertain)

Table 1 The British House of Rheged and Northumbrian kings

been quite the disaster that modern historians assume, but it does seem to have marked the beginning of the end for his kingdom of Rheged which sprawled over the northern Pennines and perhaps as far north and west as Galloway.

Urien was probably succeeded by his son Owen, also celebrated in early Welsh poetry as a champion among the 'Men of the North', and another son, Run (Rhun), was, according to the *Historia Brittonum*, responsible for the baptism of Eanfled daughter of Edwin of Northumbria (617–33) and of her royal father (See Table 1). This statement, supported by the *Annales Cambriae*, goes contrary to Bede's account of Edwin's baptism by the Roman bishop, Paulinus, in 627. Bede's dislike of things Welsh probably led him to suppress this tradition, since it was crucial to the whole saga of Northumbrian orthodoxy to show that Edwin and his court shared in an immediate way with the Roman mission from Pope Gregory. It may well be that Edwin who, in common with his British neighbours, regarded Ethelfrith of Bernicia as a great enemy, had been baptized by the Britons when in exile among them. There is no need to assume that Rhun personally baptized the Northumbrian king – the statement may simply imply that Edwin was baptized at Rhun's court, with the British king perhaps acting as sponsor. Bede's story of Edwin's conversion by Paulinus has yet to be properly reconciled with Old Welsh tradition. Edwin may have agreed to undergo a second or conditional Roman baptism at the hands of Paulinus, whose prominence in Bede's narrative springs from his undoubted role as missionary to the Anglian population of Deira and Lindsey during Edwin's reign. The tradition of Edwin's Celtic baptism and implied friendship with the court of Rheged is also supported by a note in the Saxon Genealogies in the *Historia Brittonum* which relates that Royth, son of Rhun and grandson of Urien of Rheged, had a daughter Riemmelth who married Oswiu, king of Bernicia (641– 670). Oswiu's other wife, Eanfled, was that daughter of King Edwin who was alleged to have been baptized by Rhun of Rheged.

Even accepting that this last tradition were true, it is unwise to assume as several scholars have done, that through this marriage between Riemmelth and Oswiu the old kingdom of Rheged from Catterick to Galloway passed peacefully into the possession of the Northumbrian kings. Anyone who has studied Celtic polity knows that kingdoms did not passively change hands as dowries, and that even if royal lines were reduced to sole surviving daughters, there were myriads of rival segments in the tribal aristocracy who would not sit idly by and see a Germanic warlord usurp their patrimony. All that these Old Welsh traditions point to is a state of alliance and friendship existing between the houses of Deira and Rheged in the first half of the seventh century, and between Bernicia and Rheged in the time of Oswiu. The marriage of Briton and Northumbrian may not even bespeak friendship. Traditional enemies in Ireland regularly traded royal wives across hostile borders as a matter of kingly protocol. Sometimes this may have been done to consolidate treaties, but in many cases inter-tribal slaughter continued unabated regardless of how things fared in the tribal marriage bed.

South-west Scotland and England west of the Pennines can only have passed into Anglian hands by direct conquest, though when precisely this happened is not clear. Stenton believed that on Urien's death at the siege of Lindisfarne, the Northumbrian king, Ethelfrith, followed up this opportunity by pushing across the Tyne Gap to the lowlands about the Solway. In his view, the evidence of early Anglian place-names was sufficient to show that before his death in 617 Ethelfrith 'could have ridden from the Solway to the Mersey through territory in the occupation of his own people.' All this is very much open to doubt. The survival of the kingdom of Elmet under the rule of its British king, Ceretic, into the reign of

Ethelfrith's successor Edwin (617–633) suggests that British tribes may have survived intact in the Northumbrian highlands until the end of the seventh century if not beyond, and that Anglian penetration may have been much more piecemeal and confined to valleys and accessible coastal areas. The king who may have made the most significant inroads into British territories in south-west Scotland and north-west England was surely Ecgfrith rather than Ethelfrith, or his immediate successors. In spite of Bede's claims of overlordship of the Britons attributed to Edwin, Oswald and Oswiu, it is nonetheless Ecgfrith and his warband who emerge from the *Ecclesiastical History* as presiding over the most formidable war machine in the seventh-century north. All that we know of Ecgfrith's aggressive nature suggests that his expansionist policies were directed against his neighbours in northern Britain. He failed to understand the dangers inherent in an ambition to subdue the highland massif of southern Scotland, and he met his death at the hands of the southern Picts because he had tried to push the English frontier too far north.

The contemporary *Life* of Wilfrid by Eddius Stephanus gives us an account of the dedication of the church of Ripon which was attended by King Ecgfrith and his brother Elfwini in the period 671–678. It is clear that Wilfrid's building programme at Ripon was financed by plunder and endowments from confiscated British church lands in the Pennines. The estates which Ecgfrith had granted to Wilfrid included Yeadon in Airedale which must have been in Elmet, although we have no idea at what time in Edwin's reign this territory fell to the English. The three other places mentioned – Ribble, Dent and Catlow – all formed part of the remoter highlands of Rheged in the northern Pennines. Wilfrid and his king were presiding at Ripon over the dismemberment of at least part of the Rheged kingdom. There is nothing to suggest that these British lands had lain deserted for generations: on the contrary, there is a certain immediacy in Eddius's text which shows us, incidentally, that Anglo-Saxon aggression was directed against British warriors and clergy alike. Ecgfrith's gift to Wilfrid consisted of 'a list of the consecrated places in various parts which the British clergy had deserted when fleeing from the hostile sword wielded by the warriors of our nation'. If we accept that the collapse of Rheged did not occur until Ecgfrith's reign *c.* 670–685 then this ties in with British traditions of a marriage between Ecgfrith's predecessor, Oswiu, and Riemmelth of Rheged, for such a marriage would presuppose that Rheged under Royth, grandson of Urien must have retained some semblance of British autonomy up to the middle of the seventh century. Bede offers us little help on these matters since his bias against things British renders him an unreliable source in this respect. Bede's silence, however, on churches west of the Pennines is significant and cannot be put down to the fact that he lived and worked on the other side of Northumbria. The absence of any mention of churches outside the Carlisle area in western Northumbria in his *Ecclesiastical History* brings home to us the startling possibility that the region from the Wirral to the Solway may have been in British hands almost up to Bede's own day. Not only had these places belonged to a hostile British clergy, but mention of them would have reminded men of his time that Wilfrid's campaign for orthodoxy in regard to Roman church usage involved aggrandizement and the use of violence against church lands in the old kingdoms of Elmet and Rheged.

A series of entries in the Irish *Annals of Ulster*, hitherto unexplained, may have a crucial bearing on events in northern Britain in the later seventh and early eighth centuries. Suddenly and without warning the annalist introduces roving bands of British warriors into the Irish record in the period from 682 until 709. The first reference in 682 records the slaying of Cathassach king of the Cruithne of Dál nAraide in a battle in Antrim. We next hear of them in 697 when allied with the Ulstermen they devastated the plain of Muirthemne in Co. Louth. That was an expedition against the borders of the Uí Néill kingdom of Brega, and we find that Irgalach, a king of Brega, was slain by a British warband on Ireland's Eye north of Dublin in 702. In the following year the Britons are seen to fall out with their Ulster patrons in a battle in south-east Ulster where the foreigners were defeated. We last hear of Britons fighting in Ireland in 709, by which time they were serving as mercenaries in the army of Cellach Cualann, king of Leinster, when again they were defeated in a skirmish in the Wicklow mountains.

This record shows that British warbands were active along a 160-mile stretch of the east coast of Ireland from 682 until 709. They are first heard of in Ulster which suggests they came from northern Britain rather than Wales, after which the same or other warbands worked their way down the east coast in a logical progression from Antrim, through Down, Louth, and Dublin to Wicklow. Their presence on the Irish scene must surely imply a major political upheaval in northern Britain and can best be accounted for by seeing them as part of the dismembered warband of the house of Urien. Their first appearance in Ireland coincided with a time when Ecgfrith of Northumbria was engaged in a major offensive against his northern neighbours, and when Wilfrid was busy acquiring confiscated British church lands west of the Pennines. The arrival of these Britons in north-east Ireland would fit in well with the migration of a warrior élite from Galloway or from Cumbria and the Solway plain who were driven to seek their fortune at the courts of Irish kings always in need of warriors for their own incessant warfare. Finally, if we view these warriors as part of the exiled warband of Rheged, then their earliest appearance in eastern Ireland in 682 makes sense at last out of the punitive expedition dispatched by Ecgfrith of Northumbria against eastern Ireland in 684. Ecgfrith now had not one, but two good reasons for hating the Irish. The first was that they had given refuge to his estranged and exiled brother, Aldfrith (later king of Northumbria, 685–705), and the second that they had taken in the most dangerous element in the kingdom of Rheged – those dispossessed warriors who made up the élite of the house of Urien.

If Rheged survived beyond the first half of the seventh century, even as a contracted kingdom bottled up in the northern Pennines, then Anglian penetration of south-west Scotland as far west as the Rhinns of Galloway must have been at an even slower and less intense rate. The magnificence of the two Anglian crosses at Bewcastle and Ruthwell with their thoroughly Anglo-Saxon and Romanesque associations can blind us to the tenuous hold which the Northumbrian establishment had at any time on this country north of Hadrian's Wall. The Ruthwell cross in coastal Dumfriesshire, about half-way between Annan and Dumfries, may be slightly earlier than that at Bewcastle, which dates to about 700. The Bewcastle cross was erected within the old Roman fort in the north-west corner of Cumberland, some six miles north of Hadrian's Wall. The relationship to the fort may not have been fortuitous. This was a frontier region for the Romans, whose fort here formed part of the forward defences of the wall designed to keep a watchful eye on the most northerly section of the Brigantes. For the Anglo-Saxons too, these crosses, rather than showing the strength of the Anglian hold on the north-western Britons, were most likely propaganda works on a remote frontier celebrating the triumph of Northumbrian arms and Christianity over the Britons.

If the Bewcastle cross really does preserve a dedicatory inscription to Alhfrith and his queen, Cyneburg, (or even to Cyneburg alone or to their son) then the association with that branch of the Northumbrian royal house would not be without interest. Alhfrith was that rebellious son of Oswiu of Northumbria who disappeared from history as a disloyal sub-king of Deira. It was Alhfrith, however, who championed the cause of Wilfrid to the extent of evicting the Iona community from Ripon to allow Wilfrid build his ecclesiastical empire on the ruins of the pillaged British church. The Bewcastle Cross may be a conscious celebration of the triumph of Wilfrid and his patrons over the Celtic church in the aftermath of the Synod of Whitby in 664. British Rheged probably extended westward to Dunragit in Wigtownshire if not beyond, and at the time the Ruthwell Cross was raised, that monument may have marked the limits of Anglian advance against the Britons of the north-west. It was not until about 731 that the Anglian hold on Galloway was secure enough to appoint a Northumbrian bishop (Pehthelm) to the newly constituted diocese of Whithorn.

Galloway had been Christian for centuries before the Anglian conquest. The main problem regarding our understanding of that Christianity relates to its origins and date. Bede is the earliest writer to introduce us to Ninian, a British bishop who ministered from *Candida Casa*, a place usually identified with Whithorn in Wigtownshire. Whithorn has tangible evidence for sub-Roman Christianity in the presence there of the late fifth-century *Latinus* tombstone and of an even earlier Christian cemetery under the east end of the priory. Further west, at Kirkmadrine in the Rhinns of Galloway, are three other memorial stones, one of which may be even earlier than the earliest Whithorn stone. The problem of the date and details of Ninian's early life has obscured a more important question, namely whether this Christian colony in Galloway began as an offshoot of Roman Christianity based, as some scholars believe, on Carlisle, or whether it had an independent origin. Evidence for Christians in the Roman frontier zone from the fourth century at Carlisle, Chesterholm, Brougham, Brough under Stainmore and elsewhere, all seems to support the notion that Christianity spread out from the Roman bishopric at York, first to a centre at Carlisle and later into Galloway and regions north of the Wall. This is a thesis which like many others rests on the assumption that Roman communities on the frontier had a profound cultural effect on their British hinterlands – a thesis which is very much open to challenge. Christian antiquities from Roman forts and settlements prove nothing more than the presence of Christian Romans in their own towns and forts. Carlisle as a *vicus*, however large, was probably always under the ecclesiastical jurisdiction of York, and even if we were to concede that it became a late-Roman bishopric, it would be even more unlikely to find yet another bishopric at Whithorn, given the tiny population of the neighbouring peninsula.

Thomas has rightly emphasized the essentially Atlantic character of the Galloway peninsula, not only geographically, but in the cultural affinities of its Christian memorial stones from the fifth and sixth centuries. This Atlantic connection, with the nearby Isle of Man for instance, is important since it points away from Roman Britain to an alternative Mediterranean route via coastal Gaul. This was the route along which the native Britons also received the monastic culture which so rapidly adapted to Celtic society and which owed nothing to the centuries of a Roman presence in the British Isles. The Romano-British church, like so much of Romano-British civilization (in spite of figures such as Pelagius and Patrick) seems to have had little lasting effect on the native population of Britain. Even Patrick's establishment of Roman episcopal organization in fifth-century Ireland was quickly supplanted by Celtic monasticism, and the liturgical and organizational life of the Celtic church throughout Britain was to diverge progressively over the following centuries from its Roman counterpart in continental Europe. Had the opposite been true the whole course of Anglo-Saxon relations with the Britons would have been different, and the Northumbrians under Wilfrid would have found it impossible to use Roman church organization as a political weapon with which to hammer the British and Welsh in the seventh century. For by then, the Anglo-Saxons who were newly converted to Roman ways found it politically advantageous to brand the church of their British enemies as schismatic all but in name. It is not clear whether southern Ayrshire was annexed as early as the 730s at the time when the new Anglo-Saxon see of Whithorn was established or whether none of this region had been settled before the conquest of Kyle by Eadberht of Northumbria in 750. Northern Carrick may have been infiltrated by the English at an earlier stage, but early English place-names are rare here while most of southern Carrick consisted of inaccessible forest and high ground.

The Northumbrian expansion into south-west Scotland was not of the same order as the more thorough-going Bernician colonization of the north-east. The acquisition of Kyle was followed shortly afterwards by the assassination of Eadberht's son and successor in 758, which in turn signalled a century of unrest in the northern English kingdom, eventually degenerating into anarchy prior to the Danish capture of York in 866. But the Northumbrian bishopric at Whithorn may have ceased to exist long before the Great Army of Danes toppled the kingdom. Badwulf, the fourth and possibly last bishop of Whithorn, was consecrated in 791 and he disappears from the records in 803. The obscurity of this bishopric and its short life in Anglo-Saxon records at least points to the superficial hold which the Northumbrians had over this remote territory. This conclusion is also supported by the great dearth of early English place-names in Galloway and even north of the Solway in Dumfries, compared with say, East Lothian and lands in the Tweed basin. The survival of British place-names even in Cumbria has led Kenneth Jackson to conclude that Cumbrian or northern British speech survived in the highlands of north-west England long after the English conquest. The linguistic make-up of Galloway was complicated by the settlement of Gaelic speakers from Ireland and later by Norse influence, but the overall conclusion must be that Northumbrian influence in this region was never strong, and was confined chronologically almost within the limits of the eighth century.

The attack on Catterick by Britons of Gododdin back at the opening of the seventh century marked a turning point in the history of south-east Scotland. It would be another three centuries before an army from Scotland could again travel south along Dere Street to Corbridge to do battle with their old enemies the kings of York. By then the royal participants would have changed considerably. The Northumbrian kings of Deira and Bernicia would have been replaced by Danish warlords at York, and the ancient Britons of Edinburgh replaced by a new self-confident Scottish monarchy led by Constantine II. The tenth century would see a radical shift, too, in the balance of power in favour of the men of the north, and eventually Lothian and Berwickshire would be finally secured for the medieval kingdom of Scotland. But all this was centuries in the future when Ethelfrith – known to his northern British enemies as 'Twister' – came to power in Bernicia in 593. This grandson of Ida put the Bernician kingdom on its feet and consolidated the Anglian hold on the country between the Tyne and the Tweed. The failure of Urien's coalition to drive Ethelfrith's predecessors from

Bamburgh and Lindisfarne, and the massacre of the army of Gododdin soon after, strengthened Ethelfrith's position enormously.

The possibility of a major Anglian conquest in south-east Scotland must have now seemed imminent, and to shore up the tottering British position a new protagonist entered the fray in the person of Áedán mac Gabhráin king of the Scots of Dál Riata. What Ethelfrith had done for the Bernicians, Áedán had done for the Scots. These invaders from north-east Ireland had been settling in Argyll since the fourth century, but Áedán had given this Scottish colony leadership and direction which had set its sights not just on settlement in Dál Riata, but much further afield in the Scottish lowlands. Áedán led a northern coalition, perhaps even including an Irish king from distant Ulster, against the Bernicians at *Degsastan*, an unidentified battleground either in the lower Tweed basin or perhaps, as Skene originally suggested, at Dawston (Dawstane) in Liddesdale. The English sustained heavy losses with Ethelfrith's brother among the fallen, but Áedán and his warband were decisively repulsed, and the Anglo-Saxon chronicler, following Bede and happily unaware of what future centuries might hold, could boast:

> No king of Scots dared afterwards lead an army against this nation.

Áedán may have been called in by the beleaguered Gododdin or he may have felt compelled to challenge the rising power of the Bernicians on his own account. The conflict at *Degsastan* can be viewed as a struggle between German and Scot – descendants of two major elements within the barbarian conspiracy back in 367 – as to how the invaders would share the spoils of northern Britain, and of the Votadini in particular. This conflict was to pervade the next four centuries of Scottish history, for it was only temporarily resolved in favour of the Angles in 603. It would continue, and it was to be complicated by the arrival of yet other Germanic Viking invaders, until it was finally resolved in the reign of the Scottish king, Malcolm II, in 1018.

But the immediate effect of *Degsastan* must have been to make Ethelfrith master of all the lowland territory as far north as the Lammermuirs and he was probably also in a position to extract tribute from the Gododdin in Lothian. The English push northwards, to the Forth and beyond, continued relentlessly under the house of

Ethelfrith which returned to power under Oswald in 634. The *Annals of Ulster* record the siege of *Etin* in 638 and this has been accepted as relating to the Bernician capture of Edinburgh since *Etin* is the same as Eidyn (or Din Eidyn), the northern British name for that fortress of Mynyddog the Wealthy, lord of Gododdin. While accepting that the siege of 638 was an English assault on Edinburgh, we still cannot be sure that Edinburgh fell to the English in that year, much less the lands of Lothian and Stirling to the west of it. Bede singled out Ethelfrith as an energetic king who pushed the Anglian conquest and colonization among the old neighbouring British territories and this may well refer to Anglian expansion in the eastern Cheviots rather than the Pennines, if as I believe, the kingdom of Rheged was still intact during Ethelfrith's reign and after. Bede also vouches for Bernician overlordship of the Picts and Scots during the reigns of Oswald (634–642) and Oswiu (642–71). However vague such over-lordship may have been, these statements imply that Anglian control of Lothian either direct or indirect was unquestioned at this time, and we may safely assume that the English faced the Picts across the Forth from some time in Oswald's reign.

Hunter Blair has reminded us that the Bernician annexation of Lothian was accomplished by Oswald and Oswiu, the two sons of Ethelfrith who were on the most friendly terms with the Scots, having spent an earlier exile on Iona. He reminded us also that the annexation of Lothian in Oswald's reign coincided with a marked decline in the affairs of Scottish Dál Riata culminating in the slaying of its king, Domnall Brecc, by the Strathclyde Britons in 642. Furthermore, Anglian penetration of Lothian in the mid seventh century was accompanied by intense Gaelic cultural influence introduced by the Columban clergy of Iona whose presence in Northumbria can be basically accounted for from the earlier exile of Oswald among the Scots. So the annexation of Lothian, although under English direction, was accompanied by strong Scottish Gaelic influence from the outset. As for the native Britons, Jackson believed their language must have survived in the Cheviots and southern uplands reinforced in those remote regions by the survival of Cumbric among the Strathlyde Britons in the adjoining Clyde basin. The Anglian settlers of south-east Scotland took over many older British place-names such as Peebles, Melrose and Linlithgow, while a small but significant number of early English place-names occur in East Lothian to support the conclusion that it had been overrun in the mid-seventh century. We may point to three -*ingaham* place-names, for instance, in Whittinghame and Tyninghame (East Lothian), and Coldingham (Berwickshire); as well as others in -*ingtun* (Haddington) and -*ham* (Auldhame, Oldhamstocks).

While such names vouch for Anglian penetration of the Tweed basin, the coastal lands to the south, and East Lothian to the north, Nicolaisen's conclusions on the place-name evidence point to a later Anglian advance onto the higher ground and even into the coastal areas of Mid and West Lothian. The establishment of the Anglian bishopric at Abercorn in West Lothian probably in 681 was an important landmark in the Anglian advance to the Forth and beyond. This bishopric was perhaps re-established on Roman lines on the site of an earlier British foundation, whose name *Abercorn* was preserved by the Angles. When Ecgfrith lost his life in battle with the Picts in 685, the Northumbrians were not only thrown out of southern Pictland and south to the Forth, but Ecgfrith's bishop at Abercorn, Trumwine, was forced to fly south to Whitby. In other words, the collapse of Ecgfrith's overlordship in Fife left the English position in Stirling and West Lothian untenable. Thus, while Bede may have been correct in stating that Angles and Picts faced each other across the Forth, the Angles may have held Lothian only as far as Edinburgh in Bede's time and later. Echoes of the unstable situation on the Forth after Ecgfrith's defeat by the Picts in 685 are also found in Bede's *Life* of Cuthbert where we are told that Cuthbert cured a nun who belonged to a small community of refugees 'who had fled from their own monastery through fear of the barbarian army'.

The case for early Anglian occupation and administration of East Lothian, however, seems unassailable not only on place-name evidence but on historical grounds as well. Eddius in his *Life* of Wilfrid, for instance, reveals a scenario in East Lothian some time after 680 where his hero, Wilfrid, was held prisoner at King Ecgfrith's orders in a prison at Dunbar (note the British name) in the custody of a certain Tydlin, described as a *praefectus* or reeve. Tydlin was most likely the king's representative in East Lothian, and at the time of these events, Ecgfrith and his queen were lodging at the double monastery at Coldingham further down the Berwick coast while 'making their progress with worldly pomp and daily rejoicings and feasts, through cities, fortresses and villages'. Here we have a picture of the high point of Anglian control of the Forth, but Ecgfrith's downfall was to follow shortly, and from then on East

Lothian must have reverted to a frontier region as opposed to Berwickshire which enjoyed the protection of the Lammermuirs. Further south and west, in the remote countryside of Lauderdale and Tweeddale, English communities had already established themselves by the opening of Oswald's reign back in 634 at a time when the infant Cuthbert was born. Later, in about 651, Cuthbert entered the monastery of Melrose, a monastic foundation steeped in Gaelic influence, and the anonymous *Life* of Cuthbert shows him at this early stage in his career preaching – presumably to the pagan Angles in their newly founded settlements in Teviotdale. At this time, too, Cuthbert is said to have visited Æbbe, the sister of King Oswald and abbess of Coldingham, who, according to a note in the *Breviary of Aberdeen*, had earlier shared the Scottish exile of her royal brothers under the patronage of Domnall Brecc, king of Scots. Cuthbert, too, had personal contact with lands to the north of the Forth, as his journey involving a sea voyage from Melrose to the Picts of the *Niuduera regio* must imply. The mixed Celtic and Anglian milieu of Tweeddale where Cuthbert spent his youth as a shepherd and later as a monk clearly had a profound influence on the spirituality of the man who in the heroic sanctity of his life combined all that was best in the traditions of early Celtic and Anglo-Saxon Christianity. Cuthbert, as is clear from the details of his life, was a saint of the Scottish border, and the distribution of his pre-Reformation church dedications shows that his cult flourished in northern Britain between the walls with a southerly extension across Cumbria and along the east coast into Yorkshire. In other words, his cult enjoyed greatest popularity among a population which was either northern British or Bernician.

While Cuthbert represented a happy marriage between older Celtic and newer forms of Anglo-Saxon Christianity in northern Bernicia, in time the Angles of Lothian acquired saints of their own such as the anchorite and visionary, Bealdhere (St Baldred) of Tyninghame who died as late as 756. Bealdhere's church at the mouth of the Haddington Tyne survived the worst of the Viking onslaught since we learn from Symeon of Durham that it was raided by Olaf Gothfrithsson, the Danish king of York and Dublin, in 941. The *Office* of Bealdhere in the sixteenth-century *Breviary of Aberdeen* associates him with the much earlier northern British saint, Kentigern the apostle of Strathclyde, who was a native of Lothian. The association is impossible, but the tradition, however garbled, would hardly have arisen in the later Middle Ages had not memories of early British Christianity in Lothian survived along-side those of later Anglian invaders.

The people of Gododdin had been Christian long before the collapse of their kingdom in the seventh century. The heroes in the poem who attacked Catterick at the opening of the century were seen as Christian warlords attacking heathen Angles, and archaeological surveys have produced a distribution of early Christian cemeteries extending over Lothian and north of the Forth along coastal Fife into southern Angus. These cemeteries, some of which may date back to the early sixth century, yield burials in long cists or primitive stone sarcophogi reminiscent of the earlier Celtic Iron Age, but orientated now in a Christian fashion. The Catstane, a sixth-century memorial stone in a cemetery near Kirkliston, some 10 miles west of Edinburgh and but a few miles east of Abercorn, belongs to the same class of northern British memorials as those in Greater Tweeddale and Galloway. The long cist cemeteries, too, are but a variant of the cemeteries with dug or trench-like graves in the Galloway and Carlisle region, and the archaeological evidence, however scrappy, points to a relatively unified Christian culture among the northern Britons going back to the sixth century in the north-east on the Forth, and to the fifth century in Galloway.

Other quasi-historical sources also vouch, not only for pre-Anglian Christianity in Lothian, but also for the essential Christian cultural unity spreading across the territories of Gododdin, southern Pictland and the Britons of Strathclyde. The *Lives* of Kentigern were written up in the twelfth century and drew on earlier material of Gaelic provenance dating back to the tenth century and before. This source contains hagiographical traditions, backed by detailed topographical information, linking Kentigern and his mother to Lothian. Kentigern's mother was said to have come from a northern British royal house, she is given the genuine Cumbric name of *Teneu* and is associated with *Dumpelder* or Traprain Law, the ancient hillfort of the Votadini. Kentigern, was, according to his *Life*, brought up by St Servanus (Serf) at Culross on the northern or Pictish side of the Forth in Fife. Dedications to this saint show that his cult flourished in Fife, Clackmannan and south-east Perthshire, or those areas of southern Pictland nearest to Gododdin. Kentigern later travelled south-west, crossing the river Forth somewhere near Stirling, and moving on via Carnock to Glasgow. Whether or not Kentigern ever met or even lived in the same century as Servanus does not concern us; the real significance of this Celtic hagiographical *genre* is that it reflects the essential cultural unity of the southern Picts, the Gododdin and the men of Strathclyde. Thomas has rightly pointed to the importance of the passage in Jocelyn's version of Kentigern's *Life* describing the cemetery which Kentigern found at Glasgow on his arrival there, and which was alleged to have been consecrated long before by St Ninian. This and other evidence not only points to an earlier phase of Christian activity in Strathclyde as evidenced by Patrick's letter to the Christian Coroticus, but may even, as Thomas has claimed, preserve echoes of those primitive Christian cemeteries among the northern Britons which existed before the erection of churches for the earliest Christian communities.

The story of early British Christianity between the walls is obscure due to lack of documentation and to a dearth of early hagiographical tradition. In spite of the survival of heroic traditions relating to the Men of the North as preserved by Aneirin and Taliesin, comparatively little was handed down about the deeds of Ninian, Servanus and many other holy men. What little we know suggests that the spread of Christianity among the northern Britons was probably a gradual and low-key process spreading from the Atlantic south-west of Scotland, up Liddesdale and Annandale to the Tweed and Forth, and via the west coast into the Clyde valley. It was a world which seems to have had little of the heroism of early Roman martyrs or the asceticism which characterized Celtic Christianity elsewhere. Scotland lacked a saint of heroic dimensions until the arrival of Columba in Argyll in the middle of the sixth century. On the other hand Roman Christianity organized on a diocesan basis as imposed by the Angles seems to have made little headway at either Whithorn or Abercorn, which is not surprising since the characteristic element in the population in these regions must have remained Cumbric and therefore hostile to any departure from the traditions of their Celtic clergy. This conclusion is supported by historical, archaeological and place-name evidence regarding the superficial nature of Anglian influence in West and Mid Lothian, and in Galloway. The Clyde valley under the Dumbarton Britons never fell to the Angles. With the exception of East Lothian, Berwick and Roxburgh, the dominant ethos of southern Scotland south of the Clyde and Forth remained essentially British throughout the Dark Ages until the eventual annexation of this region into the medieval kingdom of Scotland.

2

Picts: 'The Last Men on Earth, the Last of the Free'

In AD 81, Julius Agricola, governor of Britain, advanced beyond the Forth–Clyde isthmus into Caledonia, a region of northern Britain where Roman arms had not ventured before. Agricola's Scottish campaign was but one episode in the saga of the attempted conquest of Britain begun by the emperor Claudius back in AD 43 and brought to an uncertain and unsatisfactory conclusion first by Hadrian, and later by his successor Antoninus Pius in the middle of the second century. Agricola's campaign differed from all others in that his son-in-law, Tacitus, has left us an account of it. The bias of Tacitus, and the absence of any comparable record (apart from that of Dio Cassius) until the time of Adomnán in the seventh century, has caused an immense distortion in early Scottish historiography. Some of the information in Tacitus is extremely valuable if only because it is unique, but the overall emphasis on the success of Agricola's conquest and on the alleged response of the native Britons casts a great shadow over early Scottish studies to this day. Tacitus had basically two reasons for discussing the Caledonians, one because they provided Agricola with a supposed major Roman victory, and second because they provided Tacitus with an opportunity to moralize on the theme of the innocent savage uncontaminated by decadent Roman ways. We follow Agricola's army across the Forth into Caledonia striking north-east across Perth to the Firth of Tay.

Agricola chose to be led on by an enemy who refused to fight, not because the Caledonians were 'a pack of spiritless cowards', but because like Celtic warriors elsewhere, they disliked risking all on one pitched battle and preferred to make use of the natural protection afforded by the landscape. Thus, we read of the enemy sallying forth from their 'woods and marshes' to attack Roman forts and surprise legionaries encamped at night. Agricola determined to 'drive deeper and deeper into Caledonia' and to achieve the elusive conquest of all Britain. The invader marched north of the Forth through coastal Angus, with the fleet keeping abreast along the coast. The Britons eventually made a stand at *Mons Graupius*, most likely in the Mearns near Stonehaven, or perhaps further north at Bennachie in central Aberdeenshire as St Joseph suggested. Stonehaven provided a natural meeting place for tribes north and south of the Mounth to make a united stand against a common enemy but Bennachie on the other hand, would suit the conspicuous *mons* in the Romanized place-name. A close reading of Tacitus might imply that Mons Graupius was further north near the Moray Firth, but since Tacitus was trying to show that Agricola had come within an ace of the total conquest of Britain, it was in his interest to push the site of Mons Graupius as near as possible to Agricola's original objective – 'to fight battle after battle till we have reached the end of Britain'.

As things turned out, Mons Graupius was the only major battle of the campaign, and in spite of the magnificent victory which Tacitus attributed to Agricola and the inevitable carnage of defeated Britons, this battle did not make Agricola the undisputed master of Caledonia. Tacitus concedes that two-thirds of the Caledonian warriors escaped to fight another day, and among them we may assume was their overlord, Calgacus, that man 'of outstanding valour and nobility', since had he been taken or slain, Tacitus would have capitalized on the fact. The routed Britons caught on the open ground were cut to pieces, but the proximity of the forest facilitated not only escape but even opportunity for others to regroup. Lack of knowledge of this dangerous terrain is alleged in the speech attributed to Agricola to have been a cause for Roman concern, and earlier while back on the Forth–Clyde line there were those in Agricola's council who argued for a 'strategic withdrawal' from this dangerous ground. Having secured his propaganda victory at Mons Graupius, it would seem that withdrawal was precisely what Agricola resorted to. Autumn was approaching, he must have realized the impossibility of ever clearing the highlands of barbarian warriors, and he withdrew slowly and with dignity towards his base-line in the Lowlands. Significantly, it was the Roman fleet which was sent forward to sail around northern Britain, a safe move calculated to overawe the scattered tribesmen on the Isles, and to create a false illusion of total conquest. As long as the highland massif which provided the protective hinterland to

Caledonia remained unconquered, no Roman general could claim to be master of Scotland, and in spite of strenuous efforts of Tacitus to say otherwise, it is clear that the Caledonians preserved their status as 'the last of the free' long after Agricola's campaign had passed into the folk memory of the highlands.

Within 25 years of Mons Graupius, northern Britain was again aflame, with the Roman frontier pushed back firmly to the Tyne–Solway line and with Roman forward positions at Dalswinton, High Rochester and elsewhere in southern Scotland, all in ruins. But long before that northern British offensive at the opening of the second century, Roman strategists had resigned themselves to postponing the conquest of Caledonia if not, indeed, abandoning it altogether. Agricola may even have reached that decision himself, but it is impossible to be sure because Tacitus presents us with an idealized picture of a governor who excelled all his predecessors, and who was robbed of the conquest of Britain and the governorship of Syria through the jealousy of the emperor, Domitian. It was the need for extra troops to help out in the Dacian war as much as any imperial jealousy which caused the sudden about-turn in Roman policy towards Scotland. The legionary fortress at Inchtuthil was dismantled within two years of Mons Graupius, down to the detail of withdrawing the nails and rivets from the woodwork, and of hiding the scrap iron from an enemy which was still feared. Inchtuthil was abandoned before the hot water system had been installed for the all-important soldiers' bath house and the line of forts along the foothills of the Grampians was likewise abandoned. By AD 90 the last of the watchtowers north of the Forth were evacuated and the Roman presence retreated south to consolidate its hold on the southern uplands at Dalswinton and Newstead.

The results of archaeological excavation at Inchtuthil and at sites of Roman marching camps in Aberdeenshire and elsewhere in the north-east, can create, like the narrative of Tacitus, false horizons within a discipline. The imposing proportions of a Roman camp and its superior technology can blind us to its transient function as a place to protect an alien army overnight. The essentially exotic nature of these camps and forts can blind us, too, to the more elusive significance of 'native' hut circles in the hills, whose technology and material culture never approached that of the Roman military machine, but whose enduring relationship with the landscape renders them of the utmost importance as far as the early history of Scotland is concerned. For all that Tacitus and the excavation of Roman forts (Inchtuthil included) can show, the Caledonians experienced no more than five years of limited Roman military occupation in the south-east of their territory. The details of that occupation, if not implemented by Agricola, must have been planned by him, and they are instructive not only because they set a pattern for all future Roman experiments in Caledonia, but because they shed much light on later Dark Age history of the north.

To begin with, Tacitus tells that Agricola – who had a better eye for choosing his ground than other Roman generals – secured 'the narrow neck of land' between the Clyde and Forth by a string of garrisons virtually establishing a *limes* there some 63 years before Antoninus built his wall of turf across the same terrain. The Agricolan advance into Caledonia secured only a foothold in Fife, eastern Perth and perhaps south-east Angus. This corner incorporated some of the richest land of the Caledonians and its proximity to the rest of the Roman province made it attractive to hold. A new frontier road was driven from Camelon south of the Forth, north-east to Bertha on the Tay, with intervening forts at Ardoch, Strageath and elsewhere. Forward positions ran parallel to this south-west north-east orientation on a line of forts sealing off the entrances to glens leading into the Grampians. This forward line stretched from Drumquhassle Ridge, south of Loch Lomond, north-east through Bochastle, Dalginross and Fendoch, and reminds us of similar forts built to seal off the Cumbrian dales further south in Britain. Finally, the whole system was to be underpinned by a legionary fortress in the north-east corner at Inchtuthil. Although Agricola's system was not given time to prove itself, it is remarkable that the same strategy, and often the same military locations, were called back into commission in the middle of the second century. At that time, the Forth–Clyde isthmus had been given more tangible defence with the wall of Antoninus, and once more a fortified road acted as a forward extension as far as the Tay, to incorporate the rich Fife peninsula within the Roman system.

This second attempt to annex south-east Caledonia, was part of a wider plan to solve the problem of the unmanageable mountainous frontier which stretched from the Pennines to the southern uplands. While Hadrian chose to exclude most of this region from the Roman province, Antoninus decided to absorb it all, and by way of a bonus to annex the farmlands of Fife. Fife was to ancient

Caledonia what Kent was to England – a rich and vast peninsula of farmland offering a secure base to the would-be conqueror. It was essentially Fife which Ecgfrith of Northumbria lost his life in a vain attempt to hold in the late seventh century, and it was this region yet again which Kenneth mac Alpin successfully annexed in the ninth century. In the medieval Scottish kingdom ruled by Kenneth's descendants, it was Fife which constituted the premier earldom in the high Middle Ages. Any attempt to conquer Fife must have resulted in the dispossession or taxation of the wealthiest Caledonian tribes whose aristocracy was likely to retreat to the highlands to wage guerrilla war on the occupying army. It seems agreed by archaeologists that the Antonine Wall came into commission twice after it was built in the period after 143. The first Roman withdrawal coincided with the Brigantian revolt *c.* 154, but the second Roman occupation of the northern wall and of forts such as Ardoch, Strageath and Bertha may have occurred as early as the 160s or as late as AD 200. The period was clearly one of utter confusion, with the initiative lying firmly with the Caledonians while the Romans lacked both the manpower to hold Fife and the will to conquer the highlands.

The Antonine experiment in Caledonia may have lasted intermittently for a generation, but it was no more successful than Agricola's. When the emperor Severus arrived with his son, Caracalla, in an attempt to end the chaos, the older and more modest policy of Hadrian's time prevailed, namely, to hold the Roman line on the Tyne–Solway and to control the Caledonians from a distance by diplomacy and threats rather than naked force. Distribution maps of Roman finds from non-Roman sites in Scotland in the first and second centuries show an almost total absence of material north and west of the Great Glen with few artifacts also in Argyll, and comparatively little north of the Mounth. The largest concentration is immediately south of the Forth in Lothian with a scatter across Fife and (in the second century only) a spread of material along eastern Angus and Kincardineshire. The dearth of material in the north and west reminds us of Ptolemy's ignorance of geographical detail in that region at the end of the first century and confirms the view that the highlands were untouched by the Roman experience. In spite of the apparent density of Roman artifacts, trinkets, and coins found in the Scottish lowlands, J.P. Gillam conceded that the entire record looks rather impoverished compared with similar Roman finds from East Prussia, which lay far beyond the continental frontier and was never visited by Roman legions (See map 3).

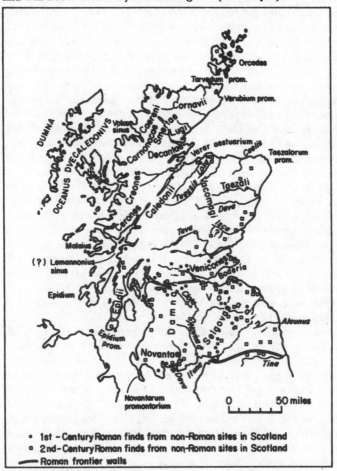

3 Scotland in the Time of Ptolemy

It was about the year 200 when a people called the Maeatae were first named along with Caledonians as barbarian enemies of Rome who were causing trouble in the north of Britain. The northern frontier had been reduced to chaos when a barbarian army crossed Hadrian's Wall in the early 180s and it took until 185 to restore the

Hadrianic defences, while forward forts between the walls (including, presumably, the Antonine Wall itself) remained out of commission until the reign of Caracalla (212–217). The situation on the frontier cannot have been helped by the civil war between Septimius Severus and Albinus the governor of Britain. Albinus weakened the province by moving south to fight for control of the empire in Gaul, and when his victorious rival Severus was free to turn his attention to Britain in 197, we learn from Dio Cassius that the Caledonians were about to break their treaty with Rome and aid the rebellious Maeatae who dwelt 'next to the cross wall that divides the island in half.' We are also told that the Caledonians (*Caledonii*) and Maeatae had emerged as the two main groupings of northern British barbarian tribes, presumably beyond the Forth and Clyde – since Dio's cross wall must refer to that of Antoninus Pius. The place-names, Myot Hill, south of the Forth (but just north of the Antonine Wall) may preserve the name *Maeatae*, as does Dumyat ('fort of the Maeatae') north-east of Stirling. Adomnán speaks of the *Miathi* – clearly the same people as the ancient Maeatae – in the late sixth century in a context which suggests that they then controlled Angus and the Mearns. So it would appear that from the third century onwards this people were overlords of south-east Scotland south of the Mounth, while the Caledonii who were 'beyond them' were another confederacy, presumably centred on the Moray Firth.

Tacitus speaks of Caledonia in the widest sense as taking in all Scotland north of the Forth–Clyde isthmus, and Ptolemy's charting of the Caledonian Ocean (*Oceanus Dvecaledonivs*) along the Atlantic coast confirms that the name *Caledonii* might be used as an umbrella term for all the *Priteni* who lived north of the Antonine Wall. It is interesting that on Ptolemy's map, the *Caledonii* are labelled as living east *and* west of the Highland massif which may well confirm that in the Roman period there was no one tribe of Caledonians as such, but that the name was used for a confederacy of individual tribes. There are several parallels from Celtic Ireland for this usage as, for example, among the Leinstermen and Ulstermen. For this reason, the place-names *Dunkeld*, and *Schiehallion*, which were called after the Caledonians do not necessarily prove that the Caledonians in a restricted sense ever occupied those regions in Perthshire as a single tribe. In Ireland, for instance, the ancient place-name, *Mount Leinster*, tells us little about the Leinstermen because there was no one tribe of Leinstermen as such – only a confederacy made up of some 35 separate tribes.

The Maeatae were on the attack c. 200 and had to be bought off by the governor Virius Lupus. The barbarians kept up the pressure so that Severus had personally to lead an expedition into Caledonia c. 208 and for the next four years we are faced with what was virtually a re-run of the Agricolan campaign. Herodian tells us of battles and skirmishes after the Severan army crossed 'the rivers and earthworks that formed the defence of the Roman Empire', while Severus, like Agricola, pushed north and east leaving marching camps in his wake to impress and confuse archaeologists much more than he did the Maeatae, in the longer term. The Maeatae came to terms without risking a major battle, but in the summer of 210 they rose again, and were visited by either Severus or Caracalla with a campaign of slaughter. This induced the Caledonians to join the rebels, but before anything decisive was achieved, Severus died in Britain and his son Caracalla, with domestic problems on his hands, made peace and withdrew from Scotland north of the Forth. The failure of Severus was caused by the same problems as beset Agricola. He initially forced the Maeatae to cede him territory, but that presumably involved the surrender of Fife, which constituted their richest land. A retreat to the high ground further north and the involvement of their powerful neighbours was inevitable, since the conquest of Fife and the building of a legionary fortress at Carpow on the Tay threatened the freedom of every barbarian magnate south of the Mounth. But Caracalla – like Agricola and Antoninus before him, and like Constantine after him – was in no position to invest the massive resources which the conquest of the barren highlands would demand, and the fortress at Carpow under construction in 212 was abandoned like Inchtuthil only three or four years later.

By the end of the third century (AD 297) we are introduced to the Picts (*Picti*) for the first time by Eumenius who associated them with Irish raiders (*Hiberni*) as enemies of the *Britanni*, and it is clear from a reference in 310 to 'the woods and marshes of the *Caledones* and other Picts', that the Caledonians were considered Pictish. Later in the fourth century, Ammianus Marcellinus confirms the Caledonian-Pictish connection by informing us in 368, that the Picts were divided into two people (*gentes*), the *Dicalydones* and the *Verturiones*. The first of these population names clearly incorporates the word *Caledonii* and the name *Verturiones* reappears in Dark Age Scottish sources as Fortriu (genitive *Fortrenn*), the name of a Pictish kingdom centred on Strathearn and Menteith which stretched from the upper waters of the Forth to the Tay, and included fortresses on Moncrieffe Hill and at Dundurn. This name *Fortriu* was used in several senses during the later Pictish period; it could signify Pictland as a whole or Pictland south of the Mounth, or it could be applied in a more restricted sense to the central and southern Pictish kingdom just described. In its more restricted sense it was synonymous with Strathearn, the heartland of the smaller kingdom. It would seem logical, too, to connect Fortriu with the tribal lands of the Maeatae. If Dio Cassius assures us that the names of all tribes beyond the wall had been merged into the names of the two greatest – Caledonians and Maeatae – and if a century and a half later we hear only of *Dicalydones* and *Verturiones*, it seems a reasonable assumption that *Maeatae* and *Verturiones* were in some way synonymous for a people who exercised overlordship south of the Mounth.

We could conclude from the statement of Ammianus in the fourth century that the *Verturiones* and Caledonians were Picts even if later Dark Age sources had never survived to identify the men of Fortriu as being Pictish. This leads us to the delicate and immensely complicated question as to what ancient writers meant by the word *Pict* in the first instance. The subject has been complicated by concepts introduced by linguists and archaeologists emphasizing distinctions between 'proto-Picts' , 'Picts', and *Priteni*, all of which deter the historian from entering a minefield of jargon and technical discussion. But the word 'Pict' is essentially an historical term, introduced by Classical writers and taken up by early medieval monastic scribes to describe an historical people from the period 300 to 900. It is the historian, therefore, who defines the term *Picti* and it is up to the linguist and archaeologist to see how language and material culture relate to that definition. The word *picti*, meaning 'painted people', was probably originally coined as a nickname by Roman soldiers, auxiliaries and *areani* who patrolled the northern frontier of Britain, and they applied this military slang to their barbarian enemies living north of the Forth and Clyde in *Caledonia* – the name of that region, incidentally, being vouched for by Tacitus as early as AD 80. The Romans called their enemies *Picti* almost certainly because they dyed or tattooed their skin, and the name stuck perhaps because of a vague likeness between it and *Priteni*, a name which the Picts were called by their Celtic neighbours if not by themselves. It seems clear that ancient writers used the word *Picti* in the loosest sense to signify those people living north of the Antonine Wall, and for those among them in particular who raided the empire. Thus, when Claudian speaks in 398 about Picts on *Thyle* (a vague word for the Northern Isles – perhaps Shetland) he can scarcely be blamed by us for imprecision. Claudian was being no more imprecise than the writer who 80 years before spoke vaguely of the 'woods and marshes' of the Picts. In other words, it is modern scholarship and not ancient writers who have invested the word *Pict* with an elaborate super-structure of argument and meaning which originally it was never intended to bear.

If we accept the word *Picti* in ancient sources to have a loose geographical meaning with reference to barbarian raiders living north of the Antonine Wall, then this puts the archaeological debate as to what is Pictish and what is not into a rather different perspective. It is not permissible on these grounds to assume that only areas covered by Pictish symbol stones, or by *pit* place-name elements, or even by both, are exclusively Pictish. It is quite pos-sible that people, say, on southern Skye, who did not carve stones and are not known to have had *pit* place-names, were just as 'Pictish' as anyone living in the mythical 'heartland' between the Moray Firth and the Forth. Of course the material cultures in archaeological terms may well have been different in eastern and western Scotland, but the historical evidence as we have it suggests that Roman writers regarded all these people as *Picti* regardless of archaeological culture and precise geographical location, provided they lived north of the Forth–Clyde isthmus in the Caledonia of Tacitus. It is just as silly to regard the people of Lewis, for instance, as living on the so-called 'Pictish periphery' as it would be to su g-gest that Munstermen in the tenth century were not fully Irish simply because they did not possess High Crosses, or that men of Somerset were not fully English in the eighth century because they did not share in that cultural milieu which produced the Book of Lindisfarne. But the terms 'English' and 'Irish' are used for Dark Age societies in the knowledge that despite local cultural diversifi-cation these two peoples had an overall identity determined by the language and culture of the warrior élite who ruled over them. When it comes to the Picts, however, things are different, because a school of thought which emphasizes the significant survival of non-Indo-European elements in Pictland would challenge the thesis that the Picts had a uniformly identifiable culture in the Roman period. This leads on in turn to a counter productive quest for the primeval dimension among the people north of the Antonine Wall.

There may well have been pre-Indo-European elements surviving in Pictish culture in the Roman period and later, but this was true of many remote regions in the British Isles. The crucial point at issue is whether the nickname *picti* as applied to the people north of the Antonine Wall was born of a Roman recognition that all or most of these people shared a common aristocratic culture in the same sense as the Britanni further south, or in the sense in which we speak of Anglo-Saxons in the later period. The emphasis must be on the culture of the aristocratic warrior élite, since ultimately this was the only class that mattered in historical sources, and it was the class which determined the dominant cultural flavour of the region at large. It was of course the warrior élite, led by such men as Calgacus and later by Argentocoxos, which raided the empire and was best known to the Romans.

A question which began life as an historical issue takes on a linguistic aspect as soon as we endeavour to show that the Picts were a Celtic or pre-Celtic people, because a people are Celtic solely on account of their Celtic speech, other 'Celtic' aspects of their culture being dependent on this linguistic criterion. Jackson concluded in 1955 that the language of the Picts was a P-Celtic Gallo-Brittonic dialect akin to Gaulish and to the language of the Britons further south. But Pictish was not identical with either Gaulish or Brittonic, and of course it was much further removed from the Q-Celtic language of the Irish Goidels. Jackson also confirmed the presence of a pre-Celtic element in Pictish which was non-Indo-European and which he believed was due to the survival of a pre-Celtic population and their speech in northern and eastern Scotland into the early Middle Ages. His emphasis on the significance of the pre-Celtic element in Pictish, was reached by way of a cumulative argument interwoven as a subsidiary theme to the main brunt of his epoch-making paper which dealt with identifying the Celtic element in Pictish as P-Celtic. When, however, we isolate the debate regarding the pre-Celtic element in Pictish from the nature of the agreed Celtic element proper, we find that the evidence for pre-Celtic survival does not stand up to close scrutiny.

Jackson's handling of Ptolemy's map of Scotland set the scene for his later conclusions. He asserted that out of 38 names on Ptolemy's map in the country north of the Damnonii and Votadini, only 16, or 42 per cent, were definitely Celtic. But he handled Ptolemy's data in a way which was bound to emphasize the pre-Celtic element, first by excluding the Celtic tribe of Epidii of

Kintyre from the list of tribes north of the Clyde, and secondly by limiting the analysis further to those tribes lying between the Moray Firth and the Forth. The Epidii were excluded from the debate on the grounds that their lands in south-western Argyll, in Kintyre and Islay, lay south of Dumbarton, and so were technically south of the Forth–Clyde line and in the domain of the Northern Britons. That was an assumption which goes against the accepted practice of regarding all lands to the north of the Forth and Clyde as being potentially Pictish or Proto-Pictish in the Roman period. It has always been assumed that Argyll was colonized by the Dál Riata Scots at the expense of the Picts, a point confirmed by Bede who believed also that Iona had been given to Columba by the Picts. There are, therefore, no grounds for excluding either the Celtic Epidii or their place-name *Epidium promontorium* (Mull of Kintyre) from the northern Scottish list, and their retention pushes the Celtic percentage up to 47. In fact the Celtic element may be much larger because Jackson seems to have excluded the Isles with such undoubtedly Celtic names as Orcades (Orkney), Dumna (Hebrides), Epidium (?Islay), as well as the Celtic probables, Malaius (Mull) and Scetis (Skye). In any event, all these statistics may be meaningless since they include names of natural features such as rivers which are likely to have retained their pre-Celtic names long after the language of origin had died.

Jackson next limited the field to what he identified as a 'Pictish heartland' between Moray Firth and the Forth, finding only one or two (*Bannatia* and *Devana*) Celtic names among the nine tribal and town names in that region. Of the four tribal names in this so-called heartland, while none of them can be proved to be Celtic, a case can be made for a Celtic origin for the Caledonii, Vacomagi and Taezali, while the fourth tribe, the Venicones, may well represent a misreading of Celtic *Verturiones* as O'Rahilly suggested. In view of mis-spellings and more serious technical errors in Ptolemy's map, it is dangerous to make a case for pre-Celtic nomenclature in the face of otherwise clearly identifiable Celtic forms. Even if the four tribal names in the 'heartland' were all pre-Celtic – and that is very unlikely – it does not prove either that the language spoken by the inhabitants of the north-east was pre-Celtic in the late first century AD or that the tribal rulers were not Celtic. Numerous Irish instances occur of tribal aristocracies taking over the names of older tribal territories they had conquered and with which they had no previous association. What is significant about the north-east, is that the Taezali – whose name may even be Celtic – who inhabited Buchan, were assigned to the Dee valley with their town at Devana. *Devana*, and its parent word *Deva* (river Dee), are thoroughly Celtic with similar examples of the place name occurring further south in Britain and Ireland. It would seem strange that an allegedly non-Indo-European people should inhabit a territory whose major river had a Celtic name – and river names, we recall, are one of the more conservative elements in the nomenclature of a landscape. We may use the same argument for the Celtic *Loxa* (either the river Lossie or the Findhorn) which flowed through the lands of the allegedly non-Celtic Vacomagi, whose territory may also have included the Celtic centre of *Bannatia*. Finally, the name *Caledonii*, one of the four names in the heartland, was probably not a tribal name at all, but a term with wide geographical and political associations, which embraced lands far to the west of the so-called heartland.

As for the heartland itself, its location is spurious, since it depends on a misunderstanding of distribution maps relating to Pictish place-names and to symbol stones. If we take the region covered by *pit* place-names as the criterion for a heartland, then we must extend the region to cover south-eastern Sutherland, Easter Ross, and the mainland opposite Skye. The same is true for P-Celtic place-name elements other than *pit*. If we are to take the Pictish symbol stones into account – which are agreed by all to be the most representative Pictish monument – then we must extend the heartland to include Caithness, Orkney, Shetland, the Outer Hebrides, Wester Ross and Skye. The only valid way to proceed is to include every area covered by features which are regarded as distinctively Pictish, but on no account may we ever exclude Easter Ross, and especially The Black Isle, since a true heartland of the Picts, if such we seek, lay north *and* south of the Moray Firth. The region where the symbol stones first came into being included those lands from Beauly to the Dornoch Firth, and this, significantly, was the home of the Decantae, Smertae, and Lugi, three tribes agreed by Jackson and others to have Celtic names with parallels in other parts of Britain, Ireland and Gaul. Further north in Caithness were the Cornavii, a thoroughly British name which occurs elsewhere on Ptolemy's map as the name of a British tribe in the English West Midlands, and on their northern coast lay the Tarvedum ('Bull-fort') promontory (Dunnet Head), once more a Celtic name, looking out on Celtic Orkney (Orcades), whose king, according to Adomnán, was subject to the Pictish overlord, Bridei, in the sixth century, and which has several Pictish symbol stones. Turning south and west Ptolemy listed four tribes between the Cornavii and the Firth of Clyde. Of these, the Carnonacae and Epidii were certainly Celtic, and the Caereni and Creones were very probably so.

If there is one definite conclusion we may reach about Ptolemy's map it is that the Pictish area included several tribes with thoroughly Celtic names related to other Celtic names elsewhere in the British Isles and in Gaul, and that *all* of Scotland and the Isles, north of the Forth and Clyde, had been permeated by Celtic speaking peoples before the end of the first century AD. Ptolemy's evidence proves nothing in regard to speculation about pre-Celtic survival: what it does prove is that regions which were regarded as Pictish from the fourth century to the ninth were already Celtic (and perhaps Gallo-Brittonic) by the first century. This is a crucial fact which must never be lost sight of in any discussion on the Picts, and in particular in any discussion of their aristocracy, which was best known to the Romans.

The next important body of evidence relating to the aristocratic warrior élite of northern Scotland is found in the names of barbarian magnates as found in Roman writers or on Roman inscriptions. When Agricola led the first Roman expedition north of the Tay in AD 83 he was confronted by a confederacy of Caledonian tribes whose outstanding leader was a certain Calgacus ('The Swordsman'). The name is Celtic, which suggests that the dominant tribal element which confronted Agricola in the north-east was a Celtic aristocracy – an assumption borne out by Tacitus's statement that apart from their red hair and large limbs the Caledonian Britons were no different from the rest of the Britons and their Gaulish neighbours, in language, ritual and religion. Had Tacitus been aware of any remarkable ethnographic differences between the wild Caledonians and the more southern Britons he would have most surely capitalized on those traits both for their curiosity value and to heighten the achievement of his hero, Agricola. But Tacitus was not aware of any exotic or bizarre element in the make-up of the Caledonians, and pictomania cannot be said to have begun with him. Dio Cassius, when describing the Severan campaign of c. AD 210 gives us the name of another Caledonian leader, Argentocoxos ('Silver Leg') whose Celtic name reminds us of the nickname of the Irish ancestor god, Nuadu Argatlám ('Nuadu Silver-Arm') who appears in the Romano-British pantheon as Nodens and whose temple was situated at Lydney Park in Gloucestershire. A Colchester inscription from the period 222–235 mentions a certain Caledonian, called Lossio Ueda, the grandson or descendant (*nepos*) of one Uepogenus. Once again the names both of this Caledonian and his ancestor are Celtic. The evidence from Classical writers is fragmentary in the extreme, but it is sufficient to prove the presence of a Celtic aristocracy among the Caledonians from the first to the third centuries. Clearly, this material is not sufficiently detailed to show the precise extent of Celtic influence north of the Antonine Wall, but equally, there is no hint in Classical sources for the survival of a pre-Celtic people ruled by their own pre-Celtic aristocracy.

When we reach the time of Adomnán, who wrote his *Life* of Columba in the late seventh century (describing events of the century before), we are again given fleeting glimpses of Pictish personalities who are mentioned by name. Adomnán shows that it was necessary for Goidelic speakers like Columba to use interpreters while conversing with some Picts at least, on Skye, but these language difficulties could easily be accounted for if the Picts spoke a Gallo-Brittonic dialect of Celtic. What is instructive is that Adomnán mentions some five people by name all of whom were most likely Pictish, and four of whose names were definitely Celtic. While the linguistic origin of King Bridei's (Bruide) Pictish name is in doubt, significantly, the name of his father, Maelchú, was certainly Celtic and the same is almost certainly true of his druid, Broichán. The sources with the most abundant supply of Pictish names are the various recensions of the Pictish king-lists, and the evidence from these is precisely the same as that which we gain from Ptolemy's map, namely, that while many names are definitely Celtic, others – in the words of Professor Jackson – 'are not clearly Celtic'. This is not to assume that all names not recognizably Celtic must be Pre-Celtic. Such assumptions are never warranted because names in the Pictish king-lists, even more than names on Ptolemy's map, have been transmitted through a garbled manuscript tradition.

Many of the names of kings who ruled according to the king-lists during the historical period from the sixth to the ninth centuries can be vouched for in other historical sources. Jackson has listed some nine instances of Celtic names in this historical section, but the majority of royal names in this section are in fact Celtic because some of them are repeated several times. As for the prehistoric section, this may have included a ragbag of improbable names from the beginning, and the poor quality of manuscript transmission renders detailed statistical analysis of doubtful value. On the other hand, several names in this section are not only demonstrably Celtic, but hark back to forms attested quite independently in Classical sources. The name of the Celtic and Caledonian magnate, *Uepogenus*, found on the early third-century Colchester inscription, may well lie behind the garbled form *Uipoig namet* in one version of the prehistoric king-lists. The name of the descendant of that Vepogenus on the Colchester inscription, Lossio Ueda, recurs in the early historical section of the king-lists in the form *Uuid* or *Wid* who fathered three Pictish kings, Gartnait, Bridei and Talorg, all of whom reigned in the second quarter of the seventh century. As for the historical Uuid, he may well be the same as *Gwid*, a leader mentioned in the *Gododdin* poem as an ally of the northern Britons in their struggle with the Angles of Bamburgh, at the opening of the seventh century. The timing is just right: the poem elsewhere implies the presence of Pictish allies in their attack on English Catterick, all of which is consistent with the thesis outlined here, that the Picts formed an integral part of the Celtic peoples of Northern Britain.

Yet another name in the prehistoric section of the Pictish king-lists is that of *Canutulachama*, regarded by Jackson as a 'non-Celtic' possibility, but even this name has recognizable Celtic elements, and was suggested by Chadwick to recall the name Cathanalachan son of Cathluan in the Pictish settlement legend in the Irish *Lebor Gabála* ('Book of Invasions'). Cathluan, who was alleged in medieval Irish legend to have founded the Pictish colony in Scotland, had a Brittonic name related to that of the Catuvellauni, a Celtic tribe located in Gaul and south-east England. Dr Marjorie Anderson has compared the name of another prehistoric Pictish king, Feredach Fingel, with Feredach Finn Fechtnach who appears in a Munster tract as king of Pictland (*Cruithentuath*). Not only are there recognizably Celtic names among the mangled lists of prehistoric Pictish kings, but some of these names also support the case for a Gallo-Brittonic origin for the Caledonian Britons, as in the case of Tarain, a name found among historical and legendary Pictish rulers who were probably called after Taranis, the Gaulish thunder god. Finally there is a king, Ciniod son of Artcois, in the prehistoric section of the lists. The name *Ciniod*, like several others in this section, is found later on as a name for historical Pictish kings, but the name of his father, Artcois, ('Bear leg') is even more interesting since it recalls that of Argentocoxos ('Silver leg'), the Caledonian chief who negotiated with the Romans during the Severan wars.

It is necessary to emphasize the overall Celtic nature of the names of tribes and individuals living between the Forth and the Northern Isles during the Roman period in order not only to counter the pre-Celtic argument but also to explore the relationship between Calgacus and his Caledonians in the time of Tacitus and the Picts of later centuries. It seems inappropriate for historians to adopt the jargon of archaeology and to describe the Caledonian chieftain, Argentocoxos, as a 'proto-Pict'. The very people whom Argentocoxos ruled are described as Picts only a century after his time, when it was not possible for any new non-Celtic invaders to have reached the Pictish region in the meantime. The name of this chieftain, and others from his time, as we have seen, are not only Celtic, but contain elements which recur in names favoured by Pictish kings in later Dark Age king-lists. If it seems reasonable to describe Argentocoxos as a Pict, then the same would seem true for the Caledonian leader, Calgacus, who fought against Agricola. The process of projection backwards is not open-ended, since the historical record of the Caledonians only begins with Tacitus. The first time the term *Picti* was used was, as Marjorie Anderson reminded us, in an anachronistic sense. In 297, a panegyrist compared the struggle between the emperor Constantius and his rival Allectus with the easier struggle between Julius Caesar and the Britons who were accustomed to enemies such as the *Picti* and *Hiberni*. In other words, the writer assumed the Picts had always existed in Britain back to the time of Caesar. The assumption is entirely justified by the evidence as we have it, and it is quite logical for historians to treat Caledonian leaders throughout the Roman period as Picts, provided it is understood that this Roman nickname, not attested earlier than 297, was used in a loose geographical and political sense to describe all barbarian Celtic tribes living north of the Forth–Clyde isthmus beyond the frontier of the Roman province.

Does it then follow from this historical argument that archaeologists may now describe an artifact or monument as Pictish even if it dates to earlier than the late third century? Provided it is found outside Dál Riata in the south-west, but otherwise between the Forth and Shetland, and provided it can be shown to be of native manufacture, then an artifact is Pictish in so far as it belonged to the historical Picts in the period AD 80–850. This is not to diminish in any way the undoubted problems facing archaeologists in trying to establish chronological sequences and precise lines of inter-relationship between material cultures within Pictland.. The fact that the broch builders who flourished from the age of Agricola to Severus were confined to the Isles and to the north and west of the Scottish mainland, while the builders of timber-laced and vitrified forts (which had a much longer life) were confined to the east and south-west, clearly suggests diverse cultural streams among the Picts which may well have political implications. But let not this important division impinge on any argument relating to the bogey of non-Indo-European survival. As far as historical documentation is concerned, no case can be made for a substantial political or linguistic distinction between the Picts of the north-west and those of the south-east. If archaeologists recognize such divisions then they must not reserve the term *Pictish* for any one of them, for that is investing a loose historical label with a restricted meaning which it was never originally intended to bear.

Even on strictly archaeological grounds, the difference between brochs and vitrified forts is culturally not at all great. Brochs and vitrified forts both ultimately derive from a common Celtic ring-fort or hill-fort ancestry. Their use of different building materials was initially, at least, due to the availability of stone, timber and earth for the construction of defences. The brochs are in essence an aberrant form of the stone cashels and cathairs of Ireland and of related Celtic Iron Age stone forts in north-western Spain. The stone fort in turn is a variant of the ring-fort with earthen ramparts, of which the *murus gallicus* technique is a further development. In short, while the distribution of brochs and vitrified forts may well point to cultural and even political divisions among the Picts of the first century, the common origin of both these forms in the Hallstatt and La Tène Celtic Iron Age supports the evidence already gleaned from Ptolemy and elsewhere regarding the essentially Celtic nature of the Pictish aristocracy.

The argument that the mutual exclusiveness of brochs and vitri-fied forts pointed to wider cultural differences among the Picts has been further undermined by the discovery that vitrified forts have had a much longer life in Scotland than the brochs. The vitrified and timber-laced forts have a chronological range from the eighth century BC to the end of the Pictish historical period. Timber-lacing, a characteristic of pre-Roman Celtic forts in Gaul, has been identified at such forts as Craig Phadraig, Burghead and Port-knockie, on the Moray Firth, and at Dundurn in Strathearn. We can be certain that all of these forts were occupied by the historical Picts – archaeological and historical evidence all support that conclusion. This shows that the Celtic *murus gallicus* had become an integral part of Pictish fortifications in eastern Pictland by the historical period. Alcock has suggested that the arrival of the builders of these Celtic timber-laced forts early in the first millenium BC may have provided the dominant aristocratic ingredient which, as it blended with indigenous cultures, produced the characteristics of Pictish society. If we add to that dominant element the later arrival of broch builders in the west, we arrive at a reasonable and accurate assessment of Pictish society as the early Romans encountered it. It consisted of an indigenous servile population ruled by a warrior Celtic aristocracy whose origins may have lain in different parts of the wider Celtic world, but whose essential cultural unity was sufficiently self-evident to draw from Tacitus the comment that these northern Britons were basically no different from their cousins in the south and further afield in Gaul.

Archaeologists have been reluctant to describe the brochs as 'Pictish' for the understandable reason that their relatively short lifespan from the last century BC to the second century AD placed them technically outside the period of contemporary usage of the word *picti*. If we accept the broch as a structure closely related to Celtic stone forts elsewhere then it follows that it was part of the cultural milieu of the Celtic Priteni of north-western Scotland in the period 100 BC – 200 AD . The existence of these Celtic tribes is vouched for independently by the presence of the Cornavii, Smertae and Lugi on Ptolemy's map. All three tribes were Celtic, and they occupied Caithness and Sutherland where the distribution of contemporary brochs is densest. To deny that the brochs were Pictish would seem to deny the title also to these Celtic tribes, and yet it was precisely the tribal aristocracy from these and related Celtic peoples in Caledonia which were described as *Picti* by Roman writers from the third century. The real archaeological problem relating to brochs does not centre on the question of their genuine Pictish status – for that in itself means far less than scholars have hitherto liked to believe – but why these impregnable forts were built in the first instance, and why they were abandoned so soon. It may be that given the great density of brochs in Caithness in particular, future excavation will show that these monuments continued in use into the fourth century and beyond. Documentation on early broch excavations is poor and much more work still needs to be done.

On present evidence it would appear that brochs were replaced in the middle of the second century by more modest circular stone-built dwellings, known as aisled round houses and wheel houses, sometimes built on the site of derelict or modified brochs and sometimes in isolation from them. The brochs and later round houses of the north and west were contemporary with a class of dwellings spread over Angus and parts of Kincardineshire and Fife, consisting of a surface building with bicellular or figure-of-eight form associated with a souterrain or large underground stone-lined chamber. Whatever the precise function of the souterrain, whether used for storage, defence, or for shelter for men and animals, the technique of souterrain building, despite the variety of form, is again essentially part of the Celtic Iron Age in the British Isles. The souterrain in various forms occurs right across eastern and north-western Scotland, and is also found in Ireland, sometimes apparently in isolation, but more usually in association with a farmstead or fort. The survival of the souterrain long after the destruction of its associated surface dwelling has caused some distortion in assessing its significance in the archaeological record. The souterrain was essentially a specialized adjunct to the more important surface building.

The radial plan of the round houses of the north and north-west may not be too far removed from the axial layout of the souterrain houses of Angus, and Leslie Alcock has stressed the important connection between the two types in the plan of the Buckquoy house on mainland Orkney excavated by Anna Ritchie. In this structure, several house forms within the early Pictish province blend together in a way which suggests an underlying material cultural unity despite so much apparent local variation. The figure-of-eight farmstead at Carlungie in Angus was occupied by a people who lived during the Severan age, while the oval house with adjoining circular cell chambers at Coilegean an Udail on North Uist dates from the later Pictish period. The variation in design of these buildings does not necessarily mean that their occupants came from widely differing cultural or ethnic backgrounds. Such variation may be due to long-established tribal custom, combined with a local response to availability of building materials and the demands of a harsh northern climate. The tradition of cellular building, whether laid out radially or axially, and the semi-subterranean siting of many houses in the north and west is connected with a need to conserve heat and afford shelter from winter gales, while the inevitable use of dry-stone walling in regions which were almost treeless put severe limits on the options open to builders. This is not to deny that deeply rooted well tried local techniques in building going back to the Neolithic cultures of Skara Brae may not still have had an influence on the dwellings of the Picts. Nobody pretends that the indigenous Neolithic and Bronze Age population of Scotland could have been wiped out by their Celtic overlords, given the demographic necessity to retain a servile population and given the complexity and natural protection afforded by the inaccessible Scottish terrain.

Dark Age fortifications are the exclusive hallmark of the warrior aristocracy, and it is the forts of the Picts, not their farmsteads, that tell us most about the dominant class in ancient Caledonia with whom the Roman armies came into conflict. Significantly, the multivallate timber-laced promontory fort at Burghead, although an obviously late La Tène fortress of a Celtic tribe, was not initially associated by archaeologists with the Picts, because structures such as this occurring in the so-called Pictish heartland on the Moray Firth were considered intrusive in an otherwise pre-Celtic region. Yet this Celtic timber-laced fortress and another at Portknockie, also in the territory of Ptolemy's *Taezali*, may, according to recent archaeological opinion, have been built by and were certainly occupied by the historical Picts, perhaps as late as the seventh century. The fact that seventh-century Pictish warlords ruled from Celtic fortresses on Burghead and Portknockie whose building techniques went back into the Scottish Iron Age of the eighth century BC is entirely consistent with the existence of Celtic names for the rivers Lossie and Dee, already recorded by the end of the first century AD. In other words, Pictland, including its heartlands, had been Celtic since documentation began, and there is little doubt that archaeology will prove in time that Calgacus and his charioteers ruled from the timber-laced and nucleated forts of eastern Scotland.

The evidence which Scottish forts provide for the presence of Celtic warlords all over prehistoric Scotland can be supplemented and confirmed by the more fragmentary historical record relating to aristocratic Pictish culture. An important observation by ancient writers on the military organization of the Caledondians relates to their use of chariots. Chariots were part of the common inheritance of the Indo-European warrior élite. They figured prominently among continental and insular Celts, and their mention not only in Irish sagas but in historical accounts suggest that they survived in Ireland as part of the royal paraphernalia up to the eighth century. Tacitus describes chariots in the van of the Caledonian army at *Mons Graupius*, and Dio Cassius vouches for the continued use of horse-drawn chariots in Roman battles with the Caledonians and Maeatae about AD 200. Such accounts do not prove that the armies of the ancestors of the Picts were Celtic, but they do show that massed armies of the Caledonian warrior élite were organized in a way that was wholly characteristic of Celtic warriors elsewhere at that time. Similarly, the argument that the name *picti* developed from a nickname for a 'painted people' who dyed or tattooed their bodies, fits in well with what little we know of the southern *Britanni* who also practised this art before the Roman conquest of Britain. The very name *Picti*, then suggests that the Picts were either a survival of barbarian British culture beyond the borders of Rome, or they represented a more archaic segment of British tribes (the Priteni) whose remote geographical location promoted both the survival of archaic Celtic customs (chariot warfare, tattooing, and the like) and independence of Rome.

Sadly, Dark Age Scottish chronicles tell us little of Pictish customs, and all too much about unidentified battle grounds, but what little information we are given is sometimes specific enough to confirm the Celtic origin of what is described. Marjorie Anderson, for instance, compared the drowning of a Pictish tribal king, Talorgen, by his overlord, Óengus, in 739 with ritual drownings in pagan Gaul. There are even closer parallels with ninth-century Ireland, where the Uí Néill highking, Maelsechnaill, executed one of his sub-kings by drowning him 'in a dirty stream' in 851 and there were other Irish examples too. Adomnán describes sacred wells and the possible connection between Pictish druids and a bull cult in pagan Pictland – all of which would have been quite at home in Dark Age Ireland. Taken on their own, none of these items from the manuscript records appear to add up to much, but when viewed in the light of evidence from aristocratic and tribal names and the archaeology of the forts, they do help to confirm the fundamentally Celtic nature of aristocratic Pictish society.

How does this assessment of Picts being essentially a Celtic warrior aristocracy fit in with the long-cherished notion that succession to their kingship was matrilinear? It is this allegedly non-Celtic element in Pictish culture which has underpinned the argument for a pre-Celtic language and for the exotic nature of Picts as a whole. We have already dealt with the linguistic evidence for aristocratic and tribal names, but we must turn finally to the two dozen odd inscriptions which are believed to be written in a non-Indo-European language. Even if the language of the inscriptions were pre-Celtic it would not undermine the case for the Pictish aristocracy being Celtic, since there are numerous examples from Dark Age and medieval Europe of barbarian warlords retaining a dynastic hold over a conquered people while adopting in part at least the language of the servile population. The case for a pre-Celtic language lurking behind these inscriptions is not proven. Many of the inscriptions are agreed to be illegible due to careless inscribing and later weathering, and the number of clearly legible inscriptions is not sufficient to provide a corpus which would identify the nature of the language beyond doubt.

There is, however the important fact that in addition to two inscriptions in Hiberno-Latin script, all of the material is presented in Irish ogham letters clearly imported from the Columban west. The Gaelic word *maqq* or *meqq* ('son of') found in several inscriptions also has a Dál Riata origin. It seems perverse to argue that this Gaelic word was borrowed into Pictish, because being a matrilinear society the Picts had no word to express 'son of a father'. Societies only borrow into a language those elements for which they have a cultural need, and if the Picts were truly matrilinear they would never have chosen to set up monuments naming unimportant fathers. Besides, they would presumably have had their own pre-Celtic word for 'son' since even Pictish matriarchs clearly had male offspring. We find too, that other northern Britons, Adomnán, and Irish chroniclers, as well as compilers of Pictish king-lists, all give Pictish royal names in a patrilinear form, as for example 'Bridei son of Máelchu'. Now in a supposedly matrilinear society, fathers are either unknown or unimportant, their place being taken for matters of identification and descent by mothers and sisters. Yet we find that the Picts used the Irish term 'son of' on their own inscriptions; that royal Pictish fathers were known to all their northern British neighbours and even to distant Irish chroniclers, and finally, that there is not one certain instance of the mother or sister of a Pictish king being named in any of the sources. This is surely a compelling argument for a radical reappraisal of the matrilinear thesis.

Basically, the whole matrilinear phenomenon rests on three supposedly unshakable supports. The first is a medieval Irish origin legend for the Picts which states in summary that they originally acquired their womenfolk from the Irish on condition that Pictish kingship should pass through the female line. The second argument is based on the recognition that one seventh-century Pictish king, Talorgen, had an Anglo-Saxon father, while another, Bridei, was the son of a Strathclyde Briton – thereby demonstrating matrilinear succession in action. The third argument is based on the valid observation that before *c*. 780 no Pictish king can be seen to be the son of another king in the king-lists. The implication of this last point is that the sons who succeeded to kingship were drawn from a lineage different from that based on a patrilinear system, and taken alongside the evidence from Irish legend would seem to confirm a matrilinear succession from the mother through a mother's son, or through a sister's son.

The legend – and it is no more than legend – of the coming of the Picts to northern Britain involves an understanding of the relationship between the words *Picti* and *Cruithin*. The Pretanic Isles, so named by the geographer Pytheas in the late fourth century BC , are related linguistically to the name *Pritani* which came to be applied to the inhabitants of Britain. A variant form *Priteni* may have been used for northern Britons, and all forms may mean 'the people of the shapes or designs', a reference to the way in which the Celtic inhabitants of Britain painted their bodies. The Welsh word *Prydain* ('Britain') and the Middle Welsh *Prydyn* ('Picts') derive from *Pritani* and *Preteni* respectively. As the Romans tightened their grip on the Celts of southern Britain, a new word *Britanni* or *Brittones* came to be used for the Romano-Britains, and their Roman Province was called *Britannia* deriving from a Latin corruption of *Pritani*. The Irish also knew of the *Priteni* not only as neighbours in northern Scotland, but as a people settled in various parts of Ireland whom they described as *Cruithin* (or *Cruithni*) – a Goidelic or Old Irish form of the word *Priteni*. It is important to recognize that the Irish Cruithin were believed in Irish tradition to be essentially the same people as the Priteni of northern Britain and *in that sense* they were rightly considered Picts.

Much has been made of the fact that Adomnán and other Irish writers never refer to the Irish Cruithin as *Picti* – the Irish group being invariably referred to as *Cruithin*. Consequently, we are told by linguists we must abandon all talk of Irish Picts. That may well be true, but not because medieval writers believed the *Cruithin* and *Picti* were a different people. The word *Picti*, as we have seen, had a politico-geographical connotation, meaning the barbarians of Britain north of the Antonine Wall. We, therefore, cannot call the Irish Cruithin 'Picts', simply because they did not live in northern Britain. But we can certainly think of them as being basically of the same stock as the Picts since as *Cruithin* they were known in Ireland literally as 'The People from Northern Britain'. We speak today of Normans in England without raising a pedantic storm about the distinction between Anglo-Normans and Normans in the Normandy homeland. Obsessions with terminology must not obscure the essential unity which existed between the Irish Cruithin and their cousins the Picts in northern Britain. How better is this exemplified than by the frequent references in Irish sources to the Picts of Scotland as Cruithin? In other words, if linguists insist that we do not speak of Irish Picts, then we most certainly may speak of the Picts as Scottish Cruithin! In short, it is very wrong to hold that medieval writers believed the Irish Cruithin had nothing to do with the Picts.

All this has an important bearing on Bede's legend about how the Picts arrived from Scythia and landed in northern Ireland, where they were refused land by the Irish and eventually seized land in northern Britain. The Picts then, we are told, sought wives from the Irish who agreed to hand over their women only on condition that the Picts should choose their kings from the female and not from the male line whenever the succession was in doubt. Bede clearly got his legend from an Irish source, and Irish versions of this tale about the origin of the Cruithin of northern Britain turn up in modified but much more extended form from the late ninth century onwards. The major difference in Irish accounts is that the bargain in wife giving involved the adoption of matrilinear succession by Picts without anything of the qualification specified in Bede. Bede's version which is, after all, the oldest, does not describe matrilinear succession as such. Indeed, Bede describes a custom in use in his own day which only involved female succession in exceptional circumstances. Some crucial features of this tale have too often been overlooked. Firstly, this is not a Pictish origin tale, but an origin tale foisted on the Picts by the Irish. Professor Duncan rightly recognized that the central point of the legend contains an Irish propaganda piece setting out Irish rights regarding Pictish settlement in Scotland and Irish rights regarding Pictish kingship. Bede's reference to that part of Britain 'which we [the Irish] often see in the distance on clear days' can only refer to the Mull of Kintyre, and betrays a Dál Riata, if not indeed an Iona origin for the whole story.

This legend was already old in Bede's day, and if it tells us anything at all, it shows that already by the end of the seventh century the Scots of Dál Riata were making dynastic and territorial claims on Pictland. This conclusion does not conflict with other findings we shall reach on similar Dumbarton and Northumbrian ambitions regarding the overkingship of the Picts in the sixth and seventh centuries. The Irish reference to matrilinear practices among the Picts may well be an oversimplification of Bede's brief but more exact account, but both versions of the legend are simply an Irish attempt to bolster contemporary Scottish claims on the Pictish kingship which had evolved through centuries of expansion and encouraged by centuries of inter-tribal marriage between the two kingdoms. This legend, unless substantiated by verifiable examples of matrilinear succession in practice in the historical period, cannot possibly be used as historical evidence. If we admit this, then so also must we admit a wealth of other legendary material relating to 30 kings of the Picts who ruled over Ireland and Scotland, and the seven kings of the Scottish Picts who ruled over Ireland from Tara.

Let us now look at two kings in the Pictish king-lists who are agreed to have come from outside Pictland. The earliest of these two rulers was Talorgen son of Enfret, the father being identified with Eanfrith son of Ethelfrith, king of Northumbria (593–617). Eanfrith went into exile among the Picts in 617 and returned as king of Bernicia in 633–4 when he was slain. The matrilinear school would argue that Eanfrith fathered a son, Talorgen, on a Pictish princess while staying in or visiting Pictland; and eventually, that son succeeded to Pictish kingship by virtue of his mother's lineage. Unfortunately the circumstances surrounding the reign of this king are so special that his rule in Pictland cannot be used to prove the matrilinear thesis. The evidence as we have it strongly suggests that Talorgen was chosen as a puppet king by his uncle Oswiu of Northumbria during a period of Northumbrian domination in southern Pictland. In other words, Talorgen ruled, not by virtue of matrilinear claims as such, but by virtue of his standing as the son of Oswiu's brother. Kirby has reminded us that after his victory over the Mercians at *Winwaed* in *c.* 654 Oswiu was free to concentrate on northern Britain. He is alleged by Bede to have subdued the 'greater part of the Pictish race', and by 669, his bishop, Wilfrid, was described as bishop of the Northumbrians and also of the Picts as far as Oswiu's overlordship extended. It makes at least as much sense to accept that Talorgen's accession to the Pictish kingship in 653 was part of Oswiu's policy of expansion and domination in northern Britain, as it does to hold it came about by a matrilinear system of succession. Kirby has reminded us also that on the death of Talorgen in 657, Oswiu may have begun an offensive against the Picts and that he may have forced an interregnum on the kingdom in the period 663–6 – that very time when as we shall see, Oswiu's bishop, Wilfrid, was victorious in pushing the claims of the Roman (and Anglo-Saxon) Church in northern Briton at the Synod of Whitby. A successor to Talorgen, called Drest, emerged as king of the Picts in 665–6, but he was expelled in 672. As far back as 1922, A.O. Anderson accepted that Drest was yet another of Oswiu's puppets who proved unacceptable to the Picts who promptly expelled him after the Northumbrian overlord died in 670.

It was almost certainly at this point that the second of the 'non-Pictish' kings of the Picts, Bridei son of Bili, entered the stage. He appears in the Pictish king-lists as the successor to Drest, and he is called in a very early poem, attributed to Adomnán 'the son of the king of Dumbarton', a title which identifies him as the son of Bili son of Neithon, king of the Strathclyde Britons. Bridei's brother, Owen (Eugein), ruled the Dumbarton Britons *c.* 645, and at the time when Bridei assumed the kingship of the Picts, Dumbarton was probably ruled by his nephew, Donald son of Owen, who died about 694. It seems logical to accept that the Picts took advantage of Oswiu's death in 670–1 to expel his puppet, Drest, in the following year, and that this show of spirit in southern Pictland drew a swift and terrible response from the new Northumbrian king, Ecgfrith. Eddius in his *Life* of Wilfrid shows us, that Ecgfrith was goaded on by bishop Wilfrid who saw in the loss of Northumbrian *imperium* north of the Forth a diminution of his own ecclesiastical overlordship. Hence Eddius's lurid tale of the 'bestial tribes of the Picts' swarming like ants 'to protect their tottering house' and being reduced yet again to slavery by Ecgfrith's terror and the alleged powers of Wilfrid, to whom the king and his queen were then 'obedient in all things'.

The true significance of the reign of Bridei son of Bili may well have been lost in the welter of comment on his rôle as yet another son of a foreign ruler who succeeded to the Pictish kingship through his mother. In Bridei's case, we have no proof whatever that he had a Pictish mother. The genealogies attached to the *Historia Brittonum* refer to Bridei as the *fratruelis* or 'cousin' of Ecgfrith of Northumbria, a reference which has invariably been taken to mean that Bridei was related to Ecgfrith through the Pictish mother of Talorgen son of Eanfrith. There is no reason why Ecgfrith's relationship with Bridei had to pass via Eanfrith, through a supposed Pictish mother of Bridei. The same Welsh source also informs us that Ecgfrith's father, Oswiu, had married Riemmelth, the daughter of Royth, a chieftain of the British house of Rheged. It is equally probable that Oswiu's father, Ethelfrith of Northumbria, had married into the powerful dynasty of Strathclyde. Such a marriage would just as easily account for the cousinly relationship between Ecgfrith and Bridei as any special pleading for a Pictish matrilinear connection. (See Table 2)

The Old Irish verse attributed to Adomnán states that Bridei was 'the son of the king of Dumbarton'. The key to Bridei's authority, then, lay in the fact that he was the son of Bili Neithons's son, king of the Strathclyde Britons, and that his brother, Owen (Eugein), was that powerful Strathclyde king who slew Domnall Brecc, king of Scots Dál Riata, in the battle of Strathcarron about 642. That battle marked a serious decline in the affairs of the Scots kingdom, which, ever since the reign of Áedán mac Gabhráin in the late sixth century, had established itself in south-west Scotland as a serious competitor for the domination of all northern Britain. Domnall Brecc's own mistakes combined with the power of Owen of Strathclyde brought a long pause in the expansion of Dál Riata. Equally, Owen's victory must have elevated Strathclyde to being the premier kingdom in the north, since Pictland was falling more and more under the influence of Northumbria. Abbot Cumméne of Iona informs us that the successors of Domnall Brecc in Dál Riata fell under the domination of strangers. The first of these 'strangers', at least, must have been the Strathclyde Britons since it was the warband of Owen, after all, which toppled Domnall Brecc. The rise of Owen's brother, Bridei, can be viewed in the context of the massacre of the Pictish army by Ecgfrith *c.* 672, which must have left the southern Picts deviod of leadership and men. The Pictish collapse must also have held out an irresistible temptation to the

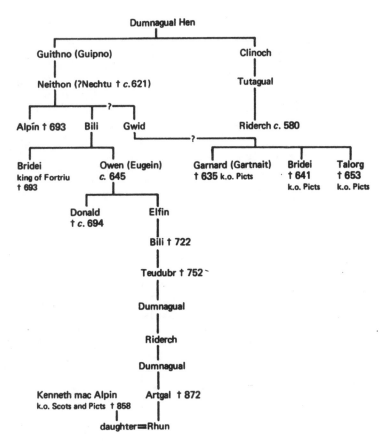

2 Kings of the Strathclyde Britons

Strathclyde Britons to assume the overlordship of that neighbouring Celtic people.

A poem describing Bridei as fighting 'for the inheritance of his grandfather' in the battle of *Nechtanesmere* suggests that unlike Ecgfrith, Bridei had some hereditary claim in Pictland. The matrilinear argument has again bedevilled this issue by drawing scholars' attention away from matters we know into the genealogical nightmare which we do not. We do know the name of Bridei's paternal grandfather, Neithon son of Guithno (or Guipno) whose name is found in the genealogy of Strathclyde, and the death of whose son Alpín is recorded by the *Annals of Tigernach* in 693 alongside that of Bridei son of Bili. The association of uncle and nephew in the same entry in the Irish annals is significant, and Alpín may, like Bridei, have held power in a southern Pictish kingdom. Neithon would have flourished as a Dumbarton ruler in the first quarter of the seventh century, and remarkably the Pictish king-lists show a *Nectu nepos Uerb* who has hitherto been doubtfully identified with a Nechtan who died, according to the *Annals of Ulster*, in 621. The Pictish king of this name would seem to have reigned from *c.* 600 to 630, and it is quite possible that he was none other than Neithon of Dumbarton with whom he was certainly contemporary.

Three of Neithon's successors in the Pictish overlordship were the three sons of a certain *Uuid* who ruled consecutively from 631 to 653 as the contemporaries of the powerful Owen of Strathclyde. Remarkably, their father, may well be the same person as *Gwid* who turns up in the *Gododdin* poem as a leader associated with the warband of Mynyddog of Edinburgh *c.* 600. This Gwid was either a northern British chief related to the Gododdin of Lothian or else he was a southern Pict – a distinction, incidentally, which is no longer so important in view of the essentially British Celtic make-up of the Pictish aristocracy. Gwid's father is named in the British poem as *Peithan* – a curious piece of information offered by the poet Aneirin, if indeed Gwid were a 'pre-Celtic Pict' whose father's name ought to be unknown or unimportant. It is possible that Gwid son of Peithan originally read as *Gwid son of Neithon* – i.e. the son of Neithon of Strathclyde – which would make the three sons of Gwid who ruled Pictland in the mid-sixth century no less than the first cousins of Bridei son of Bili. Such an hypothesis would hold that princes of the house of Neithon of Strathclyde were the true over-lords of southern Pictland in the seventh century, and that their position there was seriously challenged by the expanding North-umbrian rulers to the south-east.

We know that the kingdom of Gododdin survived the disaster at Catterick at *c.* 600, and that it was not until *c.* 640 in the reign of Oswald that the Northumbrians pushed forward to the Forth. I have suggested that their frontier with northern Britain rested near the present boundary of Mid and West Lothian. Abercorn would then have been set up as a frontier outpost to monitor the Britons and Picts of Manaw and beyond, and its new Anglian bishop would ensure the channelling of Northumbrian influence among the

Pictish clergy and their aristocracy. That, at least, was the hope of the Bernicians, but we may reasonably speculate that it was not the hope either of the Picts or of the Dumbarton Britons, who in nearby Strathcarron in 642 had put an end to Dál Riatan hopes of moving into the vacuum created by the collapse of the kingdom of Gododdin. We appear to be faced with a power struggle for the immediate control and occupation of the strategically crucial plain between Stirling and Edinburgh, in which the leading contenders were the Dumbarton Britons, Dál Riata, and the Bernicians, while Gododdin and Pictland proper were more passively involved. Whoever won control of east Stirlingshire would automatically dominate the southern Picts, and the evidence as we have it may suggest that Neithon of Strathclyde and his grandsons, the sons of Gwid, imposed their overlordship on southern Pictland in the early seventh century. Then Oswiu, whose Northumbrian dynasty had inched its way over East Lothian, succeeded in imposing his nephew, Talorgen, on southern Pictland, and this Anglo-Saxon intervention eventually triggered off a major Pictish revolt which was ruthlessly quashed by Ecgfrith in *c.* 672. The struggle continued, however, and Bridei son of Bili succeeded in rallying the Picts in the cause of the 'inheritance of his grandfather' and induced them to revert to Dumbarton overlordship. This hypothesis has the major advantage of explaining why Ecgfrith, against good advice from Cuthbert and others, set out on a second distant expedition into Pictland in 685. Clearly, a crisis had developed within that region which called for his urgent intervention – a crisis which can best be explained not by matrilinear succession, but by recognizing that Dumbarton had once more imposed a king on the Picts. The result was a disaster for Ecgfrith who fell along with the flower of his Northumbrian warriors at Dunnichen Moss (*Nechtanesmere*) in 685. It was a major triumph for Bridei, who stopped the northern English war machine dead in its tracks; drove the English warriors back across Stirling and West Lothian, and made it plain that no Anglian bishop who stood for the political intrigues of Wilfrid and his party would be welcome any more at Abercorn. For although Wilfrid had been discredited and exiled from the Northumbrian court by 685, there is no reason to believe that the expansionist policies of the Northumbrian church did not still coincide with Ecgfrith's military ambition.

Those 'Men of the North' ought not, after all, be relegated to a twilight world of heroic but hopeless deeds at Catterick and

Bamburgh. They may have been of much more consequence than we have hitherto believed, since it was the Strathclyde Britons who through Bridei mac Bili, successfully rallied the Picts and perhaps also the shattered warband of Gododdin into finally halting the Anglo-Saxon advance into northern Britain. Similarly, it was Bridei's brother, Owen, who dealt a body blow to Dál Riata, a Gaelic dynasty eager since the time of Áedán mac Gabhráin to expand into the Scottish lowlands. While Áedán was repulsed by the Northumbrian Ethelfrith at Degsastan back in 603, significantly, it was Owen of Strathclyde who acted as guardian of the Forth–Clyde isthmus in 642. It may well be, as Dumville has suggested, that early Welsh literature has created its own false horizons in its emphasis on the desperate heroism of those Britons who fought the Angles and lost, and on telescoping all of those events into the age of Urien and his circle back at c. 600. In the late seventh century the Dumbarton Britons were still at the head of a formidable warband and could lead a confederacy of Pictish and British tribes to successfully fight off pressure from both Scots and Angles.

The evidence which suggests that Strathclyde held the overkingship of the Picts in the seventh century should be assessed against a similar conclusion which A.O. Anderson reached in regard to the Strathclyde king, Teudubr son of Beli, who died in 752. Anderson concluded that during the last two years of his reign, Teudubr succeeded in ousting Oengus son of Fergus as overlord of the Picts, when the Strathclyde Britons defeated the Picts in battle and slew two brothers of Óengus. Yet Óengus son of Fergus was one of the most powerful Pictish kings on record, who had fought his way to overlordship in Pictland and overthrew the Scots of Dál Riata. All this suggests that historians have underestimated the strength and importance of the British kingdom on the Clyde.

We come now, finally, to that third major argument in favour of the matrilinear theory, namely the fact that no king in the king-lists before the time of Talorgen son of Onuist in the 780s appears to have had a father who was king of the Picts. This argument raises a question, which has never been properly faced, as to precisely what sort of kingship is listed in the Pictish sources. To understand just what Pictish kingship might have entailed we may very usefully compare the contemporary situation within Leinster, a self-contained province like Pictland with a confederacy of tribes belonging, as did the Picts, to an essentially Celtic aristocracy. While there was a king or overlord of all the Leinstermen there was no tribe of Leinstermen as such. The Leinstermen consisted of some 35 tribes some six of whom were strong enough to compete for the kingship of the province. While overlordship was largely a ceremonial and prestige affair, it did manifest itself in more tangible form in the overlord's ability to extract tribute and hostages from his tribal kings; to demand their presence on military expeditions and at assemblies; and to defend the province from attack. It would be a very rare thing for a provincial overlord to be in full possession of the loyalties of all his vassal kings at any one time, but there was nevertheless a sufficient degree of cohesion and recognition to enable him to be classed as 'king of the Leinstermen' by the annalists, and for his name to appear in Leinster king-lists. Other king-lists have survived in Leinster, however, to show that records were also kept for local tribal succession. There is in addition the most impressive collection of early Irish genealogies in western Europe, showing just how the tribal aristocracies intermeshed in any one generation. There is also a corpus of material known as the *Ban-Senchus* ('*The Lore on Women*') – a collection of genealogies of royal ladies, constructed within a rigid patrilinear system, but showing the economic and ritual importance of women in dynastic marriages. This interest in female descent suggests a strong cognatic element in Celtic royal succession – an element not to be confused with the matrilinear bogey.

Let us now apply such a model to kingship in Pictland. The fact that only one king-list survives does not mean that other tribal lists were not taken or that tribal kingship was unknown. All the evidence suggests that tribal kingship of a Celtic sort was alive and well in Pictland into the ninth century. We may begin with Ptolemy's list of tribes, in the knowledge that he did not list them all. Later additions from other sources, such as the Boresti of Tacitus and the Verturiones and Maeatae of later Classical writers, are very unlikely to represent the sum total of tribes in a country where geography conspired to consolidate tribalism and tribal loyalties. If the Maeatae and Verturiones were able to preserve their identity on the exposed lowlands until the sixth century and later, it is even more likely that tribes of the far north and west survived even longer up to the Viking Age. Pictland, like Leinster, had a natural northern and southern zone – north and south of the Mounth – a division vouched for by Bede and hinted at by Classical writers. Like Leinster too, there is evidence to show that this geographical divide induced two major tribal confederacies with the implication of two overlordships – one for each sphere of influence. This is confirmed by the reference to Dubthalorc ('Young' or 'Dark' Talorgen), as being 'king of the Picts on this side of the Mounth' who died in 782. What particular side of the Mounth Dubhthalorc ruled matters little; what does matter is the evidence this phrase provides for a duality of overlordship in typical Irish fashion.

We can assume that in addition to an overlord of southern Pictland, there was also a bevy of satellite kings in the south, locked into a confederacy involving a series of mutual obligations. This in turn is confirmed by a reference to Talorgen son of Drustan, a king of Atholl who was drowned by the Pictish overlord, Óengus son of Fergus (Unuist son of Urguist) in 739. If we concede there was a tribal king in Atholl, then why not also in Circinn (Angus and the Mearns), Fortriu (Strathearn and Menteith), Fife, Ce (Mar and Buchan) Fidach (Moray and Ross) and Cait (Caithness and south-east Sutherland) – those ancient seven regions of Pictland as described in *De Situ Albanie* and in the *Pictish Chronicle*? Indeed, the *De Situ Albanie* informs us that each of the seven Pictish kingdoms (*septem regna*) was ruled by a king who was himself the overlord of seven under-kings! This was a situation which was very closely paralleled in Ireland, not only in the proliferation of tribal kings, but even in the detail of the seven divisions. For the Cruithin, those Irish cousins of the Picts, were regularly divided into seven major groupings, wherever they occurred in Celtic Ireland.

Atholl is not the only Pictish kingdom mentioned in Irish annals. Long before the Scottish conquest of Pictland, Circinn and Fortriu also appear in early Irish records and the kingship of Fortriu appears to have had a dual meaning rather like the kingship of Tara in Irish sources. It could mean either Fortriu in the limited tribal sense of the kingdom which stretched from the upper waters of the Forth to the Tay, or it could be synonymous with the overlordship of the Picts – and of the Picts south of the Mounth in particular. By analogy with Irish evidence, this in turn suggests that Fortriu contained a major dynasty of kings which dominated the overlordship for some time, in spite of the claim in *De Situ Albanie* that Angus and the Mearns took pride of place in the list of kingdoms. The great Bridei son of Bili is described in contemporary sources as king of Fortriu, rather than king of the Picts. Fortriu was the nearest Pictish kingdom to Strathclyde, sharing a common border on the upper Forth, and Bridei's hold over Fortriu when taken along with other evidence for Strathclyde involvement in Pictland, may well point to Fortriu having become a satellite kingdom of Strathclyde in the seventh century in precisely the same way as we shall see Strathclyde became the satellite of the Scots kingdom of Scone in the tenth century.

The Pictish king-lists have been assumed by Marjorie Anderson and others to represent a single dynasty of kings who succeeded to high office through a matrilinear system. Dr Kirby abandoned the single dynasty theory, on evidence similar to that outlined above, and favoured a plurality of kings, but he settled for two houses sharing the Pictish kingship – that of Fidach (Moray and Ross) in the north, and Fortriu in the south. These scholars have constructed elaborate pedigrees illustrating how the matrilinear system might have worked, and such models are helpful in providing a working hypothesis in a subject where almost everything is uncertain. We lack the essential genealogies of the Pictish kings and no hypotheses can ever make up that lack. On the other hand, the very lack of source material has itself fuelled the matrilinear thesis. There are two major reasons – apart from a matrilinear explanation – as to why, for instance, no Pictish king in the lists can be shown to have had a father who was king. We have already dealt with Bridei son of Bili, and Talorgen son of Eanfrith. These are cases of satellite kings being imposed on Pictland by her neighbours. As the representatives of other tribes, they need not necessarily have been related to the indigenous Pictish kings through the male line at all.

There may be more examples of outsiders in the king-lists, particularly from the Scots of Dál Riata. John Bannerman has suggested that Gartnait, a king of the Picts in the closing years of the sixth century, was a son of Áedán mac Gabhráin of Dál Riata, while Marjorie Anderson considered it possible that Áedán's grandson, Domnall Brecc, was the father of two other Pictish kings, Gartnait and Drest, who reigned in the third quarter of the seventh century. It may even be that the Picts were considered a subject or client people (*aithechthuatha*), first by their Strathclyde neighbours, and later by Dál Riata as well, whose overkingship was considered a prize to be seized as a traditional right. If this were so, then many of the so-called Pictish kings in the lists were in fact Britons or Scots. Under such a system it would still be possible for indigenous kings to hold the overlordship, but they would be constantly under challenge from their powerful neighbours. This would explain the situation in 750, for instance, when Teudubr of Dumbarton toppled Óengus son of Fergus – if indeed Óengus son of Fergus was a Pict and not a Scot!

It was the Cruithin of Ulster, those Irish cousins of the Picts, who may provide the closest parallel for Pictish overlordship in Scotland. The Cruithin of north-east Ireland were regarded as a subject people in Ulster, and the overlordship of the Ulstermen was normally held by the Ulaid, or free tribe of 'genuine' Ulstermen. From time to time, however, the kings of the Ulaid failed to hold the overlordship of the province which was then seized by the Cruithin. It would of course be inevitable but quite coincidental that Pictish tribal kings were closely related to neighbouring overlords in Scotland through marriage. A detailed study of Irish tribal genealogies shows that tribal kings sought their wives outside their own tribal aristocracies and most frequently they acquired wives among their closest neighbours. Centuries of intermarriage between Pict and Scot combined with Scottish designs on Pictish overlordship to suggest to Scottish compilers of the Pictish origin legend that the Picts had surrendered their rights to overkingship to their Scottish queens. So the matrilinear myth was born. Bede had already been supplied with a version of this myth from Dál Riata in the early eighth century, but already, as we have seen, Dál Riata kings may have been ruling part of Pictland by the late sixth century.

A second and equally important reason for the absence of kingly fathers and sons in the lists may relate to the crucial distinction between overlordship and tribal kingship. The only Pictish list which survives is a list of overlords, and if Pictish overlordship was shared by several dynasties within Pictland then it would prove virtually impossible for a son to succeed his father in the kingship, for by the time the turn of his family came round again, the son would be too old to succeed or perhaps dead, and kingship would pass to the grandson or other descendant of the first holder. Such an oscillating form of kingship can now be shown to have been practised by the Leinstermen in precisely the period under discussion. A circulating or oscillating system of succession is a device whereby overlordship is shared by as many tribes as possible, the advantage being that large confederacies can be held together in 'nations' such as the Picts, with all the stronger tribal aristocracies assured a share in overlordship. We find that in Leinster from 550 to 700, some five or more tribes (out of a total of some 35) shared in the kingship of the province, and of the nine kings of Leinster in this century and a half, only once in the case of two brothers did they – and they alone – succeed a father who had been king. If all the Leinster genealogies and tribal king-lists had been lost, we might now be busy constructing a complex matrilinear system out of the surviving Leinster king-list. The reality was so much more complex than the list of overlords alone can ever show. Most kings in the Leinster list had fathers, brothers, or sons who reigned as kings of their own separate tribes, and we note, too, that the confederacy was held together in a matrix of royal marriages which not only cemented political alliances but also produced close blood relationships between otherwise separate dynasties all in competition for the same overlordship.

Returning now to the Pictish question, I believe we are in a position where we can only make some general observations because the evidence before us is so thin, but we may nevertheless develop a new understanding of the problems involved. It does seem, as Marjorie Anderson has pointed out, that the repetition of names may suggest that one or two major competing dynasties were involved in the list. On the other hand we must also allow for several intruders from outside Pictland (or satellites within it), as well as for other competitors in an oscillating system, who from time to time felt strong enough to participate in the succession. Finally, it is dangerous to assume, as has so often been done, that fathers were succeeded by sons in all agnatic systems of succession. In early Celtic society, all the descendants of a common great-grandfather were considered eligible to succeed to office. So that while sons were undoubtedly important, they might not necessarily inherit the kingship. So, for instance, while a certain Alpín who reigned as Pictish overlord in the period 726–8 may not have been succeeded by a son, we find nevertheless that his son was slain while fighting on Alpín's side in a struggle for the kingship against Óengus in 728. This information suggests that we are not dealing with a system where sons failed to inherit any political power from fathers or that fathers were either unknown or unimportant.

There is an argument which claims that evidence for eighth and ninth century Pictland is not as valid as evidence from earlier centuries, because in the later period the matrilinear system in its purest form was beginning to break down. Is it not more likely that the evidence for the later period, being more abundant, sheds enough light on the issue to show the matrilinear thesis to have had little basis in reality? The fact that fathers were succeeded by sons in the later period may have nothing whatever to do with the break-down of a matrilinear system. It could have everything to do with profound changes which were affecting Irish kingship at this time in the eighth century, when as in Leinster and elsewhere, the oscillating system of overlordship gave way to an alternating succession. Under the alternating system, kingship was no longer shared by several competing tribes, but was confined within a tighter dynastic system involving rotation between cousins. In such a system, the turn of each dynastic segment came round so frequently that fathers *were* succeeded by their sons – but usually not directly – in order to allow each major branch of the same dynasty an opportunity to participate. Such a system emerged in Leinster and among the Uí Néill highkings at the very beginning of the eighth century. In Pictland the remarkable king, Óengus I (Unuist son of Urguist), who died in 761, was succeeded perhaps by his son, Talorgen son of Oengus, who reigned *c*. 785–789. Marjorie Anderson rejected Skene's theory that Óengus had founded a new dynasty partly on the grounds that five other kings intervened in the king list between Talorgen and his supposed father. But this is precisely what we should expect if the Picts, like the Irish, had by then developed a more advanced form of dynastic succession. Such a change could only be achieved by a powerful ruler who was strong enough to exclude permanently various tribal rivals with traditional claims on the Pictish overlordship.

Óengus I was just such a king who fought his way to power in Pictland, and who having conquered all his Pictish rivals went on to subdue Dál Riata as well. Óengus's struggle for kingship is unusually well documented, and the details of that struggle strongly suggest that Pictish overlordship had not been the prerogative of one, but of several tribes. When Nechtan son of Derile abdicated his Pictish throne and retired (almost certainly under pressure) to a monastery in 724, the stage was set for a power struggle which lasted for at least five years. During that time, there were no less than four contenders for Pictish overlordship who fought each other in a league table of battles which eventually resulted in the emergence of Óengus as the final victor in 729. Marjorie Anderson believed that of the four contenders, Drest and Alpín were brothers; that a third competitor, Nechtan, was their uncle; while the victorious Óengus was their cousin – all related through matrilinear succession. Kirby arrived independently at a very similar conclusion. Inevitably, some of these contenders may have been closely related through the female line by inter-tribal marriage, but the evidence already discussed for the survival of tribal kingship in Pictland could also suggest that we are dealing here with an inter-tribal struggle rather than a family quarrel. It is true that brothers and cousins constantly quarrelled over succession to high office in the Dark Ages, but it is equally possible to recognize alliances within such family feuds. In this Pictish affair, however, all parties were competing against each other, and there is no evidence for any common ground between them. The battle roster may be summarized as follows:

726	Drest v. Nechtan (defeated)
	Alpín v. Drest (defeated)
727	Oengus v. Drest (defeated in three battles)
728	Oengus v. Alpín (defeated)
	Nechtan v. Alpín (defeated)
729	Oengus v. Nechtan (defeated)
	Oengus v. Drest (defeated and slain)

We find that while Alpín and Óengus had a common enemy in Drest, they each defeated him separately, and having done so, they then fought each other. The victorious Óengus was next challenged by Nechtan, who re-emerged from monastic retirement to finish off the defeated Alpín and regain the title of overlord. It only remained for Óengus to overthrow Nechtan in the following year, and to slay the persistent Drest who still had a warband in the field up to the end of the struggle. All this could well be an inter-tribal contest for overlordship, and this is confirmed by several key references in the annals. In the account of the battle of *Monith Carno* where Óengus won the kingship from Nechtan in 729, we are told that the *exactatores*, or tribute collectors, of Nechtan were slain. We do not expect to find *exactatores* in a family feud; besides, we are told that the *familia* of Óengus won, which might indicate that the defeated Nechtan belonged to a different kin altogether. *Exactatores* were the agents of the overlord, who in Celtic society displayed his limited *imperium* by his ability to extract tribute from subordinate kings. This is precisely what Nechtan, as the reigning overlord in 729, was trying to achieve, but his satellite Óengus refused to recognize Nechtan's claim and successfully contested the overlordship in battle. When Alpín was defeated by Nechtan in the battle of *Caislen Credi* in 728, we are told that he lost his *cricha* or 'territories'. He had already lost the overlordship of the Picts to

Óengus earlier in the same year, but presumably had retained his own tribal kingdom. This was now seized by Nechtan who, returning from monastic retirement, seized Alpín's kingdom and then claimed the overlordship against Óengus. Finally, for those who are not yet convinced of the multiplicity of kings in Pictland, we may move on briefly to the period 780–784 when we find three Pictish kings recorded during this period – Drest son of Talorgen, Talorgen son of Drostan, and Talorgen son of Óengus (Unuist). One of these men was Dubthalorc who died in 782 as 'king of the Picts on this side of the Mounth.' Their relationship to each other is problematical, but we shall not solve that problem by forcing the evidence under great pressure to yield a matrilinear pedigree for one unhappy family of Pictish kings.

Nechtan son of Derile, who was worsted in the power struggles of the late 720s, is the central figure in that episode in Bede's *Ecclesiastical History* relating to Pictish attitudes to Anglo-Saxon Christianity and Roman usage. It was Nechtan who applied to Ceolfrith, abbot of Jarrow, for advice on the controversy which raged between Iona and Northumbria on the matter of reckoning the correct date of Easter, and Nechtan also asked for masons to build him a stone church 'in the Roman fashion'. This incident has enjoyed a disproportionate prominence in Scottish historiography simply because it appears in Bede, in spite of Bede's otherwise lack of knowledge and, indeed, interest in Pictish affairs. A detailed examination of the last five years of Necthan's reign shows him hovering uncertainly between kingship and monastic retirement, warring with no less than three determined rivals, and finally being toppled by Óengus I. Viewed in this light, Nechtan's plea for help to Jarrow, and his expulsion of Columban monks 'across the spine of Britain' in 717 may not have been the actions of a strong ruler about to implement radical cultural reforms, but those of an insecure king about to be swamped by those very influences he sought to curtail. The expulsion of the Columban clergy was clearly a political move, since they had already conformed in part at least to the Roman Easter a year previously. Nor can we assume that they never came back since Nechtan's attitude towards the Columban clergy was essentially eccentric – hence the fact that it was recorded by annalists in the first place. When Bede tells us that the Picts had adopted Catholic rites in his own time, he does not necessarily imply that the Picts had imported Anglo-Saxon clergy. By then Iona had long conformed to Roman ways, and it is likely to have recovered any ground lost among the Picts. Besides, whatever Nechtan had hoped to achieve politically must have come to nought in 729, while in the next century Dál Riata eventually succeeded in annexing its Pictish neighbours. As for Bede, it was in his interest to stress the Pictish desire to follow a Northumbrian lead in church matters, since the most important theme in his *History* dealt with the triumph of Anglo-Saxon Roman Christianity over its Celtic neighbours. Nechtan's part in this long saga was deliberately exaggerated just as Bede also suppressed, as much as he decently could, the hostility which must have existed between the Picts and Northumbrians ever since the reign of Talorgen son of Eanfrith back in the 650s. Nor had the enmity ended in Bridei's victory at *Nechtanesmere* in 685. A slaughter of the Picts by the Northumbrians in the plain of Manaw in 711 shows that the frontier was far from peaceful in Bede's own time, in spite of his closing remarks about a peace treaty between the two peoples.

Our understanding of Pictish kingship and dynastic politics will always be limited by the dearth of manuscript materials from within Pictish society itself. But the Picts have left us a wealth of alternative documentation, in the form of symbols and naturalistic art incised and carved on stone slabs distributed throughout the north and east of their territories (see Map 3). When we look at the fineness of drawing, the firm lines and realism in, say, the Dunrobin fish or the Burghead bulls we realize that we are dealing with an artistic tradition which at some levels at least takes us back to the palaeolithic painters of Lascaux. The association of the symbolic animals with the hunt is confirmed by actual hunting scenes such as those depicted at Aberlemno or Hilton of Cadboll. While these scenes may owe much to oriental or Mediterranean influence, they must reflect nonetheless indigenous cultural traits. Of course the hunt depicted at Hilton of Cadboll and elsewhere is that of the aristocratic warrior rather than the palaeolithic gatherer, and the people who engaged in the Pictish hunt were the Iron Age warrior élite who elsewhere in Pictish art are seen riding in pomp across the surfaces of such stones as Meigle no.2 (see cover) or Aberlemno no.2. These helmeted horsemen, accoutred with swords, spears and shields, and accompanied by the birds of battle would be perfectly at home, stylistically and culturally, among the Celtic or indeed Germanic warrior élite anywhere in the British Isles. Nor is there any constituent of Pictish art, symbolic or otherwise, which cannot be derived from the sub-Roman Iron Age of

Celtic Britain and the earliest Christian art of Ireland. It is the achievement of Pictish artists to have welded these various constituents into a genre which is at once distinctive and masterly. For two of the most outstanding qualities of Pictish art are its archaism and highly developed regional style – characteristics which distinguish it sharply from its Anglo-Saxon and Gaelic neighbours. As for the enigmatic symbols, they may have served one or several of the many functions which have been plausibly suggested for them – boundary stones, grave markers, totems, talismans and so on. Whatever their precise function, these devices bring us back to the dawn of Celtic history in Britain. It can scarcely be coincidence that the *Cruithin* – 'People of the Shapes or Designs' who were perhaps nicknamed *Picti* or 'Painted People' by Roman frontier troops, did in fact possess a whole repertoire of symbols or designs in their art. Nor is it too fanciful to suggest – given the evidence that the ancient *Britanni* dyed or tattooed their bodies – that the Picts once displayed the devices of the symbol stones on their own bodies also.

Art historians who argue for direct borrowing between Pictland and Northumbria as the major way in which to account for the close similarity between Pictish and Anglo-Saxon art fail to set this artistic exhange into a credible historical setting. It is true that much of the interlace on Class II stones in Pictland relates to Anglo-Saxon patterns, and that various key patterns, vine scrolls, and bosses in high relief, also have close Northumbrian, and even closer Mercian affinities. It is equally true, however, that all of these Pictish elements have the closest parallels in Irish art, and it is in Ireland, furthermore, that we find close similarities in the materials and forms of this sculpture. We find, for instance, the technique of carving crosses in relief on stone slabs as at Gallen (Co. Offaly) and Fahan (Co. Donegal), and in Ireland as in Pictland the stones may or may not be dressed. Ireland also offers the closest parallels to the pictorial scenes on Pictish monuments, as in the case of the horsemen and trapped deer on the Banagher pillar; the animal-headed men and other creatures depicted at Moone; and above all by the pictorial scenes showing riders and animals on the bases of the high crosses at Ahenny and Monaincha. The most impressive point about the relationship between early Pictish and early Christian Irish Art is that it is only in these two regions within the British Isles that we find parallels between such a wide range of motif and form, particularly in regard to cross structures and design. But ultimately, the historical sources must point the way for the art historian, since artistic evidence alone is not sufficient in itself to show us the circumstances in which craftsmen and their patrons shared in the exchange of ideas.

Artistic motifs depended on the Pictish aristocracy for their acceptance or rejection, and ultimately the borrowing of art forms depended on the political relationship between the Picts and the Irish and Northumbrians. A people who so eagerly drove the Anglian bishop at Abercorn to seek refuge further south in 685, and who drove out Anglian nuns in terror to the safety of Cuthbert, do not appear as the most likely candidates for welcoming Anglo-Saxon craftsmen north of the Forth. We might argue, of course, that Nechtan did make Columban clergy equally unwelcome in 717, but we would have to balance that statement against Bede's admission that Iona 'was for a very long time chief among all the monasteries of the northern Irish and the Picts, exercising supervision over their communities.' In other words, Iona provided the parent culture for Pictish Christianity and the burden of proof clearly lies with those who would argue for an alternative major Anglo-Saxon influence. If Pictland closed its doors to the Anglo-Saxon cultural and ecclesiastical drive after Bridei's victory in 685, it is even more unlikely that the Picts wished to absorb Anglian influence in the years when they were subject to the Northumbrians. True, Wilfrid might temporarily impose an Anglian style of worship on the southern Picts, but it is unlikely that a people would absorb too much culture from an enemy eager, as Eddius tells us, to choke the rivers of the lowlands with the bodies of Pictish dead.

Later on, Nechtan son of Derile may or may not have had time to build his Roman church in honour of St Peter, perhaps at Restennet in Angus or elsewhere. But this ruler did not last the pace and was in no position to launch Pictish art in a new direction. Isobel Henderson has convincingly argued that the earliest Pictish symbol stones occur around the Moray Firth, in the very area where, as we shall see, Adomnán shows us Columba making his first contacts with the Pictish king, Bridei son of Maelchú, who had a stronghold in that region in the late sixth century. It is no coincidence that Pictish art first flowered in that corner of the north-east where it was first contacted by the Columban church by way of the Great Glen. The conclusion seems inevitable that the earliest symbol stones, whether Christian or not, began life as a result of contact with Iona, and it was surely Iona which acted as the great disseminator of ideas and motifs throughout Pictland in the centuries that followed. The centre which supplied the Picts with Irish insular script and the ogham alphabet as well as Gaelic loan words for their inscriptions clearly must have had the most profound effect also on Pictish art.

Iona has too often been seen merely in terms of a cultural transit camp where early Irish learning and art was passed on to the Picts and Northumbrians. This was party true, in so far as Iona and its Dál Riata hinterland represented an extension of the Gaelic world in northern Britain. Iona, however, must be taken seriously as one of the greatest centres of monastic civilization in its own right. It housed a whole series of able spiritual leaders throughout the Dark Ages under whose patrongage annalists, writers, calligraphers and craftsmen flourished to a degree almost unparalleled elsewhere, both in terms of individual achievement and of the great length of time in which all this happened. The Picts, then, in looking to Iona for a lead in Christian affairs, were drawing on the resources, not just of any Celtic neighbour, but on one of the greatest monastic centres in Dark Age Europe. Not only would future leaders within the Pictish church have gravitated towards Iona, but that centre in turn would have introduced them to the wider world of Gaelic Christianity beyond. Adomnán mentions a Pictish priest wandering around Leinster in the late sixth century carrying a psalter of Columba's – the earliest historical reference, so far as I am aware, to Picts actually using the books of a neighbouring people – and we are reminded of those close parallels between the animals in the *Book of Durrow* and those of the Pictish symbols. The implications are obvious, for whatever direction we may wish to see the borrowing take, a case can be made for Hiberno–Pictish artistic contacts at the most important political and cultural levels through the church of Iona from the late sixth century onwards.

The Irish origin of the Dál Riata Scots tends to obscure the close cultural ties which the ancient Irish also recognized to exist between their own tribes of the Cruithin and their Pictish cousins. A feud between the descendants of Áedán mac Gabhráin and the family of a certain Gartnait of Skye came to a head in 668 when we read of the 'voyage of the sons of Gartnait to Ireland with the populace of Skye' and of their return two or three years later. This Gartnait, whose name was borne by several Pictish kings seems to have been a Pictish ruler, and Skye was an island which in Columba's day was almost certainly Pictish. In 699, another Pictish king, Taran, who had lost his throne two years before, went into exile in Ireland, and we can be quite certain, as in the case of his contemporary Aldfrith of Northumbria (who also spent a long exile in Ireland), that such magnates travelled with a sizeable following. The concept of a court in exile is important, because several of these influential people no doubt eventually returned to their homeland with ideas, books, and artifacts, which influenced Pictish and Anglo-Saxon art. Of course ideas travelled in more than one direction, and we may cite the case of the Anglo-Saxon Egbert who soon after this time persuaded the monks of Iona to reject the old reckoning of Easter. Yet Egbert's itinerary has much to tell us about the way Anglo-Saxon ideas and art motifs especially from, say, distant Mercia might have reached Pictland. Egbert had left his Anglo-Saxon homeland for Ireland as a young man in the 660s. He became a monk in Ireland, and later a bishop renowned for his holiness of life. He eventually turned up at Iona as an elderly man *c.* 712 and persuaded the Columban church in Scotland to accept Roman usage on Easter. The companion who had persuaded Egbert to undertake his Scottish mission (while they were still in Ireland) had once been a monk at Melrose under Abbot Eata. Eata was in turn one of the 12 English boy pupils of Bishop Aidan of Lindisfarne, and it was during Eata's abbacy at Melrose that Cuthbert joined that community as a young man. Finally, in Professor Duncan's opinion, Egbert may have journeyed on from Iona to the court of Nechtan, king of the Picts. At any rate, Egbert very probably had contact with the Pictish clergy before his death at the age of 90 at Iona in 729.

The second half of the seventh century saw an immense flowering of scholarship and art in the Irish schools among a people whose Christianity was coming to cultural maturity and who had much to offer Anglo-Saxon and Pictish Christians whose Christianity was still emerging from the first generation and conversion phase. It is against this wider cultural and historical background that we must view the arrival of Anglo-Saxon and Pictish kings and clerics in late seventh-century Ireland. Clearly, as the eighth century advanced, and as the churches of northern Britain came of age, they were less dependent on Irish influence, particularly in Northumbria where the English church was organized on a Roman diocesan system. But in Pictland, where Celtic monasticism survived, Ireland and Dál Riata must have continued to exert a prime influence. Aristocratic Pictish contact with Ireland continued into the eighth century. In 733, Brude, the son of the powerful Pictish king, Oengus I, was staying on Tory island off the Donegal coast in the territory of the northern Uí Néill where he was dragged out of sanctuary there by a Scots prince of Cenél Loairn. A detailed survey of Irish annals would no doubt yield several other examples of Pictish clerics and warriors in Ireland and some may be lurking behind the names of individuals whose deaths alone are recorded without comment on their place of origin.

The evidence for sustained Hiberno–Pictish contacts in the seventh and eighth centuries does not mean that the Picts borrowed everything slavishly from their Gaelic neighbours. The vitality of Pictish art with its strength of line and confidence in its own indigenous motifs shows this was not true. Nor must we view the borrowing of Irish learning and ideas in the same sense as an import trade across modern national frontiers. When the Picts are restored to their rightful place within the wider Celtic world, their frontier with the Britons and Scots can be viewed in the light of one Celtic people vis-à-vis another. Mutual friendships and hostilities must all be seen against the background of a common Celtic heritage, while the common cultural background in turn was offset by tribal attitudes which promoted a strong sense of localism. There is one important characteristic of that Celtic world which had a crucial bearing on cultural exchange and which does not seem to have been shared by its Germanic neighbours, and that was the freedom with which the learned throng of poets, antiquaries, and genealogists, passed from one tribe to another. This was a world in which all the Celtic aristocracies of northern Britain participated, and indeed it is thanks to this freedom of movement of the learned caste that the ancient records of the Picts are now preserved in such unlikely sources as the *Book of Ballymote* or that poems such as the *Gododdin* eventually found a safe refuge in Welsh manuscripts.

Jocelyn's *Life of Kentigern* is a later medieval compilation which reflects well the spirit of that Dark Age Celtic commonwealth in Britain. This is a work which contains traditions of the ninth century and earlier, but which describes events of the late sixth century. Kentigern was, as we have seen, of the royal house of Gododdin in Lothian, and he had earlier served a spiritual apprenticeship in south-east Pictland before settling at Glasgow. According to Jocelyn's *Life*, the saint was recalled to Strathclyde from a lengthy visit to Wales by Riderch Hen, who established Kentigern within his kingdom. This king, we learn from Adomnán, was

'Rodercus son of Tothal (Tutagual) who ruled at the Rock of the Clyde' and who was in personal contact with Columba. According to Kentigern's *Life*, Riderch had been baptized in Ireland, and a folk-tale in the *Life* shows an Irish minstrel playing at Riderch's Christmas court. The iconoclast will doubtless argue that we have no proof of those last two statements or of many others, and dismiss them as later Gaelic 'influence' on the compilation. Yet the real value of this work is that a writer sometime in the eighth or ninth century considered it normal for the Strathclyde court to have contacts with every Celtic realm in the British Isles.

It is in this wider Celtic context that we ought to view Pictish traditions in the king-lists which state, for instance, that the church of St Brigit at Abernethy was founded by a Pictish king, Nechtan, in the presence of Darlugdach, abbess of Kildare. Traditions such as this have always been ignored if not rejected by those scholars who pursue the essentially introspective approach to Pictish studies in their relentless quest for the elusive matriarchy. Yet this is a tradition which it was in nobody's interest ever to invent – not even for Columban clergy – and its presence in so many versions of the king-lists demands comment. Some versions of the Pictish king-lists suggest that the *Nechtonius Magnus* who established Kildare nuns at Abernethy was Nechtan, who ruled as overlord of the Picts in the early seventh century. I have already suggested that this Nechton was the same ruler as Neithon, king of Strathclyde, who was, incidentally, a cousin of Riderch Hen, and however this identification is received, a strong case can be made for Strathclyde influence on southern Pictland in the seventh century. A date sometime about 625 for the founding of the Kildare colony at Abernethy would suit the Irish evidence very well. This was the period when Kildare advanced in status from a local tribal nunnery to that of a great house and the seat of the chief Leinster bishopric. It was also the time when Kildare was taken over by the kings of Leinster in the person of bishop Áed Dub, a cousin of Fáelán, king of Leinster. The Leinster royal house had several marriage ties with Scots Dál Riata in the sixth and seventh centuries. King Fáelán's grandson and successor in the kingship, Bran (d. 693), was married to a princess of Scots Dál Riata. A Leinster princess, Caintigern, daughter of Cellach Cualann, settled on Loch Lomond on the border of Strathclyde where she died in 733. Her father Cellach was that king of Leinster who, as I have shown, welcomed the exiled northern British warband of Rheged as mercenaries at his court. In the tenth century,

Kenneth II of Scotland had a Leinster queen.

None of these genuine historical connections can verify a Pictish tradition which is in essence unverifiable: yet the abundance of the material relating to south-east Irish contact with Scotland provides us with the essential context in which to view the Abernethy tradition. The Strathclyde kingdom – just as much as Dál Riata – must have acted as an intermediary between the Irish and southern Picts. The kingdom on the Clyde occupied a crucial medial position in Viking contacts between Ireland and Britain in the ninth and tenth centuries, and there is no reason to suppose that this was not the case also in earlier Celtic times. It is the wealth of documentation relating to Adomnán's Iona and to Bede's Northumbria compared with the poverty of surviving sources from Dumbarton and Pictland which blinds us to the undoubted importance of the northern Britons in the pre-Viking period. This lack of Strathclyde and Pictish documentation, has created a great gap in our understanding of northern British society, resulting in a tendency to treat the Dál Riata Scots as being somehow very different from their neighbours in Scotland. And yet the conclusion of this study on the Picts is fundamentally the same as that which we have already reached on the peoples south of the Antonine Wall, namely that northern Scotland was essentially a Celtic land in the Dark Ages occupied by northern British Cumbri in Strathclyde, by an older British or Pritenic people whom we call Picts, and by Goidelic Celtic immigrants from Ireland. The essentially Celtic make-up of Dark Age Scotland from Hadrian's Wall to the Northern Isles goes a long way to explaining how this exposed land survived the terrible events of the Viking Age and was capable of being forged eventually into a united medieval realm, under the house of Kenneth mac Alpin.

3

Columba: Holy Man Extraordinary

Columba is remembered as the father of Scottish Christianity; the missionary of the Picts; one of the three patriarchs of the Irish Church and the founder of Iona, whose monks built up a brilliant Christian civilization 'on the edge of the world' and eventually introduced the benefits of their Christianity and learning into northern England. All these claims have some substance and any one of them would have been sufficient in itself to ensure a man immortality in the folklore of the Middle Ages. It is not surprising then that a holy man of these heroic dimensions should appear larger than life in the mythology that already surrounded his memory within 50 years of his death. King Oswald of Northumbria could inform Abbot Ségéne of Iona (d. 652) that he had seen 'Saint Columba in a vision, radiant in angelic form, whose lofty height seemed with its head to touch the clouds . . . and standing in the midst of the camp he covered it with his shining raiment'. That incident was reported to Adomnán by his predecessor Abbot Failbe, who had himself heard King Oswald tell the tale to Ségéne of Iona. The apparition was alleged to have been seen by Oswald on the night before his decisive battle with Cadwallon near Hexham in 633. That was about 60 years after Columba's death, while by the time Adomnán was writing in the 680s Columba's cult was firmly established and claims were being made for his miraculous powers which vied even with those of Christ in the Gospel narratives. Adomnán introduced his subject as one who raised the dead to life, had control over winds and seas, changed water into wine, foretold the future, was bathed in heavenly light and enjoyed angelic visions. As centuries passed the legend became more diffuse and in the traditions of later medieval Ireland Columba, like Patrick, was seen as a super-wizard who had joined the ranks of those irritable Irish saints who had become vending machines for curses and gloomy prophecies. In Scotland, Columba's cult survived the onslaught of the Viking wars in spite of the destruction of Iona, and was even absorbed into Scandinavian society there. In later Scandinavian tradition the old Celtic patriarch was seen as the defender of the Southern Isles and its Gaelic-Norse inhabitants. According to *Hákonar Saga*, when Alexander II of Scotland was lying in the sound off Kerrera Island in Argyll in 1249 on his way to attack King Haakon's fleet in the Hebrides, the Scottish monarch saw Columba in a dream. Of enormous stature and repulsive appearance, he appeared in the company of Olaf the Saint of Norway and St Magnus of Orkney. Columba in Norse imagination had taken on something of the awful and sinister qualities associated in Viking times with visions of the war god, Odin.

Adomnán, writing in Latin, and well versed in a Christian Classical tradition, speaks to us from the seventh century with a voice of confidence and authority and the overall quality of his historical writing towers above the welter of Celtic saga and heroic poetry of his age which, like a willow pattern, offers no sense of perspective and no fixed points to the historian. But Adomnán was writing for a monastic community and for pious Christians who accepted direct divine intervention in human affairs as normal. His task was to tell good miracle stories which would reinforce the belief already established in mens' minds that Columba was a saint. What is discouraging for the historian is the discovery that already within a century of Columba's death, miracle stories which were no more than folk tales were in circulation in Scotland. Adomnán has the earliest documented reference to the Loch Ness monster, for instance, which his hero Columba cowed but did not slay. This monster 'with gaping mouth and with great roaring' had an insatiable appetite for human prey and pursued Lugne, one of Columba's monks, in the river Ness during a journey in Pictland. A magic 'spear of plenty' given by Columba to a poor man in Lochaber in Argyll, is basically a fairy tale with Columba playing the role of a wizard. Adomnán, and Columba before him, lived in a world where the Christian supernatural and survivals from the Celtic Otherworld lived side by side with the physical realities of everyday life. Thus Adomnán accepted that unless a milk pail in Iona had the sign of the cross marked on it before filling, a demon might leap in and hide under the milk. Columba viewed his own death in terms of angels dispatched from God's throne to collect his soul at Iona, and these emissaries perched like supernatural vultures on the Mull side of the sound awaiting final instructions from Heaven.

Having sounded these warnings, it is still possible to discover some new and exciting insights into the career of Columba from Adomnán's account of him and from early Irish tradition. Amidst the welter of marvellous tales we are almost startled to find that Adomnán was near enough to Columba's life to have spoken with the 'very aged' Ernéne who remembered the night the saint died in June 597, when, while fishing in the dark on that Sunday night in the Finn river in Donegal, he claimed to have seen the eastern part of the night sky lit up with a pillar of fire. I have already mentioned how Abbot Failbe (Adomnán's predecessor on Iona) passed on the tale of King Oswald which he had heard in the presence of Abbot Ségéne. Yet another tale was transmitted from Ségéne via Failbe concerning Ernéne, a monk of Clonmacnoise, and Abbot Ségéne is cited yet again for passing on a story which he had heard from Silnan, a monk of Columba's on Iona who had once been dispatched on a mission to Ireland. Adomnán also cites Finán, an anchorite from Durrow, a daughter house of Iona in Co. Offaly, and a certain Comman the Priest who related stories to him which they had heard from men who had known Columba. Certain elders in the Columban community on the Scottish island of Hinba passed on a tale to Adomnán which they had heard from Virgno, a monk of Columba's who later became abbot of Iona and died in 624. That was the only story which Adomnán claims he heard orally and also saw in writing. Many more of Adomnán's anecdotes – where no source for the information is cited – may have been derived from written records. We know that his predecessor Cumméne, who died in 669, had written a work on the miracles of Columba and a small section of that work was added verbatim to Adomnán's *Life*. It is reasonable to assume that Adomnán borrowed heavily from Cumméne's work, which was compiled some 60 years after Columba's death. Adomnán does tell us, after all, that he had written sources to follow, and Cumméne's work must have been the most important of these. A detailed account of Columba's last days on Iona must have been written up by someone who witnessed those events, very probably Diarmait, Columba's personal attendant, and this account either survived independently or Adomnán found it incorporated into Cumméne's work. Adomnán tells us that the information he picked up orally was passed on to him by earlier abbots and by 'informed and trustworthy aged men'. This does not prove that their information was correct but it does show that Adomnán had a unique advantage in his efforts to recover information on Columba.

The most crucial element in the transmission of information on Columba over the century from his death to the time of Adomnán's writing was the geographical isolation of the island monastery. This sense of isolation was heightened by the inhospitable climate, and Adomnán's writings reflect this with accounts of contrary winds preventing monks and indeed Adomnán himself from reaching Iona. In another passage Adomnán describes 'a day of crashing storms and unendurably high waves' around Iona which prompted a monk to remark: 'On this very windy and too-perilous day, who can cross in safety even the narrow strait?' Columba's funeral took place in total isolation, because a high gale, blowing across the sound, prevented mourners arriving from Mull. Elsewhere in a storm at sea, Columba is shown joining the crew in a desperate attempt to bail out water when

> 'the whole body of the ship was violently shaken, and heavily struck by great masses of waves, with a mighty storm of winds that pressed on all sides.'

Travel to and from this remote island community must have been frequent, but also very perilous, and such dangers ensured that the rank and file of the monastic family on Iona were less inclined to wander abroad than monks on other mainland monasteries. We have independent evidence from contemporary annals kept on Iona which shows that Adomnán's (and perhaps Cumméne's) dread of the surrounding seas were fully justified by the toll which they took on human lives. In 641, during Ségéne's abbacy, the annals record the shipwreck of a boat 'of the family of Iona', while on 16 October 691, at the very time when Adomnán was writing his *Life* of Columba, 'a great storm overwhelmed six persons of the community of Iona.' Such were the harsh realities that lay behind Adomnán's anecdotes of crashing winds and heaving seas, and such realities, too, consolidated the Iona community in its sense of isolation and created an environment conducive to the transmission of oral traditions about their founder, Columba.

Adomnán specifically mentions that apart from monks and trustworthy men, he also obtained information from former abbots of Iona. Not only were these men direct successors of Columba in an unbroken line, but all of them, with the possible exception of

Suibne (d. 657), are known to have been of Columba's kin. Adomnán as ninth abbot was no exception. These men must have been in a strong position to pass on reliable information as members of a closed aristocratic and priestly caste whose lives of exile or 'pilgrimage' on a remote island must have served to intensify their consciousness of literally following in the footsteps of their founder. Columba's deeds were handed down through an eternal family of monks, by men like his attendant, Diarmait, who had been among the first 12 of his companions who sailed to Scotland in 563 and who outlived him. A cross on the roadside between the corn barn and the monastery was believed to mark a spot where Columba sat down to rest on the last day of his life; in Adomnán's time, Columba's pillow-stone stood beside the saint's grave; and yet another cross was believed to mark the spot where Columba's uncle died on his way to meet his nephew. The presence of such man-made memorials must have reinforced memories in a Celtic society remarkable throughout the Middle Ages for the transmission of oral traditions. Other natural features on the small island were associated in the late seventh century with events in Columba's life. A little hill overlooking the monastery was believed to have been a favourite place for Columba to sit and gaze out to sea; he is described as sitting on another hill at Dún Í looking out towards the northern sea, and the Hill of the Angels in the western plain on Iona was so called from Columba's meeting with angelic visitors there. An anecdote which has all the hallmarks of a genuine tradition shows the ageing saint being drawn around the western plain of Iona in a wagon during the last summer of his life, when the monks were busy building stone enclosures in that part of the island. These particular details may well derive from an eye-witness account, and most likely formed part of Diarmait's account of Columba's last days. Having restored our confidence somewhat in Adomnán's narrative, it is now time turn to his account to see if there is anything new we can learn about Columba himself.

Adomnán gives us very little factual information on Columba, such as the place of his birth, of his schooling, and so on. This was largely because his work is a collection of miracle stories which are neither biography nor history. It is clear, too, that far more information was available on Columba's associations with Iona and Hinba than on scenes from his earlier life. The obvious reason for this was that Columba spent his last 34 years in south-west Scotland and it is a strong point in favour of Adomnán's narrative that

Columba's later years are most vividly described. One remarkable point about Adomnán's *Life*, however, cannot be explained away, and that is the noticeable dearth of miracle stories relating to Columba's earlier life in Ireland. Miracle stories were grist to Adomnán's mill, and had Cumméne left him a ready-made supply of these for Columba's youth he would surely have pressed them into service. All the evidence suggests that neither Cumméne, who flourished in the 650s, nor Adomnán, who wrote after 688, had access to much information which testified to Columba's sanctity in his earlier Irish existence. This is all the more remarkable when we realize that Columba's sanctity was the central point at issue in Adomnán's work, and both Adomnán and Cumméne were in a strong position to gather miracle stories, if there were any, on Columba's Irish days since they both grew up in Columba's tribal homeland of Tír Conaill within the same aristocratic kin. Furthermore, Columba spent 42 years in Ireland before his pilgrimage to northern Britain, allowing ample time for his saintly power, real or imagined, to pass into hagiography.

The vast majority of Columba's Irish miracles were performed by remote control from Iona or elsewhere in Scotland. A woman is helped in childbirth; a plague is averted; travellers are helped on the open sea; in angel is dispatched to save a monk falling from a roof in Durrow; and so on. Columba is also able to 'see' events in Ireland from his distant Scottish retreat, such as the death of Brendan of Birr and of a Leinster bishop, or the drowning of monks of Bangor in Belfast Lough. Numerous other miracles are performed by Columba in Ireland, but by then he was a visitor who had already chosen Scotland as his home. Columba's prophecies concerning future Irish kings, his prophecies about the battle of Dún Cethirn in 629, and tales connected with his visit to the church of Coleraine, were all associated by Adomnán with his attendance at the Convention of Druim Cett in Co. Derry in 575. Several other tales with an Irish setting also date to a time 'when Columba was staying for some days in Ireland', and so like the Druim Cett episode belong properly to his Scottish career. These include Columba's warning to Áed Sláne, highking of the southern Uí Néill; his visit to Brega and to Trevet in Co. Meath; and his chariot-drive in Ireland with Colmán the founder of Slanore near Lough Oughter. There are three other tales with Irish settings, one at Kilmore, and two near the River Boyle where it enters or leaves Lough Key, but no indication of time is offered by

Adomnán. All three anecdotes clearly relate to one period in Columba's life, 'while', as Adomnán says in one of the stories, 'the saint was staying for some days beside Lough Key'. A Latin *Life* of St Munnu suggests the year 579 for the timing of this Roscommon episode, or 16 years after Columba had settled in Scotland. Anderson believed that Columba's fishing expedition in the river *Sale* referred to a pre-Scottish phase in his career and that the river must have been the Co. Meath Blackwater in Ireland. The story of the *Sale* fishing is told alongside the Lough Key fishing, not because they both occurred in Ireland, but because Adomnán grouped his miracle tales according to type without much regard for chronology. It is much more likely that the *Sale* in this tale refers to the river Shiel which marks the boundary between Argyll and Invernessshire. Adomnán does, after all, tell another story about a river *Sale* which beyond all doubt refers to the mouth of the Scottish Shiel. In this second anecdote, Adomnán tells us that he himself took part in an expedition to tow oak timbers out to Iona from the mouth of the river Shiel around Ardnamurchan Point. Finally, Adomnán makes the remarkable statement that Columba founded Durrow in Co. Offaly during the abbacy of Alither of Clonmacnoise. Alither ruled Clonmacnoise from 585 to 599 and so we must conclude that Columba founded Durrow at a very late period, long after he had settled in Scotland and 'when', as Adomnán says, 'the blessed man remained for some months in the midland district of Ireland'. Adomnán's testimony here is not necessarily at variance with an Irish tradition which says that the land for the Durrow foundation was granted by Áed, king of Tethba who died in 589. All this evidence points in one direction, namely that traditions available to Adomnán showed Columba active as a holy man in Ireland at a time when he had already settled in Scotland.

Adomnán was of course obliged to tell us something of Columba's 'hidden life' in Ireland before his Scottish mission, and what he tells us is of crucial importance. He confirms Irish traditions that Columba was born into the royal house of Tír Conaill in Donegal, the son of Fedelmid mac Fergusa and the grandson of Conall Gulban who gave his name to the dynasty of Cenél Conaill, a dynasty which survived as one of the premier royal houses in Ireland down to the seventeenth century. Columba's great-grandfather was the half-legendary Niall of the Nine Hostages (*Noígiallach*) who gave his name to the *Uí Néill* warlords and who was remembered in later Irish tradition as a pagan king who raided Roman Britain. Adomnán does not mention Columba's birthplace but the *Old Irish Life* and centuries of uninterrupted Gaelic tradition point to Gartan on the edge of the Derryveagh Mountains in Donegal. This countryside, associated with Columba's childhood in medieval tradition, although lost in the wilderness of central Donegal, does have easy access through a series of rivers and lakes to the Atlantic coast around Lough Swilly, Mulroy Lough and Sheephaven, and these shores in turn look out on Iona, Tiree and the Outer Hebrides – that very region where Columba was destined eventually to settle down as the holy man of Scotland.

Adomnán names three men who played an important role in Columba's early development. One was the priest Cruithnechán ('Little Pict') about whom we know nothing except that he was Columba's fosterfather; another was 'the aged Gemman' under whom Columba studied as a young deacon in Leinster; and the third was the bishop, Finian. Adomnán tells us that Columba lived with Finian while he was still a deacon and it is likely but not certain that this was Finian of Clonard who died of the great plague in 549, by which time Columba would have been 28. The early traditions regarding Columba's education in Leinster are supported by the Leinster origin of his mother, and the fact that Leinster housed the leading scholars and the best libraries in sixth-century Ireland. Columbanus, the evangelist of Merovingian Gaul, was a Leinsterman.

Adomnán tells us absolutely nothing of Columba's early manhood or of his life in Ireland until, as a middle-aged man of 42, he sailed for Britain. Indeed, he was by then *senex* or 'old' by Dark Age standards, when anyone was fortunate to see the age of 40. The handful of miracles which Adomnán offers for the young Columba have nothing whatever of an authentic flavour. A vision foretelling to Ethne the future greatness of her son, the claim that Columba turned water into wine for his master, Finian, and Finian's account of Columba walking in the company of an angel have nothing circumstantial or convincing to offer. Similarly Cruithnechán's vision of a ball of fire over the head of the sleeping Columba, like Finian's angel, is a typical motif used to show how teachers or parents were made aware of the precocious sanctity of their charges. The only tale concerning Columba's Irish existence that has anything circumstantial about it tells how a girl ran for protection to Gemman and his pupil, Columba, and how she sheltered under their cloaks from the wrath of her pursuer. This man speared the girl to death under the clerics' cloaks and Columba accurately foretold his immediate doom. The story is too close to Adomnán's own preoccupation with the protection of women from violence to carry any weight in an historical debate on Columba. It may tell us much more about Adomnán's personal interests at a time in that author's life when he was preparing to introduce his famous *Law* for the protection of women and children all over Scotland and Ireland.

Adomnán does provide us with one crucial detail relating to the last year or two of Columba's 'hidden life' in Ireland which may well hold the key to understanding Columba's amazing success in later years. This is not a miracle story. On the contrary, it is a tale of startling indictment of any medieval man:

> After many years had passed, when on a charge of offences, that were trivial and very pardonable, Saint Columba was excommunicated by a certain synod (improperly, as afterwards became known in the end).

This was a painful subject for Adomnán – it was painful for a man of great integrity to have to resort to whitewashing his saintly hero. Excommunication was the ultimate weapon of every Christian establishment and was not resorted to lightly in any church, not even among the puritanical Celts. To claim, therefore, that Columba's offence was 'trivial and pardonable' is a nonsense, particularly when the author felt obliged to conceal the misdemeanour, and when he offers no evidence to substantiate his claim that the decision of the synod to excommuniate was later shown to be improper. It appears that Columba was publicly excommunicated by one synod and pardoned by another held at Teltown, Co. Meath – the assembly of the Uí Néill highkings, the most important assembly in Ireland. Adomnán informs us that the attitude of the Teltown synod to Columba was hostile, and he has to invoke supernatural means to clear Columba's name. Clearly Columba's excommunication triggered off a major crisis in his career, and one which Adomnán chose to dispose of as discreetly as possible. Anderson has shown that Adomnán's original narrative followed up the account of this synod with the sentence:

> In those days the saint sailed sailed over to Britain, with 12 disciples as his fellow soldiers.

It is impossible to escape the obvious conclusion that Columba's departure for Scotland, marking as it did, such a radical change of direction in his life, was in some way connected with his pardon at the Teltown Synod. Clearly, that assembly needed more than Brendan's vision of angels and a pillar of fire to convince it either of Columba's innocence or of his repentance. Such an assembly would most likely impose a penance after readmitting Columba into the church, and with this in mind, Columba's voyage to Scotland could well have been a penitential journey either imposed on him by his superiors or undertaken voluntarily.

Columba was himself a hard-liner when it came to doling out penance. It was only at Baithene's intercession that he allowed an Irishman who had slain his brother and slept with his mother to land on Iona. When he eventually gave the sinner a hearing, the penance Columba decided on was 12 years exile among the Britons and permanent exile from Ireland. Other penances were no less severe: Libran of the Reed Plot, who came on a penitential journey to Iona after escaping from bondage where he was held for a man-slaying, was given 7 years penance on Tiree. This evidence is important. It shows that already before Adomnán's time, Iona and Columba's cult were associated with fugitives and exiles fleeing from enemies or undertaking penitential journeys. Not long after Columba's death, the sons of Ethelfrith of Northumbria were also to seek out distant Iona as a safe refuge far removed from the fury of Edwin in 617. The fact that Adomnán shows Columba imposing penitential exiles of 7 to 12 years, and even permanent exile from Ireland on penitents, may lend substance to persistent later Irish traditions that Columba's voyage to Scotland was itself of a penitential nature of this sort. Later Irish traditions even claimed the Scottish phase in Columba's life was an enforced permanent exile from Ireland, and although Adomnán clearly shows that Columba must have returned to Ireland at least twice, that in itself might not necessarily contradict the overall issue of permanent settlement in northern Britain. But penances of this sort were fixed to match crimes of a correspondingly gross nature, such as manslaughter or incest as mentioned elsewhere by Adomnán. What is the evidence for such a crime having been committed by Columba, the 'Dove of the Church'?

Adomnán did not date events by AD reckoning, nor by indictional methods used by contemporary annalists. Instead, he sometimes used a battle as a chronological landmark, as for instance

'Ecgfrith's battle' against the Picts at Dunnichen Moss in 685, after which he tells us he went himself to Northumbria. Twice in his book Adomnán tells us that Columba sailed to Britain in the second year after the battle of Cúl Drebene. In both cases he repeats that the voyage was in the nature of a *peregrinatio* – a pilgrimage in the penitential sense, which might or might not be undertaken voluntarily. Adomnán does not use battles merely as a crude chronological guide, especially if they occurred two years before the major event he wished to discuss. Just as Ecgfrith's defeat at Dunnichen Moss was intimately connected with Adomnán's journey to the court of his successor, King Aldfrith, so we are entitled to assume that the repeated association between Columba's sailing to Scotland and the battle of Cúl Drebene must underline a well known connection between the two incidents. When we turn to the account of the battle of Cúl Drebene at the year 561 in the *Annals of Ulster* we find that Columba was indeed connected in Irish tradition with that victory of the northern Uí Néill, for 'through the prayers of Columba they conquered'. The victors in the battle of Cúl Drebene consisted of Columba's first cousin, his uncle, his more distant cousins of the Cenél nEogain, and the king of Connacht. This formidable alliance defeated the highking, Diarmait mac Cerbaill, ruler of the southern Uí Néill, who is remembered in Irish tradition as the last of the highkings to rule from the pagan sanctuary on Tara. The pagan attributes of Diarmait's kingship are alluded to in the earliest account of the battle of Cúl Drebene, where we are told that Diarmait had engaged the services of a druid to erect a magic fence or wall of mist around his army. Unfortunately the account of this battle in Irish annals is not contemporary, and clearly relies on a well established saga tradition. But the connection of Columba with the battle, which was clearly his family affair, is interesting in view of Adomnán's stressing that Columba sailed to Britain in the second year after it took place. The phrase: 'they conquered through the prayers of Columba' may be special pleading on the part of the later compiler who worked over this entry. It may have been inserted to contradict other traditions, which we do know were circulating, to the effect that Columba either personally fought at Cúl Drebene or incited his cousins to attack the highking Diarmait in the first instance. If Columba as an ordained priest had personally taken part in a slaughter as early as 561 that would have been regarded as a sufficiently grave offence by the more fervent Irish Church of the sixth century, and would explain his excommunication as vouched for by Adomnán. When we recall that Columba's two first cousins, Ainmere and Báetán, who fought at Cúl Drebene, were both in their time highkings of the Uí Néill, we realize how close Columba himself was to high office. Had he not been a churchman, he would have been a front runner for the highkingship, and certainly for the kingship of his tribe of Cenél Conaill. By Old Irish law he was well within the kin relationship to make him eligible for election to both kingships.

Adomnán, and presumably his predecessor Cumméne, vouched for Columba's fiery personality, his great interest in battles, and for a well developed cult in the seventh century where Columba figured as the giver of victory. Adomnán tells us of a Scottish magnate, Ioan of Cenél Gabhrain, who had been plundering Columba's friend, near Ardnamurchan or Loch Linnhe, and whom Columba encountered as he was loading his booty on to his ship. The saint's entreaties failed, and scoffing at Columba, the aristocratic robber sailed off. Adomnán continues:

> The saint followed him down to the sea, and entering knee-deep the glassy waters of the ocean he raised both hands to heaven, and earnestly prayed to Christ, who glorifies his chosen ones.

Columba then retreated out of the sea on to high ground and brooded over the nasty fate that was about to befall his enemy. This was not the action of a saint as we conceive of sanctity but – as the Andersons have noted – an outburst from one who had the blood of countless Uí Néill warlords rushing through his veins. Elsewhere, Adomnán shows Columba in his Scottish career as a man who still had a great interest in battles, albeit a prophetic one, and as a saint who frequented the company of kings in Scotland. Already, after being only a few months in Scotland in 563, Adomnán shows us Columba in the company of the Scottish king, Conall mac Comgaill, relaying an account to him by supernatural satellite as it were, of the battle of Móin Daire Lothair, then being fought in Ulster. Both Columba and his new royal patron would have had a keen interest in that battle, for it was an Uí Néill victory by which Columba's relatives pushed the Ulstermen back east behind the Bann, thereby bringing Columba's dynasty uncomfortably nearer to Dál Riata. If we are to believe Adomnán, Columba was eventually ordered by an angel to ordain Conall's first cousin, Áedán mac Gabhráin, to the kingship of Scots Dál

Riata, which was another way of saying that Columba, and of course his successors, had a major say in the election of the Scottish king.

In addition to his involvement with Scottish kings, Columba was in friendly contact with Riderch, king of the Strathclyde Britons, and with Bridei son of Maelchú, king of the Picts. Nor did Columba cut himself adrift from Irish power politics after his 'pilgrimage' to Scotland in 563. His interest in the outcome of the battle of Móin Daire Lothair can be matched by Adomnán's tale of how, when Columba was trudging through Ardnamurchan with his companions in 572, he informed them of the violent end of his distant cousins, Báetán and Eochaid, joint highkings of the Cenél nEogain. At the Convention of Druim Cett in 575 Adomnán shows us Columba back in Ireland extending his friendship to the future highking, Domnall son of Áed mac Ainmerech, and to a future king of Ossory. Columba was probably the key figure who set up the conference at Druim Cett in the first instance, since he was uniquely qualified to establish an alliance between his kinsmen of the northern Uí Néill and his royal patron, the Scottish Áedán, whom he had ordained king only a year before. We know that Cumméne, who wrote about Columba only 60 years after his death, believed that Columba had a deep personal commitment to that alliance. Adomnán also shows us Columba lecturing the future highking, Áed Sláne, in a friendly way, and he gave refuge in Scotland to Óengus Bronbachal, a future king in Connaught, along with his two brothers, when they were forced into exile in their youth. On another occasion Columba anticipated news reaching Iona of the slaying in mutual combat of two men of royal blood in Mugdorna in southern Ulster. Columba grieved at the news, the implication being that the magnates were his friends.

Columba, then, was not only a member of the warrior aristocracy, but he continued into the holy part of his life to maintain an abiding interest in the affairs of these warlords, advising them how to behave, predicting how they would die, and even showing a warrior's own fascination with the outcome of their battles. Equally significant for this warrior aspect of Columba's life is the early evidence for his cult procuring victory in war. With the suppression of the pagan war-gods, such as the Celtic Babd and Germanic Woden (Odin), the warrior caste desperately needed a substitute for their old victory gods. Saints of Columba's hot blood fitted the bill for this role much more comfortably than the figure of Christ who preached mercy and dissociation from violence. Already by the 650s, Cumméne the White believed that Dál Riata could sustain its military victories only if it kept faith with Columba, and Adomnán shows us Columba securing victory by his prayers for the Scots king, Áedán, in his battle against the Pictish Miathi. Adomnán's most dramatic picture of Columba as the giver of victory is described in his apparition to Oswald of Northumbria on the eve of his crucial victory over the Welsh invader Cadwallon. 'The Lord has granted to me', said Columba 'that your enemies shall be turned to flight and your adversary Cadwallon shall be delivered into your hands'. Thus spoke the towering spectre of Columba as he covered the English war camp with his heavenly mantle. Adomnán considered Columba's special gift as victory-giver so important as to spell it out as one of the chief overall attributes of the saint at the beginning of his *Life*:

And in the terrible crashings of battles, by virtue of prayer he obtained from God that some kings were conquered, and other rulers were conquerors. This special favour was bestowed by God on him, not only in this present life while he continued but also after his departure from the flesh, as on a triumphant and powerful champion.

Adomnán also informs us that already in his day, certain ritual chants were in circulation in the language of the Scots (*scoticae linguae*) which invoking Columba's aid were powerful enough to deliver even 'guilty and blood-stained men' from dangerous situations. In the centuries after Columba's death, a psalter which may well be from his own pen was enshrined in a metal case which might never be opened. This reliquary was known as 'The Battler' (*Cathach*) and was preserved in the O'Donnell clan down to the sixteenth century. This potent relic was used to secure victory for armies before battle. In later times, it had to be carried sun-wise thrice around the assembled host by a hereditary warden who was, to the best of everyone's knowledge, free from mortal sin. Parts of the Cathach's shrine are almost as old as the psalter itself, and we have evidence from annals that Columba's crozier was carried before Scottish armies to win them victory against invading Vikings in the early tenth century. Clearly, the cult of this warrior saint was intimately connected with affairs of war.

According to Adomnán, Columba had 'a livid scar, which remained on his side all the days of his life'. He explained its origin by linking it to the tale of how Columba ordained Áedán mac Gabhráin king of Scots Dál Riata. Columba was visited by an angel who carried with him 'the glass book of the ordination of kings' which also carried instructions to choose Áedán as ruler. Columba preferred Áedán's brother, Iogenán, and the angel had to insist on the choice of heaven by lashing out at Columba with a scourge. It took three visions on three successive nights to convince the saint that Áedán was the right man. We may begin with the virtual certainty that the scar had a real existence and the tale of the angel's scourge was invented to explain it. The scar remained with Columba until his death, and we know that traditions from the end of his life tend to be much more reliable than earlier ones. Such a scar would have been noticed when the saint was laid out for burial, if not earlier in life while bathing. His attendant Diarmait, who seems to have written an account of Columba's last days, could easily have passed on this remarkable and curious feature. A 'livid scar' on the body of a man of royal kin with a lifelong association with battle is much more likely to have been an old battle-wound inflicted in earlier life than anything associated with angels and glass books. If we look for an appropriate battle, we need search no further than the dreadful slaughter of Cúl Drebene, believed in Irish tradition to have been caused by Columba and believed by some to have witnessed the clash of his sword. Furthermore, if the slaughter of Cúl Drebene had brought about his excommunication and permanent 'pilgrimage' to Scotland, then the scar which he received there could indeed be seen as a scourge from heaven which had given his life a radically new direction.

Not all the evidence suggests Columba was either responsible for, or fought in, the battle of Cúl Drebene. Adomnán shows us Columba in an apparently friendly relationship with Áed Sláne, the son and successor of Diarmait mac Cerbaill who was defeated by Columba's kin at Cúl Drebene. Adomnán also stresses Columba's aversion to violence as, for instance, in the story of the Ulster king, Áed Dub, 'a very bloody man and a slayer of many men', who visited Columba on Iona. Columba had an instinctive dislike of this pilgrim and he forecast that he would 'return like a dog to his vomit, and he will again be a bloody killer.' Columba's dislike of Áed was heightened by that king's ordination to the priesthood, and when Adomnán tells us that Áed was the man who assassinated the highking, Diarmait mac Cerbaill, we seem to have a tailor-made argument against any involvement of Columba in a battle against Diarmait. Here after all, in one anecdote, Adomnán shows Columba fulminating against a royal cleric like himself who had assassinated that king who in Irish tradition was supposed to have insulted Columba and fought in battle against him. Whatever the purpose of this anecodote, we cannot dismiss Adomnán's own admission of Columba's excommunication and of some connection between that and a battle against Diarmait – a connection which was probably all too clear to many of Adomnán's readers. This story of Áed's blood-lust may well be special pleading on Adomnán's part to show that in spite of rumours to the contrary, Columba was not by nature a man of violence, and that whatever momentary lapse he may have been guilty of in an earlier life at Cúl Drebene, he later made full recompense and sought a reconciliation with Diarmait and his son Áed Sláne.

We seem to be dealing with a classic conversion story, involving not necessarily the conversion of a great sinner to repentance, but the giving at least of a new intensity to a life already dedicated to the church. For Columba, like Paul, or even like Christ or Muhammad, seems to have waited to translate his fervent sense of mission into action when he reached middle age, and from then on his life took on a radically new direction. There is no evidence whatever to suggest that Columba was remarkable as a holy man before the battle of Cúl Drebene in 561 or that he had even founded a monastery before then. He was involved in a slaughter either directly or indirectly, and as a result he was excommunicated (or at least threatened with excommunication) and was finally reconciled with the Irish ecclesiastical authorities at a Synod held in King Diarmait's own assembly in 562–3. A direct result of this synod was the departure of Columba for Scotland, either voluntarily or as a penance imposed by the Synod. Either way it was the *hijrah* in the life of this remarkable churchman whose physical removal to Scotland coincided with the dedication of his life to the well-being of his new monastic *familia* which was to spread from Scotland far and wide across the British Isles. All the great achievements for which he was later remarkable still lay in the future – the foundation of Iona and other Scottish houses; the foundation of Durrow with its reputation for scholarship and art; the moral support for the dynasty of Dál Riata and the legacy of his missionary zeal which eventually left such an impression on Pictland and Northumbria.

We know much more about the Scottish phase of Columba's life

due to the survival of Iona's records and the strength of its traditions, but Adomnán, perhaps deliberately, concentrated on the
humdrum activities of his founder and tended to ignore what are,
for the historian at least, the more important biographical details of
his life. We have a detailed picture of Columba, sitting in his
writing office, copying and proof-reading manuscripts; praying in
chapel or in some lonely spot; and supervising the daily chores of
his monks in the fields. Yet we are not certain where Columba
spent the first 10 years after he came to Scotland or precisely how
much time he spent on Iona after he founded it; and – most crucial
of all – we are not certain whether Columba saw himself as later
generations liked to see him, in the positive role as missionary
extraordinary to the Picts. Early Irish tradition – and the *Old Irish
Life of Columba* in particular – have reinforced the popular assumption that Columba founded Iona as soon as he reached Scotland in
563. It is just possible to infer from Adomnán, however, that while
Iona did eventually become the headquarters of Columba's mission, it may have been a relatively late foundation, begun as late as
573. A close reading of Adomnán suggests that Columba's earliest
base in Scotland was on the unidentified island of Hinba and that
he moved from there at the beginning of the reign of Áedán mac
Gabhráin to take up permanent residence on Iona in 574.
Adomnán understandably associated the majority of Columba's
Scottish miracles with Iona, that island monastery where
Adomnán himself wrote and where Columba died, but in spite of
that it is clear that Hinba was an important early base for
Columba's Scottish career, and that it continued to be a monastic
centre down to Adomnán's own day.

Iona and Hinba were not the only Scottish monasteries founded
by Columba. His foster-son, Baithene, who sailed with him on his
voyage of pilgrimage to Scotland in 563, seems like Columba to
have been associated first with Hinba, and eventually succeeded as
abbot of Iona: But sometime before Columba's death, Baithene
was the *praepositus* or prior of the monastery of Mag Luinge on
Tiree, and it is implied from a tale of Adomnán that Mag Luinge
may have had some kind of ecclesiastical jurisdiction over Coll, the
nearby island to the north. Mag Luinge was not the only monastery
on Tiree. Adomnán relates how a pestilence ravaged the island
and how while the Mag Luinge community escaped unharmed
under Baithene, 'many in the other monasteries of the same island
died of that disease'. We have here, and elsewhere in Adomnán, a

strong hint of bitter competition between these rival communities which were clearly overcrowding Tiree. He tells us of Findchan the priest, who founded *Artchain* on Tiree and who displeased Columba by inveigling a bishop into ordaining that violent king, Áed Dub, to the priesthood. The consequences were dire: Áed was later drowned in a lake while pierced by a spear, and Findchan, who died on his bed, paid for his misdeeds and for his 'earthly love' of the king by forfeiting his right hand. There must have been a lot of tension, if not between these holy founders then certainly between their seventh-century successors in these remote corners of Argyll and the Hebrides.

If we are to believe the Latin *Lives* of Brendan of Clonfert and Comgall of Bangor, then these saints, too, founded monasteries on Tiree. There is nothing implausible in that since Adomnán vouches for the visit which both men paid to Columba while he was on Hinba, and he describes them as 'holy founders of monasteries'. Brendan was otherwise remembered as the great navigator who explored the islands of the North Atlantic and the Scottish Isles in particular. His most important Scottish foundation was probably Ailech, convincingly identified by Watson with Eileach an Naoimh in the Garvellochs in the mouth of the Firth of Lorn. Comgall and Columba appear from Adomnán to have been good friends: we are shown the two men travelling together past Dún Cethirn on the road from Limavady to Coleraine in Co. Derry, and elsewhere we are told how Columba, through a vision on Iona, came to the aid of Comgall's monks who had drowned in Belfast Lough.

Elen was another island monastery which was subject to Iona but which still eludes identification. It had as its prior a certain Lugne, who as a young man had been cured of a nose-bleed by Columba. The most southerly Scottish monastery mentioned by Adomnán as having been founded by Columba (and ruled by a prior) was *Cell Díuni* on the shores of Loch Awe in Argyll. The most northerly point on the west coast of Scotland to which Adomnán takes his saintly hero is the Isle of Skye. Adomnán mentions Skye twice, and in both cases he says that Columba spent 'some days' there. He also tells us that Columba was accompanied by monks or 'brothers' on Skye and that the saint baptized an old man who died there and whose cairn was still visible on the coast in Adomnán's own time, at a place called *Dobur Artbranani* ('Artbranan's stream') called after that convert. The clear implication of Adomnán's tale is that Artbranan was a Pict: he was a pagan, and Columba had to

converse with him through an interpreter. The mention of
Columba's 'brothers' on Skye and the suggestion of contact between
that particular area where Columba was staying, with later writers on
Iona including Adomnán, may hint at the possibility of there being a
Columban community there from Columba's time or soon after.

This brings us to one of the greatest enigmas surrounding
Columba's life, namely the extent of his involvement with the Picts
and the justification of the claim that he was the Apostle of Pictland.
If we start from the few known and certain facts at our disposal we
notice that all the monasteries mentioned by Adomnán as being
under Columba's rule (with the exception of a possible foundation
on Skye), lay not only to the west of the highland massif and in Dál
Riata but were confined within a relatively small area of the territory
which we normally identify with the Cenél Loairn. (see Map 4)
These monasteries were not very far from each other and most were
easily accessible by sea. It is abundantly clear from Adomnán that

4 Northern and Central Scotland AD 550–850

Columba's main theatre of pilgrimage in Scotland centred on the shores of Ardnamurchan, the Firth of Lorn, the Sound of Mull and the waters between Tiree and Iona. Columba was from first to last a saint not even of the ruling Cenél Gabhráin territory but of the Cenél Loairn. It is true that he enjoyed Cenél Gabhráin patronage but expeditions outside Cenél Loairn seem to have been exceptional rather than the rule, and it is from this starting point that we must view his contacts with the Picts.

Adomnán does not mention a single monastery founded by Columba among the Picts with the possible exception of a base which is merely hinted at on Skye. But Skye lay to the north of Columba's Scottish mission field and to the west of the 'Spine of Britain' – Adomnán's term for the Grampians, or the highland massif as a whole, which from an Iona standpoint divided Scotland into an eastern and western zone. King Bridei's main strength on the other hand clearly lay as overlord of those Picts to the east of the Spine and north of the Mounth. Adomnán mentions a young follower of Columba called Finten who was taken ill on a journey to Pictland proper, across the Spine of Britain, who was cured by Columba and who afterwards founded the monastery of *Kailli au inde*. We cannot assume that this place was in Pictish territory, since Finten presumably returned with Columba to Iona. Watson believed that Finten's monastery is now Killundine in Morvern near the shores of the Sound of Mull. That location, although not certain, would fit perfectly with the distribution of early Columban monasteries which we have already recognized in Cenél Loairn territory. We learn from Adomnán that Columba did visit King Bridei's Pictish court to the east of the Spine of Britain, which was probably located in the hillfort at Craig Phádraig near where the River Ness flows into Moray Firth, or less probably at Urquhart. Columba's journeys to Pictland, however, are referred to more in the context of expeditions rather than visits to territory which was considered within Iona's sphere of influence. The Picts are consistently shown to us in the guise of pagan barbarians whose magicians or 'druids' are hostile to Columba and his companions, and most significant of all, there is no evidence in the pages of Adomnán either for the conversion of King Bridei or for the mass conversion of his Pictish subjects. We must balance this evidence in turn against the more positive record in Adomnán's account, to the effect that Columba did seek out the Pictish king; that he left a marked impression on him and his court; that he effected a few conversions and that he clearly paved the way for subsequent missionary work by his monks throughout Pictland.

Adomnán makes seven major references to Columba's travels among the Picts. Anderson believed that all of these accounts related to one single expedition undertaken by Columba to Bridei's court, and he explained away the reference to Columba's 'first tiring expedition to King Bridei' by taking that phrase to refer to the first tiring climb to Bridei's fortress on the top of Craig Phádraig! There is indeed ambiguity in Adomnán's account, but it is clearly distorting the evidence and Adomnán's Latin to follow Anderson's interpretation of this passage. Surely a 'first tiring expedition' presupposes at least a second, and it is evident from the context that Adomnán was thinking in terms of a long period of years rather than days. Thus, he tells us that on the *first* journey, Bridei refused to admit Columba to his fortress until the saint forced the locks of the gates by his miraculous powers 'and from that day onwards, throughout the rest of his life, that ruler (Bridei) greatly honoured the holy and venerable man'. The implication is that Adomnán at least believed Columba and Bridei were in personal contact over a long period of time.

The account of what we may call the major Pictish expedition shows that Columba travelled to King Bridei by way of the Great Glen, and this route is also implied for 'the first tiring expedition' and for the visit to negotiate terms for hermits on Orkney, since these too were directed to Bridei's fortress near the Moray Firth. The tale of the River Ness monster clearly fits into the same geographical context, as indeed does the tale of the burning village. That hamlet lay 'on the journey across the Spine of Britain' at a point where 'a stream flowed into a lake' – a vague enough phrase, but one which echoes other descriptions in Adomnán of journeys through the Great Glen. Finally, in another anecdote, Adomnán tells us how Columba 'while making a journey on the other side of the Spine of Britain beside the lake of the River Ness' baptized an old pagan called Emcath on his farm at Urquhart on the northern shores of Loch Ness. It is impossible to be certain whether we are dealing here with seven or more journeys to Pictland or with only two, since all of them are set along the same route through the Great Glen. The fact that they were confined to the Great Glen does not necessarily suggest that few journeys were involved, since the route from Argyll to the Moray Firth was determined by the formidable physical geography of the Scottish highlands.

The evidence from Adomnán which suggests that Columba's foothold in eastern Pictland was pretty tenuous hangs not on the number of journeys which he made through the Great Glen but on the results achieved, and here we must agree with Anderson that the results were far from dramatic. Adomnán sets the scene for Columba's encounter with the Pictish king in the context of a classic conversion story. Just as Irish hagiographers dramatized the clash between Patrick and the fierce pagan highking on Tara, and just as Bede confronted his hero Augustine with the pagan court of Ethelberht in Kent, so too Columba had to overcome Bridei's royal anger and the powerful magic of his druids. Most conversion stories of this sort involve a miracle contest and Adomnán was not found wanting in his account of Columba's confrontation with the Picts. During the first encounter, Bridei refused to meet the saint and remained closeted within his locked fortress. When Columba forced his way in, he earned the 'veneration' of his host. Bridei may have been impressed, but he did not become a Christian – at least Adomnán does not tell us so, which amounts to the same thing. It is in the miracle contest proper that Adomnán clearly reveals the limitations of Columba's success in Pictland. We are told that Columba forced Bridei's foster-father, Broichán, the court magician, to release a Scots slave-girl by having an angel shatter a glass which he held in his hand, and by bringing the druid to the point of death. Columba eventually took pity on his victim and restored him to health, but Adomnán concedes that far from becoming a pious Christian, this Pict was unrelenting in his hostility right up to the end of Columba's visit. Broichán raised a magic mist and a contrary wind to prevent Columba sailing home down Loch Ness. While Columba sailed miraculously against the storm, we are left with the decided impression that the expedition ended in stalemate. Columba's magic may have been stronger, but King Bridei and his druids stuck to their pagan guns.

In spite of Adomnán's declaration that Bridei mellowed towards Columba, numerous other incidental remarks strongly suggest that the pagan priests of the Picts treated the saint with open hostility and that in this they may have had political support from their military leaders. Even Adomnán's bare statement of Bridei treating Columba with respect is outweighed by more positive accounts of the king hiding behind locked gates and his druids trying to disrupt the Scottish vespers. Pictish territory was, on the whole, hostile terrain for Columba, and at times that hostility broke into violence as in the case of those 'hostile pursuers' who fired a village in the hope of destroying Columba and his companions. Adomnán's accounts of Columba's miracles in the Great Glen suggest that he met with as little success there as he did at Bridei's court – in spite of the outlandish nature of the miracles supposed to have been worked. When Columba saved his monk Lugne from the jaws of the Loch Ness monster, 'the pagan barbarians. . . . magnified the God of the Christians', but we are not told of their conversion. Adomnán, in what he himself regarded as a key miracle story which placed Columba in the same class as the prophets and apostles, relates how Columba raised a Pictish boy from the dead. This boy fell seriously ill a few days after the conversion of his parents and all their household, and his death encouraged the Pictish magicians 'to taunt his parents, . . . and to magnify their own gods as the stronger, and to belittle the Christians' God as the weaker.' Columba's restoration of the boy to life meant that 'the God of the Christians was glorified'. The pagan party was confounded but not necessarily converted. Indeed, while all these stories in Adomnán's *Life* present the appearance of conversion stories they are in essence conversion stories which do not end in conversion.

The question as to whether we should view Columba as the apostle of the Picts and consequently as a 'national' rather than merely a Dál Riata saint raises another more fundamental issue as to whether Columba saw himself as a missionary at all. Was he, like his friend, Cormac, merely seeking 'a desert place in the sea' rather than positively setting out to preach the Christian message to pagans who had never heard of Christ, and to believers in need of pastoral care? Adomnán does help us answer these questions. Although he makes no positive claims for mass conversions among the Picts, he does mention certain individual converts who were baptized by Columba. These include the old man on Skye; the conversion of the entire household in the Great Glen; and the conversion of another household on a farm at Urquhart. We are told that on Skye and at Urquhart, Columba preached the 'word of life' through an interpreter, and the use of the word *predicante* ('preaching') is a crucial reminder that in spite of Columba's limited success in Pictland, Adomnán (and presumably his sources) did believe that the saint preached the message of Christianity to the Picts. When Columba visited Bridei, he clearly had other objectives in mind above and beyond the immediate task of converting his host. Adomnán shows us Columba negotiating with Bridei for the safety of Christian monks who were seeking a retreat in the Orkneys, and Columba petitioned Bridei in the presence of his subject-king of the Orkneys, whose hostages were in his possession. In other words, the main purpose of Columba's negotiations with the Picts to the east of the Spine might have been to ensure the safety of hermits and the Christian church at large in its expansion northwards among the Picts of the Isles and the Atlantic coast of Scotland. If this were true, then we must agree with Anderson in accepting that Columba may not have made many journeys up the Great Glen, and the limited success of his preaching in the east can then be explained by seeing it as a secondary consideration limited by time and by the diplomatic nature of those expeditions to eastern Pictland.

It would be unwise to assume that a mass conversion even of the north-western Picts took place within Columba's lifetime or indeed that Iona ever had jurisdiction over the early churches in that region, although Adomnán might have wished to give that impression. The fragmentary evidence which survives suggests that the coastal territories to the north of Skye were not evangelized by Columba and did not indeed become Christian until at least a century after his time. An attempt to evangelize the north-west was made quite independently of Columba, but during his time on Iona, by his younger contemporary, Donnán of Eigg. Church dedications are a dangerous guide to the actvities of a missionary saint, but in the case of the obscure Donnán, they do confirm the western and north-western Scottish location for this saint's activities. Place-names and church sites called *Kildonnan* occur on Eigg; in Kilpheder Parish on South Uist; on Little Loch Broom in Wester Ross; at Kishorn, where *Seipeil Dhonnáin*, ('Donnan's Chapel') looks out on Skye; while on Skye itself we have Kildonnen in Lynedate at Loch Snizort in the north of the island. There is also *Eilean Donnáin* ('Donnán's island) on Loch Alsh not far from Kishorn, and yet another *Donnan's Chapel* on Little Bernera in north-west Lewis. All of these dedications, with one exception at Auchterless in Aberdeenshire, emphasize a strong north-western Pictish location for Donnán's northern monasteries. Donnán's origins are obscure, but he belonged to that band of 'holy founders' who sought their spiritual fortune in western Scotland. Donnán, like Columba, came to stay and a few dedications to this saint in Kintyre, Arran, Wigtownshire, and Ayrshire, either point to his place of origin or more likely to an earlier phase in his career before moving from Ireland into north-western Pictland. The brief record in the *Annals of Ulster* of 'the burning of Donnán of Eigg with 150 martyrs' on 17 April 617 gives us a contemporary record of the massacre of this saint and his monastic community, probably at the hands of the Picts. It was far too early in the seventh century for his assailants to have been Vikings, and unthinkable, even given the violent conditions of the age, for so many monks to have been butchered by Christians. 17 April 617 was a Sunday and that detail supports a medieval Irish tradition in the martyrologies to the effect that Donnán and his monks were slain after the celebration of Mass. A note in the *Martyrology of Óengus* states that the destruction of the community on Eigg was brought about by a queen on the mainland who objected to her flocks of sheep on Eigg being disturbed by the intrusion of the monks. This legend may also suggest that Donnán's assailants were pagan Picts, which is supported by the chronology of the event; by the fact that Columba encountered a pagan on Skye only a few decades before; and by the evidence for general Pictish hostility towards Columba and his Christian monks as vouched for by Adomnán. Donnán was associated with Eigg in contemporary and later Irish tradition, and medieval Irish records also associated him with eastern Sutherland and Caithness. His church there was Kildonnan beside the Helmsdale River, and the rock of 'St Donnán's Seat' (Cathair Donnáin) was in the same parish. Eigg recovered or was re-established after the Pictish onslaught in 617, for it is Eigg rather than other churches dedicated to Donnán which reappears in the pages of the *Annals of Ulster*. We read of Oan, the *princeps* or superior of Eigg who died in 725, and of Cumméne, a religious who died there in 752. Irish martyrologies record the feast days of holy men associated with Eigg, but their names alone survive: we know nothing of their origins or the age in which they lived and prayed there. These include Berchán, Congalach, Conán and Enán – all of them probably flourished in the eighth century before the Viking onslaught put paid to the monastery. The mention of a *princeps* in 725 is suggestive of an important and wealthy foundation, for that title was used at precisely this time by Irish annalists for 'royal abbots' of wealthy monasteries that had fallen under royal control. Eigg may have become a royal monastery by the early eighth century, either of the expanding Dál Riata or of a local Pictish tribe, no doubt having exploited the reputation of its founding martyrs to full advantage among the newly converted Picts. The massacre of Donnán's community was prompted by political fears among the Picts at the prospect of Gaelic expansion into Skye. We find evidence for just such Dál Riata expansion in 668 when the people of Skye fled to Ireland for a time. It may be, therefore, that the recovery of Eigg in the early eighth century was due to Dál Riata patronage and protection.

The distribution of churches dedicated to Donnán and that of churches considered by Adomnán to have been founded by Columba are mutually exclusive. Donnán's churches lay either south of Columba's group or, more particularly, to the north of it. This evidence suggests that although Columba and Donnán were contemporaries, they worked quite independently of each other, and that while Columba chose to give leadership and coordination to the already Christian community within northern Dál Riata, Donnán opted for a more hazardous life among the northern Picts. A later entry in the *Martyrology of Oengus* claims that Donnán once sought out Columba with a view to making him his confessor, but Columba refused saying he had no wish to become confessor to a community of martyrs! The tale is of course apocryphal, but it does show that later Irish monastic tradition considered the activities of Columba and Donnán as two quite separate and rival enterprises. Columba was prudent to choose a life of 'white martyrdom' (i.e. a life of exile from one's kin) among the Scottish Christians of Dál Riata, for it seems clear from Adomnán that the Picts were not ready for conversion to Christianity at the close of the sixth century. And so Donnán's enterprise, whether it was a missionary campaign among the Picts or merely the seeking of a monastic retreat, was doomed to a real or 'red martyrdom'. The butchering of Donnán's community in 617 supports evidence gleaned independently from Adomnán that Skye was the furthest limit of Columba's activities, and accords, too, with other evidence that the conversion of the north-western Picts may not have been possible without the political backing of Dál Riata.

The first real breakthrough in the conversion of this section of Pictland was most likely achieved under Maelrubai of Applecross, who founded his monastery there in the late seventh century. Maelrubai sailed from Ireland in 671, and quite independently of the Columban enterprise on Iona he founded Applecross two years later. Like Columba, Maelrubai lived to a great age, dying in his eightieth year in April 722. The geographical position of

Maelrubai's monastic headquarters at Applecross, looking out on Skye and not far to the north of Eigg, would suggest that he was consciously trying to rebuild on the ruins of Donnán's missionary activities among the northern Picts. This point is confirmed if we compare the distribution of ecclesiastical dedications to Maelrubai with those of his predecessor Donnán. As in the case of Donnán's dedications, those of Maelrubai's are again mutually exclusive to those early monastic sites of Columba, and significantly, the distribution of Maelrubai's dedications broadly coincide in northern Scotland with those of Donnán. Thus, Applecross and Clachán Ma-Ruibhe on Loch Carron are quite near the dedications to Donnán at Kishorn and Eilean Donnáin in Loch Alsh, while the dedication to Donnán on Little Loch Broom is paralleled by that to Maelrubai (Eilean Ma-Ruibhe) on Loch Maree (Loch Ma-Ruibhe). These dedications in Wester Ross are echoed by others across the Inner Sound on the Isle of Skye where we have already noted the dedication to Donnán at Loch Snizort. Maelrubai's activities put the seal on the Christianization of north-western Pictland. In 737 we read in the *Annals of Ulster* of the shipwreck of his successor, Failbe mac Guaire, at Applecross with the loss of 22 sailors. It is no coincidence that this is also the time when we hear of holy men back in business on Eigg in 725 and 752. Christianity was enjoying a brief period of success in the north-west between the conversion, if not the conquest of the Picts, and the coming of the Vikings. It is remarkable that Adomnán, who wrote in the late 680s, did not mention Maelrubai who was then active in northern Pictland, nor did he refer even once to the martyr, Donnán of Eigg, who was the contemporary of Columba. It was not to Adomnán's purpose to mention either of these important northern monks who operated outside the sphere of influence of Iona. Donnán in particular, who had paid for his monastic ideals with his life, may have caused some embarrassment to Iona monks of Adomnán's time who were anxious to read of the power of Columba's spirituality and of his authority all over northern Britain. The reason why we know so little about Donnán and Maelrubai is that, unlike Columba, they did not earn the official patronage and esteem of that particular Dál Riata dynasty from whom later kings of medieval Scotland claimed descent; and unlike Columba, they never found anyone of Adomnán's stature to write up their lives of toil among the Picts. The outcome of the Viking invasions also had an effect on the development of saints' cults in

Scotland, for while the ecclesiastical inheritance of men like Donnán and Maelrubai sustained a shattering blow in the exposed north, Iona managed to preserve its organization by the prudent evacuation of the island by most of its monks in the early ninth century.

In our search for a balanced assessment of Columba's contribution to the early Scottish church, we have allowed for his limitations as a missionary among the Picts; we have recognized that he was not alone as a monastic founder with pastoral authority in western and northern Scotland, and that chance also played a significant part in the later phenomenal growth of his cult in northern Britain. Yet, after all these things have been said, we are still left with works such as the obscure *Amra Coluim Cille* written but a few years after his death which testifies to Columba's sanctity and scholarship; and with Adomnán's *Life* which shows that belief in Columba's saintly powers had already spread far across the British Isles before the end of the seventh century. It is important that we do not allow Iona's political power and great wealth of later centuries to obscure the true greatness of Columba, for it may have been largely on the achievement of her founder that so much of the success of later centuries was built. We must balance all the evidence for Columba's apparent lack of involvement with Pictland against what Adomnán had to say of Columba's ecclesiastical missionary labours in general and against what he had to say of the achievements of the Columban confraternity in his own day. Columba's mother was alleged to have heard a voice in a dream foretelling that Columba was 'predestined by God to be a leader of innumerable souls to the heavenly country', a prophecy which echoed that of Brendan of Birr who was alleged to have saved Columba from excommunication by persuading an Irish synod that he was 'predestined by God to be a leader of nations into life.' Adomnán, and presumably Cumméne before him, considered Columba to be 'the father and founder of monasteries', while Adomnán also cites a disciple of Patrick, a British holy man called Maucte, foretelling that 'Columba will become famous through all the provinces of the islands of ocean'. Columba himself is made to speak 'of these islands of ours' over which he exercised ecclesiastical jurisdiction, which is echoed by Adomnán's reference to Iona as 'this our principal island'. Whatever we may think of these supposed prophecies, they show us at least what Adomnán liked to think was true in the late seventh century. Clearly these statements must have meant more than the obvious fact that Columba as a founding abbot had helped generations of monks to find salvation. We are given to understand that entire nations were led by him to God, and that his cult and spiritual authority had spread far and wide throughout northern Britain by the late seventh century.

Adomnán makes it quite clear that by his day Columba's church had firmly established itself throughout Pictland to the east of the Spine of Britain. Adomnán, in referring to the plague which he experienced at first hand during his visit to Northumbria in 688, informs us that this pestilence spared both the Picts to the east of the Spine and Dál Riata to the west of it. This he attributed to a miracle of Columba 'whose monasteries placed within the boundaries of both peoples, are down to the present time held in great honour by them both.' In other words, Columba may not have personally converted the Picts of eastern Scotland, but within about 50 years of his death, his followers must have been busy organizing an infant church in Pictland which initally was probably centred about the shores of the Moray Firth. Viewed in this light, the enquiry as to whether Columba personally converted many Picts or not becomes quite irrelevant. If through the power of his own personal zeal and sanctity, his followers claimed to carry the banner of Christianity to the eastern Picts, then it was natural for writers like Adomnán to see Columba as the apostle of northern Britain. Bede believed that Columba, 'a true monk in life no less than habit' had come to Britain specifically to convert the Picts who lived north of the Mounth, and elsewhere he speaks of Iona as the chief monastery 'for a very long time', not only of the northern Irish but also of the Picts. Bede was probably fed this information by Iona clergy, but propaganda or not, it makes even greater claims for Columba and his successors than those put forward by Adomnán.

In contrast to the unlucky Donnán, Columba founded all his monasteries within the territory of Dál Riata whose political star was in the ascendant. As an Uí Néill prince, he could talk to the Celtic warlords at Dunadd, Dumbarton or the Moray Firth, on equal terms, and his experience and strong personality put him in a position to offer valuable advice to aspiring Dál Riata kings. Columba had founded a church which was designed to serve the pastoral needs of the Gaelic colony in Scottish Dál Riata. Everything we know of the monastic communities founded by the saint supports that, although this church was inevitably monastic in view of its Irish origin, and although it may have lacked Roman episcopal and parish organization, Adomnán's frequent references to 'priors' on Hinba, Tiree and elsewhere, is clearly suggestive of organization with a well planned network of monasteries serving the needs of northern Dál Riata. In one important anecdote, Adomnán shows us Columba busy baptizing an infant in Ardnamurchan at a spring which later became a cult centre. The boy was clearly not a pagan Pict, but a child in Cenél Loairn territory, and Columba is seen here going about his duties like any country priest. We get other glimpses too, from Adomnán, of Columba travelling through 'the rough and rocky district of Ardnamurchan'; of travelling along the shores of the Firth of Lorn; and of staying with friends who were laymen and small farmers, like Nesan of Lochaber or Colmán of Ardnamurchan, who struggled to make a living in a hostile environment. These men gave food and shelter to Columba and his monks as they went on their rounds ministering to local communities. Adomnán gives us the impression that Columba's contacts with northern Dál Riata and its inhabitants extended far and wide, embracing all classes in society from men like the thief on Coll, to Feradach, a rich Gaelic magnate on Islay, and extending physically from the shores of Skye to Loch Awe in Argyll. The fact that Adomnán does not dwell on this pastoral role of Columba and his monks does not necessarily mean that it was not important. On the contrary, we may assume that Adomnán took that role for granted, and no case can be made for viewing Columba as a recluse locked up on Iona or Hinba.

It is still possible, within those special limits imposed by the nature of Adomnán's *Life*, to recognize three distinct levels at which Columba's Scottish career unfolded. There is firstly Columba, the founding abbot who ruled from Iona over an entire network of monastic houses in northern Dál Riata, and who was the close friend of Scottish kings. Columba was in this respect no different from the founders of other great mission churches in Britain – Augustine, archbishop of Canterbury, and Aidan, bishop of Lindisfarne. For although Columba lacked the sacramental authority of a bishop, as the leader of a monastic confederation within the Celtic church he exercised the powers that went with metropolitan status elsewhere in the Roman world. Secondly, the key to Columba's success lay in his founding a monastic organization which took pastoral control of the Christian colony in south-west Scotland which had hitherto lacked coordination and may well have been only half-Christian in its ethos. The subsequent and rapid spread of Columban Christianity to the Picts and Northumbrians was clearly due to the solid organizational structure which Columba had created and due to his own personal reputation for holiness. In addition to Columba the metropolitan abbot, and Columba the baptizing priest, Adomnán concentrated his talents as a writer of miracle stories in affording us glimpses of Columba the holy man – the humble monk, who divided his time between supervising the activities of his followers and devoting himself to writing and prayer. But even this monastic vocation which pervades every page of Adomnán's narrative is intimately connected with Columba's role as a church leader and as a pastor. We see him supervising the humblest chores of his labouring monks at milking time, at harvest and while fishing; thinking of building programmes at far-off Durrow; interviewing guests who arrive from the mainland; hearing confessions of visiting penitents; receiving deputations from the king of Strathclyde; praying alone in the chapel at night; celebrating Sunday Mass; travelling on the Scottish mainland and visiting his Irish monasteries. In short we get the impression of a man with boundless energy for organization and of great strength of character, who lived long, and was remembered by his own monks as an unflinching champion in spiritual combat, who regarded evil as something to be fought with all the strength of his warrior ancestors.

For Adomnán at least, Columba's spiritual warfare reflected the violence of the physical world dominated by the warrior aristocracy from which he and Columba had sprung. We are told that Columba fought all day in a wild part of Iona against an array of black demons armed with iron spikes who sought to impale him and his monks. Iona tradition had a firm belief in a widespread medieval mythology which considered that the souls of the just might not be safe even after death. Columba is credited with visions of angels struggling with devils in the sky over Iona for the soul of a deceased Briton who had died as one of Columba's monks. At another time Columba relayed a vision to one of his Anglo-Saxon monks, where, rather as at a rugby match, a dead man struggling for his soul against demons was aided by his pre-deceased wife and a team of angels. Columba himself could influence the outcome of these salvation battles, as when, on Iona, he retailed a struggle between demons and a band of monks from Bangor who had just been drowned in Belfast Lough. Clearly, whatever his part had been on the battlefields of Ireland, in his Scottish life Columba was seen as the champion against the spiritual violence of the devil and his alert warband of demons.

Adomnán's description of the closing hours of Columba's life is the longest continuous passage in his work and it follows the movements of the ageing saint with the precision of a modern film director's camera. This account constitutes one of the most moving narratives in the whole of Dark Age historical literature. Its strength lies in its simplicity and its circumstantial detail. We are presented with a picture of the closing moments in the life of a great monk who had guided the destinies of men in his own time and who from beyond the grave would shape the destinies of others for centuries to come – and yet we see him, quite convincingly, pottering around his beloved community. On that Saturday in June, 597, he went with his attendant Diarmait and blessed two heaps of grain in the nearest barn where he confided that this was to be his last day on earth – literally his Sabbath or 'rest'. Halfway back to the monastery he was forced to sit down, 'weary with age', and there the white horse who carried milk from the cow pasture trotted up and took his farewell by weeping on his lap. He then climbed the little hill overlooking the monastery and blessed it and returned to his writing hut where he worked for a while transcribing a psalter. When he reached the line 'But they that seek the Lord shall not want for anything that is good', he said:

> Here at the end of the page, I must stop. Let Baithene [Columba's relative and successor] write what follows.

Columba went from his writing hut to vespers (evensong) and from there returned to his private cell, where on his bed of stone he delivered his final wish for his community in the presence of Diarmait alone. It was a message of peace and love: then he fell silent. The midnight bell tolled out the coming of Sunday morning, 9 June, and on hearing it the old man ran ahead of his monks to the church. Diarmait and other monks followed closely and saw the building filled with light; but as Diarmait entered all was dark again, and the grief-stricken servant cried out in the darkness: 'Where are you, where are you, Father?'. Stumbling forward, he found his master slumped before the altar. Columba was now dying and too weak to speak. The community gathered round; their torches lighting the gloom to show Columba's face glowing, with eyes looking round in joy. Diarmait raised the master a little and moved his enfeebled right hand through the movements of a blessing. *Columb Cille*, the Dove of the Church, was dead.

4

The World of Adomnán: 'In the Midst of Ecclesiastical Cares'

Iona had been founded by Columba within Dál Riata, a territory ruled by a dynasty of kings whose immediate ancestors had migrated across the North Channel from Co. Antrim to settle in south-west Scotland in the post-Roman era. This dynasty took charge of a Gaelic population which had already infiltrated Argyll from perhaps as early as the third century. Up until the Convention of Drumceat in 575 the kings of the Scottish colony ruled the territory of their Ulster homeland direct. The purpose of the convention was to sort out the constitutional position of Dál Riata's Irish home territory vis-à-vis the Uí Néill highking Áed mac Ainmerech and the king of all Dál Riata, Áedán mac Gabhráin, who resided in Scotland. Columba attended this meeting as the chief cleric in Áedán's Scottish territories, and as the cousin of Áed mac Ainmerech. The outcome seems to have been that while Irish Dál Riata was regarded as formally subject to the Uí Néill highking, it continued to yield tribute to the king of Scots Dál Riata. This treaty between the Uí Néill overlord and the kings of the new Scottish colony survived for some 60 years, sustained no doubt by the good offices of the abbots of Iona who themselves constituted a dynasty of clerics from the house of Uí Néill.

The Scottish dynasty suffered a major setback in the reign of Domnall Brecc, a Scots king who began his fighting career in 622. In 637, Domnall Brecc took part in a disastrous battle at *Mag Rath*, in Co. Down in which he lost control of the Irish Dál Riata homelands. He also brought his dynasty into a head-on confrontation with the Uí Néill highkings – that dynasty to which Columba and his successors on Iona belonged, and on which Scottish kings relied for moral and political support ever since that day when Columba was said to have ordained Áedán mac Gabhráin king of the Scots. At *Mag Rath* in 637 the Dál Riata king was backing his traditional ally and perhaps also his nephew, Congal, king of Dál nAraide and of all the Ulstermen. The Scottish kings chose the Dál nAraide, a people of the Cruithin, as their Ulster allies, and supported them in their bid for the kingship of Ulster, presumably in return for the protection of Dál Riata lands in Ireland. This close relationship between the early Scottish kings and the Irish Cruithin ought to be seen in the context of the proximity of the Scottish kingdom of Dál Riata to the Picts – those cousins of the Irish Cruithin. But in 637, the Scottish king, Domnall, allowed himself to be dragged into a quarrel on the side of Ulster Cruithin against the Uí Néill highking, Domnall son of Áed mac Ainmerech. This Uí Néill Domnall was a kinsman of Adomnán who relates that as a boy at Drumceat, Domnall received Columba's blessing and the benefit of the saint's prophetic powers.

While the Irish Domnall was believed in Iona tradition to have enjoyed Columba's blessing, for the first time a Scottish king (Domnall Brecc) was believed to have incurred his curse, and the evidence for this is earlier than Adomnán, coming as it does from the only surviving fragment of a *Life of Columba* written by Cumméne the White, seventh abbot of Iona (657-69). According to Cumméne, St Columba had promised the kingships of Dál Riata to Áedán mac Gabhráin and his descendants provided they were loyal to his successors on Iona and loyal to the kindred of Columba in Ireland. If they should prove false in this, divine retribution would follow. Cumméne continues:

> This prophecy has been fulfilled in our times in the battle of [Mag] Rath when Domnall Brecc, Áedán's grandson, without cause wasted the Province of Domnall grandson, of Ainmere. And they are from that day to this still held down by strangers; which fills the breast with sighs of grief.

Cumméne, who wrote sometime after 661, believed that Dál Riata power collapsed after Domnall Brecc's defeat in Ulster in 637 and that the Scottish dynasty remained in a shambles for the next 30 years. Domnall Brecc's reign in Scotland seems to have been an unqualified disaster. He suffered several other military defeats, most likely at the hands of the Picts in 635 and 638, and he was finally slain in battle against Owen, king of Strathclyde, at Strathcarron in Stirlingshire about AD 642. A British bard at the court of Dumbarton celebrated the Strathclyde victory over the

Scottish hosts of Kintyre in a poem which gleefully conjured up images of the raven gnawing the head of the unfortunate Domnall (*Dyfnal Frych*).

The overthrow of Dál Riata power in 642 was followed some 22 years later by a similar setback for the church of Iona when it was deprived of its influence over the emerging English church in Northumbria, at the Synod of Whitby in 664. The decline of Dál Riata kings and that of their holy place in the Inner Hebrides were intimately connected with each other and with those 'strangers' (*extranei*), who according to Abbot Cumméne were 'holding down' the Scottish kingdom in his time. The identification of those strangers leads us into the wider world of northern British politics where Scots, Strathclyde Britons, Picts and Angles were desperately competing for control of east Stirlingshire in the middle of the seventh century. The conquests of the Bernician Angles, who had gradually tightened their grip on the coastal lands between the Tees and the Forth, had attracted the hostile attention of Dál Riata kings as early as the time of Columba. Áedán mac Gabhráin had feared the advance of Ethelfrith to the Forth and attempted to block English penetration of the central lowlands which were still in the hands of the northern Britons and the Picts. Áedán failed to stop the Angles and was defeated by Ethelfrith at (Degsastan) in 603. In 617, however, Ethelfrith was slain by his rival Edwin who had returned from exile in East Anglia, and in the endless cycle of 'exile-and-triumphant return' – which was to dog Northumbrian politics until the Vikings reached the walls of York in 866 – it was the turn of Ethelfrith's sons in 617 to seek refuge among the Scots and Picts.

Of Ethelfrith's exiled sons, Oswald was to have the most profound influence on the destiny of northern Britain. Oswald's conversion to Christianity while he was exposed to the influence of Iona resulted in his introduction of Columban missionaries into Northumbria when he regained his kingdom in 634. The Northumbrian church was ruled for the next 18 years by the saintly Aidan, whose bishopric at Lindisfarne was founded from Iona and which (as we gather from Bede) was clearly answerable to Iona in matters of major ecclesiastical importance. The slaying of Oswald in 641 in battle against the Mercians provided Northumbrian Christianity with its first martyr. Oswald's brother and successor, Oswiu, was yet another veteran of the Scottish exile and he was naturally sympathetic to Iona influence in his realm. But things began to go badly wrong after the death of Aidan in 651. His successors in the see of Lindisfarne – Finán (d. 660) and Colmán (resigned 664) – found themselves embroiled in an ecclesiastical dispute known as the Easter Controversy which affected all the Celtic churches throughout the British Isles in the seventh century. This dispute involved not only the question of calculating the correct date of Easter, but included other matters such as the correct form of tonsure, baptismal rites and procedures for the consecration of bishops. The problem arose in the first instance as a result of the geographical isolation of the Celtic churches from the mainstream of developments in Mediterranean liturgical practice. Among the Celtic communities of the British Isles, the dispute developed along the lines of a contest between a progressive Romanizing party who argued for uniformity with what they saw as universal church practice, and a conservative opposition which included Iona, and which argued passionately for the retention of old Celtic ways. In Northumbria, however, the situation was more complicated, because here the battleground was not Celtic but rather English, and the lines were drawn between those in the king's circle who favoured the Celtic party who ruled from Lindisfarne, and those in the circle of Oswiu's Kentish queen and his rebellious son, Alhfrith, who backed the Roman party led by Wilfrid. In other words, in Northumbria the Easter Controversy was an ecclesiastical dispute which was complicated by rival factions within the Northumbrian royal house, and complicated too, by Oswiu's political ambitions vis-à-vis the Celtic peoples of northern Britain.

The Northumbrian episode in the Easter Controversy reached its climax in 664, when a synod was held at Whitby to resolve the dispute, which was attended by the leading ecclesiastical and lay magnates involved. Ultimately, it was Oswiu who decided the issue in favour of the Roman party, and the complete collapse of Iona influence on Northumbrian ecclesiastical administration is clearly seen in the withdrawal of Colmán and his entire Irish contingent from Lindisfarne to Iona (and afterwards to Ireland). The real issues at stake at Whitby were neither Easter nor the tonsure, but rather the problem of political and ecclesiastical control. Would the Northumbrian church come of age and constitute a political province in its own right? – and this could best be achieved under Rome – or would it continue to be ruled by bishops and clergy appointed and controlled by the abbot of Iona? Oswiu, although by nature sympathetic to the Celtic rite, had to consider his position vis-à-vis the Mercians and his disloyal son who backed Wilfrid in following Roman ways. Would not Oswiu's adherence to Celtic ways undermine his authority in the kingdom of Deira where Alhfrith was in control, and would it not ultimately work against Northumbrian ambitions for overlordship south of the Humber and north of the Forth?

We know little of the all-important political relationship between the kings of the Scots and Northumbrian rulers at this time. Obviously the antagonism between Áedán mac Gabhráin and Ethelfrith at the beginning of the seventh century had given way to alliance and friendship – otherwise Ethelfrith's sons would never have fled north for refuge among the Scots from 617 until 633. That was a time when I have suggested the Pictish overlordship had been seized by the kings of Strathclyde under Neithon and his grandsons, the sons of Gwid. In 642, Owen, another grandson of Neithon of Strathclyde, slew Domnall Brecc, king of Scots, in Strathcarron, thereby showing the northern Britons to be the most formidable power in the north. It is very likely that the Britons on the Clyde were the first of those 'strangers' who Cumméne of Iona claimed were holding down Dál Riata ever since the defeat of Domnall Brecc on his Irish expedition in 637. If that were true, then it would have made sense for the Scots to exploit their friendship with the sons of Ethelfrith and to seek an alliance with distant Northumbria to help keep Dumbarton at bay. Oswiu had made himself overlord of southern England after his decisive victory over Mercia and East Anglia back in 654, and from then on he seems to have concentrated his efforts on northern Britain, where according to Bede, he 'overwhelmed and made tributary' the Picts and Scots. Bede also speaks, but with less force, about Oswald's overlordship of Picts and Scots, and Adomnán described Oswald as 'ordained by God as emperor of the whole of Britain'. Oswald had spent some time on Iona, and Adomnán writing about 50 years later must be taken seriously when he describes the king in these grandiose terms. It is very likely, then, that Dál Riata accepted Oswald's overlordship during the period after 637 if not before, when the Scots kingdom was vulnerable to the domination of its stronger neighbour in Strathclyde.

Oswald's death in battle in 641 and the collapse of Domnall Brecc's warband in Strathcarron within the year, must have compelled the Scots to renew their submission to the new Northumbrian ruler, Oswiu. By 653, the Strathclyde hold on the Pictish overlordship may have been broken. It was at this time that Oswiu succeeded in imposing his nephew, Talorgen, as overlord of the Picts. This was a development which may well have caused the Scots to rethink their alliance with Northumbria. Talorgen's reign in Pictland as a Northumbrian puppet brought Oswiu's influence uncomfortably nearer Briton and Scot alike, and upset the complicated checks and balances within the Celtic confederacies of northern Britain – not least Scottish and Strathclyde British ambitions for Pictish overlordship. A close reading of Bede suggests that while Oswald ruled with tact and humility, Oswiu was made of sterner stuff, and his relationship with his northern neighbours was more aggressive. We shall never be certain whether Oswiu's relationship with the Dál Riata kings had already turned sour before Whitby – and hence his decision to back Wilfrid – or whether his aggression towards the Scots was a later development. But whatever the answers to these questions, there is no doubt that the real issues at Whitby were primarily political. Arguments about the date of Easter and set speeches on St Peter were little more than a smokescreen to hide more pressing issues exercising the minds of the Bretwalda, of Alhfrith, and of course of Wilfrid.

In the light of these happenings, we can glimpse the circumstances which inspired Abbot Cumméne to write what was probably the earliest *Life* of his founder, St Columba. Cumméne's rule on Iona saw the continued collapse of the Scottish dynasty, which Columba had once blessed and was believed to have prophesied of its future greatness. The political shambles was a minor worry compared to the body-blow which the Synod of Whitby had dealt to the Columban church in England. As the demoralized missionaries returned to Iona from the farthest corners of northern and eastern England, Cumméne must have decided to write up the *Miraculous powers of Saint Columba* as a counterblast to Wilfrid and his party who had poured scorn on the Father of Scottish Christianity, and who as Bede put it, rejected the teachings and despised the principles of Bishop Colmán's superiors. Whitby had been a personal triumph for Wilfrid, who became sole ruler of the Northumbrian church in the very year in which Abbot Cumméne died in 669. Works such as Cumméne's account of Columba were often written not when a cause was secure, but when it was under attack. Iona and Columba were in full retreat in 665 and Cumméne most probably wrote his account after the Synod of Whitby, during the last four years of his life, which were spent in retirement perhaps on Rathlin island. We shall see that Adomnán wrote his *Life* of Columba also at the close of his life and under crisis circumstances very similar to those of Cumméne's time.

I began this discussion on the Synod of Whitby with an account of the Convention of Drumceat, and both these gatherings although far removed in time and place had much in common. At Drumceat in Ulster in 575, the Uí Néill highking had to sort out his relationship with the new Scottish colony in Argyll, while almost a century later, the English Bretwalda convened a conference with a very similar purpose in mind. At both assemblies Iona played a central role, for Columba attended at Drumceat in person, and one of his successors, Colmán, led the defence of the Celtic Church at Whitby. There were of course differences in issues and outcomes, and while Scots Dál Riata seems to have achieved something approaching recognition as a separate kingdom at Drumceat, at Whitby Oswiu prevented the growth of an alien Scottish ecclesiastical establishment on English soil. But in some ways the Scottish defeat at Whitby ought not to be viewed as final, any more than Áedán's defeat at Degsastan in 603 or Domnall Brecc's slaughter in Strathcarron in 642 can be said to have marked the downfall of Dál Riata. Rather, all these events from Drumceat to Whitby show us a new kingdom in the throes of extricating itself from the remoter world of Irish politics and testing the ground in an effort to find a place for itself within the scheme of things in Britain. It is a sign of the vitality and strength of the young Scots kingdom that it made such an impact on the politics and religion of both Ireland and Britain, and that it was capable of surviving the apparently endless series of setbacks it endured in the seventh century. Those historians who glibly write off Dál Riata after Áedán's defeat by Ethelfrith in 603 fail to take the interaction of politics and other cultural matters into account. The military setbacks of the seventh century do not tell the whole story. The tract known as the *Senchus Fer nAlban* ('Tradition of the Men of Scotland') provides us with evidence of a very different kind. This tenth-century edition of a seventh-century work provides us with the earliest, and indeed a very rare instance, of a Celtic civil survey which also provides details of army and navy musters for the three major tribal divisions within Dál Riata. Columba and the great intellectual, spiritual and artistic effort that surrounded his cult may in the longer term have provided the Scots kingdom with a cultural superiority which ensured its political dominance and survival in northern Britain long after neighbouring dynasties had passed into oblivion.

Adomnán did not serve as a monk under Abbot Cumméne of Iona, but he seems to have joined the community soon after Cumméne's death in 669. He tells us very little about himself in his *Life of Columba* apart from a few miracle stories which he claims to have witnessed and apart from two journeys which he says he made to Northumbria and which we can date independently to 686 and 688. The first miracle which he personally claimed to have witnessed on Iona concerned a spring drought which occurred 14 years before he wrote, i.e. sometime between 671 and 678. Failbe, the eighth abbot of Iona, is the earliest abbot cited by Adomnán who provided information directly to him on Columba. Failbe began his rule on Iona in 669 and he may well have invited Adomnán to join the community there soon afterwards. Adomnán eventually succeeded Failbe as ninth abbot in 679. He was born in about 624 and he was in his late 40s when he moved from Ireland to Iona – even older than Columba was when that saint migrated to Scotland almost a century before. Adomnán was born at a time when Northumbria was still a pagan land before Paulinus arrived at York; his youth coincided with the time of Aidan's mission on Lindisfarne and he was already an elderly man by Dark Age standards when the practices of Iona were outlawed at Whitby in 664. He did not land on Iona out of the blue some five years after the synod of Whitby. He was a member of Columba's royal kin in Donegal; his grandfather, Tinne, had probably been a tribal king; while his great-great-grandfather was a first cousin of Columba. Adomnán's contemporary and kinsman, Loingsech, reigned as highking of the Uí Néill and died a year before Adomnán in 703. These aristocratic connections meant that this priest of the Columban *familia* in Ireland must have been clearly recognizable as a front runner for the abbacy of Iona long before he arrived there. All of Adomnán's predecessors on Iona (with one exception) had come from Columba's kin, while his holiness of life, scholarly ability, and powers of diplomacy made his succession to his kinsman Failbe inevitable.

If Columba's reputation for sanctity was confined solely to his later life in Scotland, then Adomnán's migration to Iona seems to have given scope to his ability as a writer – or at least it is only those works from his Scottish career that have survived. Those high winds and raging seas so frequently mentioned in Adomnán's *Life* of Columba marooned a Frankish seafarer on Iona sometime between 679 and 686 and this happy accident provided Adomnán with material for his earliest surviving work. The shipwrecked traveller was Arculf, a Gaulish bishop returning from the Holy Land, who provided Adomnán with the information he needed for his work on *The Holy Places*. Arculf 'most willingly dictated the facts', while Adomnán 'diligently asked him to tell of his experiences'. So, as the bishop dictated his story, Adomnán made notes on wax tablets, and later wrote up a fuller account on vellum. Adomnán was in charge of Iona when Arculf arrived, for he tells us he wrote his book on *The Holy Places*

> although placed in the midst of laborious and nearly insupportable ecclesiastical cares, which come upon me the whole day from all sides.

This work has value as a detailed account of the Holy Land as it appeared to a Frankish traveller in the early 670s. Arculf spent no less than nine months in Jerusalem and he gave Adomnán a detailed account of the layout of its walls and shrines, sometimes even drawing plans of buildings and often, too, giving fascinating glimpses of social conditions. Adomnán's book on *The Holy Places* forms but a small part of a genre of early and later medieval literature on the homeland of Christ, but the fact that it was based on an eye-witness account in the century which saw the Persian massacre in Jerusalem in 614 and the Islamic domination of the Holy City which began under Caliph Omar I in 638, makes it particularly interesting. When Arculf visited Jerusalem, Islamic influence in the city was still at an early stage, and it was only when Adomnán had finished writing, for instance, that the caliph, Abd al Malik, commissioned the Dome of the Rock, which was not finished until 691. Arculf travelled widely outside Jerusalem, visiting Bethlehem, Jericho and the Dead Sea region in southern Palestine, while in the north he sought out Nazareth and the Sea of Galilee, and he seems to have explored the source of the Jordan. He reached Damascus, where 'the king of the Saracens had seized the government' and where he noted a mosque had been built. Finally, Arculf returned to Jerusalem and left Palestine from the port of Joppa.

Adomnán's interest was not confined to Palestine: he followed the traveller on a 40-day voyage from Joppa to Alexandria, giving a description of that city and of the Nile with its legendary crocodiles and irrigation systems. We are next taken back via Crete to Constantinople where Arculf spent about eight or nine months from

Easter to Christmas. Here we are treated to a description of Hagia Sophia, rebuilt by the Emperor Justinian in the middle of the sixth century. We are told of the relic of the Holy Cross; of an icon of the Virgin Mary; and treated to tales from the cult of St George. Adomnán's miracle stories of St George are the earliest accounts of this saint's cult which survive in Britain, and they are interesting, too, in that a horse, which was characteristic of that cult, figures prominently in the two stories which Adomnán offers. Arculf sailed from Constantinople to Rome, and from there he visited Sicily, where, from somewhere near Messina, he told Adomnán how he had seen Mount Vulcan on the most southerly of the Lipari islands. Elsewhere, in his description of the Jordan and the Dead Sea, Adomnán refers to salt mines which Arculf had visited on Sicily. Adomnán's interest in places other than Palestine shows that he did not intend to write a stereotyped account of the Holy Land. He tells us that he edited Arculf's account and so did not slavishly transcribe it, and he had access to other works on the East:

> Arculf's narrative about the situation of Alexandria and the Nile does not differ from what we have learnt in our reading in other books. We have, indeed, abbreviated some excerpts from these writings and inserted them in this description.

Iona's library, therefore, contained works on Near Eastern topography, presumably part of a wider genre on oriental hagiography and biblical exegesis. This suggests that the reason Adomnán took the trouble to write on the Holy Places in the first instance was because a well developed interest in the subject already existed in Iona.

The necessity of setting Adomnán's much neglected work on the Near East into the context of early medieval Scottish intellectual and art history scarcely needs stressing. Adomnán was writing at a time when Iona's political power was waning, but when at another level it was entering a golden age of artistic and literary endeavour. Other writers in addition to Adomnán, were active on Iona at this time, such as Cú Chuimne the Hiberno-Latin poet and canonist, and the compilers of what may have been the earliest set of annals in the Gaelic world. The surviving fragments of Dark Age sculpture from the monastery and its dependencies testify to the ability of seventh-century Columban craftsmen in stone, and the *Book of Kells* was begun on Iona not long after Adomnán's death.

Adomnán's interest, therefore, in the Byzantine and Coptic worlds has much to tell us about his own educational background and about artistic taste on Iona in the late seventh century and its contacts with oriental Christendom. D.A. Bullough recognized Adomnán's use of biblical criticism in the *Holy Places* as being characteristic of seventh-century Irish schools of exegesis. This observation supports my own conclusion that Adomnán must have received his early education at Durrow, the most important Columban house in Ireland and situated in the centre of a whole network of Offaly and Westmeath monasteries all renowned for the study of biblical criticism. While Adomnán mentions Derry only in passing in his *Life of Columba*, he shows a detailed knowledge of the topography and monastic buildings at Durrow. Considering Adomnán's family connections and the long time which he had spent in Ireland it is quite likely that he held a senior position at Durrow before he sailed to Iona.

Adomnán's concern with the East went far beyond the limits of biblical scholarship. He was interested in the wider Byzantine and Coptic sphere of influence as shown for instance by his discussion on the tomb of the Virgin in the Holy Land and of an icon of the Virgin in Constantinople. His interest in this subject can scarcely be put down solely to the stimulus received from a wandering Gaulish pilgrim. The cult of the Virgin appears rarely in the Christian art of the West including the Celtic world in the Dark Ages in contrast with its popularity in the Eastern Empire. Representations of the Virgin differ from other biblical motifs in that icons of Mary were intended for popular veneration rather than illustrations of strictly historical biblical matter. Françoise Henry and other art historians have noted that while the Virgin and Child motif does not appear on Irish high crosses, it is found on Iona sculpture, such as St Martin's Cross, and further east in Pictland, on a slab at Brechin. Other early instances of this rare motif occur on the wooden reliquary of St Cuthbert made at Lindisfarne about 698, and in an illuminated page in the *Book of Kells*. The Kells version of this icon may well be later than that at Lindisfarne, but the presence of the Virgin and Child both in the sculpture and manuscript art of Iona rightly prompted Henry to suggest that the monastery possessed a Byzantine icon dealing with this subject. Remarkably, Adomnán mentions an icon of the Virgin seen by Arculf during his visit of Constantinople, and Adomnán's younger contemporary Cú-Chuimne the Wise of Iona (d. 747) was almost certainly the author of that fine Hiberno-Latin hymn which bears his name and which testifies to devotion to the Virgin Mary in the early eighth-century Irish church. This of course does not prove that Arculf ever carried an eastern icon of the Virgin and Child to south-west Scotland in the seventh century, but it does show that an Iona abbot, writing more than a decade before the making of St Cuthbert's reliquary, was sufficiently interested in Byzantine icons of the Virgin as to include a mention of them in his book on the Holy Land. Art historians are of the opinion that a Coptic or Syriac original inspired the Virgin and Child page in the *Book of Kells* which was begun on Iona perhaps within a generation of Adomnán's death.

The Virgin and Child motif provides but one example of several oriental influences at work on Celtic art in the Dark Ages, but its particular interest to us lies in the fact that it centred on Iona. Iona had its own close contacts with the eastern Mediterranean either by way of academic knowledge through its library or at first hand through travellers like Arculf. This knowledge of eastern Christendom was inevitably transmitted in artistic form to other Columban monasteries in Dál Riata and Pictland. Byzantine and Coptic influence has been seen on the St Andrews sarcophagus as well as in hunting scenes on Pictish Class II cross slabs at Nigg and Hilton of Cadboll, together with individual Classical motifs on several other Pictish monuments. Art historians have challenged the plausibility for any direct oriental contacts between Pictland and the Eastern Empire, and have sought instead the inspiration for Pictish art in seventh-century England. But why must we look to Jarrow, to the Canterbury Psalter and to the Lichfield scriptorium for the origins of Pictish Christian art? On the contrary, it is straining the historical evidence beyond all prudent limits to wander south of the Humber in search of mentors for the earliest Pictish craftsmen. Are not the Hilton of Cadboll and the Nigg slabs – which most probably date from Adomnán's time – situated in precisely that region of the Moray Firth where Adomnán himself envisaged Columba journeying in search of Bridei, king of the Picts? Adomnán's contemporary, Curetan bishop of Rosemarkie, was almost certainly the bishop of that name who helped promulgate Adomnán's *Law of Innocents* at the Synod of Birr in 697. Rosemarkie, on the Black Isle, lay in the heart of that region to the north of the Great Glen where evidence for medieval dedications to Curetan survive – along the shores of Loch Ness, in

Glen Urquhart and Strathglass, as well as Glen Glass and the valley of the Alness, north of the Cromarthy Firth.

According to hagiographical tradition, Curetan evangelized the Picts from his base at Rosemarkie which lies in the centre of that distribution of symbol stones around the Moray Firth, and Rosemarkie itself has one Class II monument and several of Class III. We have then a reliable historical context which connects the Class I monuments about the Moray Firth with early Columban Christianity, and significantly, Isobel Henderson has concluded on other grounds, that the Class I monuments originated in this area rather than further east and south. Adomnán and his colleague Curetan were contemporary with Class II monuments in the same area and although the Class II monuments may well have begun life outside the Moray Firth region, nevertheless, there is clearly continuity, artistically and historically, between the earlier and later group of monuments. The decidedly Christian iconography of Class II cross-slabs, including their oriental motifs, testifies to the flowering of Columban Christian culture among the Picts of the north-east in Curetan's time in the late seventh century. Contact between the Iona region, as an extension of the Firth of Lorn, and the Moray Firth on the other side of the Spine not only makes sound geographical sense, but Adomnán offers us abundant proof that he considered the Great Glen to be the major route between Iona and Pictland. As for artistic impulses, those scholars who reject direct oriental influence on Iona and Pictland out of hand overlook the fact that Adomnán was so knowledgeable on the eastern Mediterranean that Bede thought fit to devote two whole chapters of his *Ecclesiastical History of the English Church* to extracts from Adomnán's work on the Near East!

We know that Adomnán had finished the story of Arculf's voyage before he began work on Columba. In Columba's *Life* he mentions two visits to the court of his friend, King Aldfrith of Northumbria, – one 'after Ecgfrith's battle' at *Nechtanesmere*, and another visit two years later in 688. Adomnán mentions his journeys to Northumbria in connection with the plague which was raging in northern England during those years, and Bede takes up the story by telling us that during Adomnán's visit to Aldfrith's court, he presented the king with a copy of his book on *The Holy Places* and that Aldfrith had the work copied for widespread distribution in his kingdom. Aldfrith (685-705) was the last of the Northumbrian rulers who had been brought up in sympathy with the

Scottish and Irish tradition, for like his father, Oswiu, and his saintly uncle, Oswald, this king, too, was exiled among the Irish before he came to power. Aldfrith was known in Irish tradition as *Flann Fína* ('Wine Red') the son of an Irish Uí Néill princess, Fína, and the Northumbrian, Oswiu. When Oswiu died in 670 Aldfrith was passed over in favour of his brother Ecgfrith either on grounds of youth or illegitimacy, or he may then have been preparing for the priesthood. When Aldfrith's interest in Northumbrian politics became too obvious, he was forced, according to William of Malmesbury, to seek exile in Ireland. He did not finally return to Northumbria until he was summoned by the *witan* to become king after the defeat and death of Ecgfrith at the hands of the Picts in 685. According to the *Anonymous Life of Cuthbert*, Aldfrith was staying on Iona in the year before his brother's death. Adomnán knew the Northumbrian king well enough before his visit of 686 to describe him as his 'friend' and later Irish sources call Aldfrith the *dalta* or 'pupil' of Adomnán. This would imply that Aldfrith had known and studied under Adomnán earlier in his youth in Ireland and that, too, is in keeping with other Irish traditions concerning Aldfrith's great learning in the Irish language and his ability as a poet in that tongue. It is highly unlikely that Aldfrith became an accomplished writer in Irish during a short exile on Iona when he was already early middle-aged. It is quite possible on the other hand, that he had studied under Adomnán in Ireland most likely at Durrow as a youth, and that later when he was forced into exile, he sought out his old master who was then abbot of Iona.

Adomnán, with typical modesty, does not tell us why he set out to Aldfrith's court in 686, but we learn from Bede and from a letter written by Abbot Ceolfrith of Jarrow (*c.* 706), that the Iona leader 'was sent on a mission from his people to the king'. Irish sources make it clear Adomnán travelled not merely as an envoy of Iona but as a representative of the Irish Uí Néill king of Brega, whose territory had been invaded by an army of Ecgfrith of Northumbria in June 684. The Northumbrians carried off captives on that raid, and it was to secure their release that Adomnán set off in 686. Ecgfrith had fallen in Pictland a year before and with news that he had been succeeded by his half-Irish brother Aldfrith, the time was considered ripe to seek the release of the captives. If Aldfrith really had been Adomnán's pupil in his youth, and accepting the English evidence that he was staying on Iona in 684, then clearly Adomnán was the obvious choice to lead an embassy to negotiate with the new king. It cannot have been difficult to persuade Aldfrith to release the prisoners of his hostile brother, and the *Annals of Ulster* inform us in 687 that 'Adomnán brought back 60 captives to Ireland.'

The Irish *Three Fragments of Annals* and Bede mention only one visit of Adomnán of Aldfrith's court, but Adomnán tells us himself that he returned two years later in 688 and it was probably on this second visit that he was persuaded to abandon the Celtic Easter as reported in the letter from Ceolfrith of Jarrow to the Pictish king, Nechtan. Adomnán's friendship with Aldfrith of Northumbria and his eventual conversion to Roman ways opened up old wounds inflicted at Whitby in 664, only this time the 'Roman' party, through Adomnán, would carry the war into the heart of Iona's camp. Adomnán was personally aware from his youth of the Easter dispute in Ireland since as a Columban monk he may have celebrated Easter at a different time from the other churches there. He must have been well informed on the history of Aidan's mission on Lindisfarne and he was 40 when the Iona party retreated in defeat from Whitby. It is highly unlikely that a man of his integrity could have been bullied into abandoning the Celtic rite simply to secure the release of captives as later Irish tradition implied. Besides, he was willing to suffer rejection at the hands of his own community for the sake of his convictions and he devoted the rest of his life in trying to persuade the Columban *familia* to accept the Roman order. It is clear from his own writings that Adomnán was a man of broad outlook who had nothing of the provincial in him. He shows us in his *Preface* to the *Life of Columba*, for instance, that he regarded Latin as the international language of learning, and he looked on his vernacular 'Irish tongue' as a 'poor language' of little use to those who did not understand it. That is not to say that Adomnán could not write fluently in Irish or appreciate its special qualities, but a man of his catholic taste was a bad choice to rule a provincial church steeped in a conservative tradition. A scholar who was fascinated by the layout of Alexandria or the appearance of volcanoes in Sicily was very vulnerable to the argument that 'he in company with a very small band of followers, living in the remotest corner of the world, should not presume to go against the universal custom of the church'. Such an argument, put forcibly by Ceolfrith, was irresistable to a man of wide learning who had great gentleness and humility to boot. This was the old argument, which Cummian and the southern Irish used against Ségéne of Iona in 632, and it was the same argument which Wilfrid hammered home at Whitby. Adomnán was won over at Jarrow, and by accepting the Roman order of things he created great difficulties for himself and for his community.

Bede oversimplified Adomnán's career after his acceptance of the Roman rite. He implied that Adomnán returned to Iona, and failing to convert his own monks to Roman ways, he crossed over to Ireland and persuaded many who were not under the rule of Iona to abandon the old ways. Finally, according to Bede, after celebrating the Roman Easter in Ireland, he returned to Iona and mercifully died there before the next Easter, thereby avoiding a bitter clash in the heart of his own community. The vague implication of all this is that Adomnán returned to Iona in say, 689, celebrated Easter in Ireland in that year or in 690, and died in 690 or 691. Far from ending his career with this failure, Adomnán still had two major achievements ahead of him when he left Aldfrith's kingdom in 688. He had yet to write his *Life* of Columba and to convene a major synod regulating the conduct of warfare throughout Scotland and Ireland. Instead of Bede's single account of one visit to Northumbria, Adomnán made at least two; and he did not die until his seventy-seventh year on 23 September 704, and not as Bede implied in 690. Nor can we accept Bede's statement without qualification that Adomnán converted those Irish who were not under the ecclesiastical jurisdiction of Iona. It seems clear that the major part of the Irish Church outside the Columban *familia* had already accepted the Roman Easter and tonsure back at the Synod of Mag Lena in 630. Bede's bungling of these major facts relating to Adomnán's career is all the more remarkable when we bear in mind that he may well have been present as a youth at Jarrow when Adomnán visited there. Nor was Adomnán of merely fringe interest to Bede, who relied heavily on his work on the Holy Places, and his account of Adomnán's conversion to Roman ways was an important part of Bede's rounding off the victory of Northumbrian Roman Christianity in Britain. If Bede could get his facts so wrong on an important contemporary churchman and scholar, how much less ought we trust his judgement on earlier and more sensitive matters such as the baptism of Edwin or the survival of the northern Britons?

Iona monks were not prepared to follow the decision of their own abbot in the matter of the Roman rite, as both Bede and Ceolfrith assert. This is supported by the amount of time we know Adomnán spent away from Iona after 692, presumably in exile from his own community, and by the contemporary statement in the *Annals of Ulster* to the effect that Iona did not change to Roman ways until 716, when according to Bede, they were finally converted by the English bishop, Egbert, who had come over from Ireland. That was during the abbacy of Dúnchad, a cousin of Adomnán, who died in the following year. All does not seem to have been well at Iona even after 716, and there are hints of strife in the community beyond the middle of the eighth century. The tension generated by Adomnán's conversion to Roman ways must have been great. Here was the successor of Columba and a member of his kin, pledged to lead his community in the tradition of their saintly founder, now abandoning the Celtic rite which in the years after Whitby must have come to symbolize much of what Columban monasticism stood for. It was this emphasis on the Celtic rite which Adomnán must have seen to be misplaced, and with this in mind he devoted his time on Iona from 688 to 692 in writing a *Life of Columba* which would show the saint, not as a champion of either Roman or Celtic ways, but as a man of God whose spiritual integrity and simplicity of life mattered above all else. And so, just as Cumméne turned to writing the *Life* of Iona's founder after the crisis of 664, now his successor set himself the same task. There was a significant difference between Cumméne's situation in 664 and Adomnán's in 688. Cumméne, in spite of the setback to Columban Christianity in England, still had the respect and support of his Iona monks, and Iona was still a power in the land. Adomnán, although abbot, saw his authority flouted by his own monks and the Iona community now faced dissension on its own doorstep.

Viewed against a background of controversy within Iona itself, Adomnán's *Life of Columba* is an even more remarkable document than has hitherto been supposed. We should expect that Adomnán would have used all his gifts as a writer and 'his excellent knowledge of the scriptures' – vouched for by no less an authority on biblical studies than Bede – to show his hero Columba as a champion of orthodoxy, and to use his own position and family background to hammer the opposition into silence. But there is no polemic in the *Life of Columba* in spite of the storm its writer was weathering in those years after 688. Only once is the Easter controversy referred to, and Adomnán does not use it to his advantage. He simply tells us that Columba once prophesied during his stay at Clonmacnoise 'concerning the great dispute that after many years arose among the churches of Ireland over the diversity in the time of the Easter festival'. We are not told what the prophecy was, and the cynic might well speculate that Adomnán was tampering with the earlier *Life* of Cumméne in order to erase a tradition which did present Columba as the champion of the Celtic Easter. I doubt that, since all the evidence suggests that Cumméne's *Life*, too, reflected the other-worldliness of Columban spirituality, and besides, Easter had not been a contentious issue in Columba's lifetime. It seems certain, for instance, that Cumméne's *Life* did not boast of the initial success of the Columban mission in England, which would after all have been grist to its mill. Adomnán never mentions Lindisfarne or the phenomenal spread of Columban communities over England. To read his *Life* and to have read nothing else about Columba, simply gives the impression of a tiny and remote island community following the rule of a saintly founder who spent his life supervising the humblest chores in the monastery and we sense little of Iona's enormous political power and prestige as the holiest place in northern Britain. Instead of concentrating on the great political stories of his day, Adomnán was much more interested in telling us about an injured crane driven by a storm to seek refuge on Iona. Rare instances where Adomnán may be trying to make a point, as in the case of Columba's last wish for charity and love within his community, only serve to reinforce our sense of Adomnán's own integrity. Seen in this light, the *Life* is an even greater witness to the gentleness of spirit and the sanctity of the writer than it is for the miraculous powers of Columba.

Adomnán seems to have spent not one but four years with his Iona monks after returning from Northumbria in 688. The Iona annals record in 692 that he went to Ireland in the fourteenth year since the death of his predecessor, Failbe. This backward glance to Failbe may be suggestive of a community looking back on happier days. Adomnán lived a life of exile self-imposed or otherwise during the years that followed, but he was still publicly recognized as abbot of Iona. He was back in Scotland, and almost certainly at Iona, before 697 when he accomplished the crowning achievement of his long career. This was 'The Law of Innocents' which he negotiated with Irish, Scottish and Pictish kings, and which he promulgated at the Synod of Birr (Co. Offaly) in 697. Irish annals tell us that Adomnán came to Ireland in that year to proclaim his Law, and it is reasonable to assume that he came from Iona. The location of the Synod at Birr, which was a traditional venue for

Irish inter-tribal assemblies, meant that it was conveniently placed near the borders of no less than five of the major Irish provincial kingdoms and strongly suggests that most of the Irish delegates turned up in person. Adomnán travelled there with his Scottish followers, based no doubt at nearby Durrow. The Law of Adomnán was ratified by Bridei son of Derile, king of the Picts, and by Eochaid son of Domangart king of Scots as well as by Adomnán's bishop, Coeddi of Iona, and by Curetan who was almost certainly bishop of Rosemarkie.

It is very unlikely that the Scottish and Pictish kings attended the Birr synod, but Adomnán must have consulted with them personally during his stay in Scotland prior to 697. Adomnán's Law is remarkable not only for its content but for the fact that it gained royal approval in both Ireland and Scotland, and the participation of the Pictish king in this venture confirms yet again that the Pictish aristocracy regarded itself and was regarded by others as an integral part of the Celtic world. The list of guarantors of Adomnán's Law is remarkably consistent, and there are no anachronisms to suggest it is a forgery. No less than 40 leading churchmen and 51 kings and tribal rulers gave their public assent to Adomnán's proclamation. This was a remarkable tribute to his own powers of diplomacy and to the continued prestige of Iona in spite of the Easter bogey, and it says something, too, for the ability of Celtic leaders of the late seventh century to assemble for a common purpose and to bring a new law into effect which had far-reaching social consequences going beyond the interests of any one particular tribe. The Law of Adomnán was not confined to Ireland: 'its enactment was imposed upon the men of Ireland and of northern Britain, as a perpetual law till Doom, by command of their nobles clerical and lay.' Bede may have misled us once more not only in regard to Adomnán's implied early death, but by exaggerating the heat generated by a postscript to the Easter question, Bede has obscured the fact that Iona held on to its unique role as peacemaker and arbiter between kings throughout the Celtic world up to the end of the seventh century.

Adomnán's Law was designed to protect the 'Innocents' or non-combatants (women, children, clergy, etc.) from the horrors of Dark Age warfare, and there may even be some truth in the later Irish tradition that it sought to exempt or even prevent women from participating in battle. This law can be seen as a forerunner of the 'Peace of God' proclaimed throughout Burgundy and Aquitaine in the late tenth century. The Frankish Peace and Adomnán's Law were both ecclesiastical in origin; both relied on the cooperation of the warrior aristocracy; both were proclaimed at synods, and they both dealt with the protection of non-combatants. None of these enactments ever completely banished violence from medieval society where warfare was an essential way of life for the barbarian aristocracy. Celtic warlords were as loath to abandon their brutality and head-hunting as their clergy were loath to turn away from their time-honoured observance of Easter. An apocryphal medieval Irish account of the circumstances which prompted Adomnán to seek protection for women introduces us to a grotesque world where the violence, even if it were not real, offers us a chilling perspective on mens' attitudes in a society dominated by a warrior caste:

> Now Ronait, Adomnán's mother, saw a woman with an iron reaping hook in her hand, dragging another woman out of the enemy host with a hook fastened in one of her breasts. For men and women went equally to battle at that time. After this, Ronait sat down and said: 'You shall not move me from this spot until you exempt women forever from being in this condition.'

The renewal of Adomnán's Law throughout Ireland in 727 suggests that those in authority considered it worth reviving, even if they could not hope to enforce it all the time. Besides, the public renewal of the law provided a valuable source of income for Iona and by 929 we read of a *procurator* for the Law of Adomnán established at the Columban monastery at Derry. Adomnán may have become an embarrassment to his own community in life, but in death his relics and his Law became an extremely valuable asset.

As ruler of the church of Dál Riata, Adomnán had little difficulty in gaining the cooperation of Eochaid son of Domangart, king of Scots. Taran, king of the Picts, was expelled from his kingdom in the year in which the synod was convened at Birr, and the Pictish king who gave his assent to Adomnán's Law was Bridei son of Derile. Since the law was stated to apply to northern Britain we may presume that it was also adopted by the Strathclyde Britons. Later traditions from Adomnán's own *Life* claim that he was a friend of Bridei son of Bili, that Pictish king who overthrew Ecgfrith's army at Dunnichen Moss in 685, and who was the son of the king of Strathclyde. According to a legend in the *Life* of Adomnán, Bridei's body was taken out to Iona for burial and

Adomnán kept vigil beside his friend's body all night. With the coming of dawn, the corpse began slowly to come alive, but a prudent visitor warned Adomnán that if he were to revive the dead king, he would set impossibly high standards for his successors on Iona! Bridei was then allowed to pass on without further incident. This obviously late tale may have been inspired by a very early fragment of verse which forms part of an elegy on Bridei and which may be a genuine fragment of Adomnán's writing which has survived in his own Irish vernacular:

> The king that is born of Mary performs many wonders
> giving life to a *scuapan* in Mull,
> death to Bridei son of Bili.
> It is strange, it is strange
> That after being in the kingship of the people,
> A block of hollow withered oak,
> Should be about the son of the king of Dumbarton.

This early evidence for the friendship between Adomnán and Bridei and the fact that Adomnán persuaded his successor Bridei mac Derile to abide by the Law of Innocents, suggests that Adomnán had visited Pictland several times. Medieval dedications, and churches otherwise associated with Adomnán in early Scotland have a surprising distribution. Apart from Sanda, off the Mull of Kintyre and Killeunan on Kintyre itself, which were set in the extreme south of Dál Riata and on Adomnán's well-trodden route to Ireland, almost all the other church sites connected with him were in the heart of the Pictish kingdom. The *Breviary of Aberdeen* mentions Adomnán's church at Furvie near the Ythan estuary in Aberdeenshire. Further north at Forglen in north-east Banffshire the church dedicated to Adomnán once contained the *breacbannach*. This reliquary, known as the Monymusk shrine, may date from the closing years of Adomnán's rule on Iona. It probably housed a battle banner associated with Columba. Aboyn on the Dee in central Aberdeenshire was a centre of Adomnán's cult, with a church, holy well and tree sacred to the saint. Further south, at Tannadice on the South Esk in Angus, a large rock once bore the name of *St Adomnán's Seat* while the church there was dedicated to Columba. More southerly dedications occur at Campsie and Loch Lomond, while those in Glen Lyon, Loch Tay and Strath Tay may mark staging posts on Adomnán's route from Iona across the Spine of Britain into southern Pictland. Finally, there were two dedications to Adomnán in the Firth of Forth, one

doubtful at Inchkeith and another at Dalmeny near the Forth Bridge
in West Lothian, which may mark foundations of Adomnán when
he visited this region on his journeys to the court of Aldfrith of
Northumbria. Both centres were at that time near the Anglian
frontier and Inchkeith lies but a few miles to the west of Inchcolm
which may well have been a regular staging post for those Columban
monks engaged in constant travelling between Iona and Lindisfarne
through the Scottish lowlands in the seventh century. This same
region in the Forth–Clyde isthmus assumed renewed importance in
the ninth and tenth centuries when it provided a major route for
communication between Scandinavian York and Dublin. Reeves
once pointed out that many of the churches associated with
Adomnán had either connections with Columba or were near
Columban churches, which is what we should expect if Adomnán
were visiting Pictland in his capacity as head of the church of Iona.

We have seen how Adomnán was on friendly terms with Bridei
son of Bili, and how later in 697 he won the cooperation of Bridei
son of Derile for the enforcement of his Law. As abbot of Iona,
Adomnán must have had great influence in Pictland by virtue of
his authority in the Columban monasteries there, and if Bede has
any value whatever in this discussion, then we may at least accept
his general and reasonable statement that Adomnán tried to persuade 'those who were in houses subject to his monastery' to convert to the Roman Easter. And so we reach the simple deduction
that it was Adomnán who must have first approached the Pictish
aristocracy in an effort to gain support for the Roman party
within the Columban *paruchia* in Pictland. This may well have
happened before the death of Bridei son of Bili in 693, or more
accurately before Adomnán left Scotland for Ireland in 692.
Bridei son of Derile died two years after Adomnán in 706, and he
was succeeded by his brother Nechtán in the kingship of the
Picts. Much of our understanding of Pictish history is limited by
our ignorance of the true nature of Pictish kingship, and inevitably we must resort to hypothesis in making sense of the facts at
our disposal. If that kingship rotated between several tribal dynasties as I have suggested, then the immediate succession of a king
by his brother, although not unprecedented in Pictland, would
cause immediate tension within the system. The succession of
brother by brother was an understandable development, since a
family power base was already established, but if the process went
unchecked it would lead away from older rotational succession

systems to a narrower dynastic arrangement.

That being so, we may surmise that Nechtán's succession in 706 was resented by many Pictish leaders from the outset. Besides, the anarchy which surfaced in the last years of Nechtán's reign clearly took several years to evolve. Nechtán's request for advice on the matter of Roman Easter to Ceolfrith of Jarrow was a political move by an insecure king, but Nechtán was not necessarily hostile to Iona, as has too often been rashly assumed. He latched on to the Easter controversy between two Iona factions within his kingdom, and what was earlier a strictly religious squabble was transformed, in Pictland as in Northumbria, into a political issue. Nechtán, like Oswiu at Whitby in 664, had to consider what sides his rivals for the kingship might take in his dispute. Ceolfrith's rambling reply to Necthán's request for advice may well conceal the fact that the Pictish king sent his *legatorios* to Northumbria not just to be lectured on the Roman Easter but primarily to win some political backing in the form of a non-aggression treaty on his vulnerable southern border. We know that fighting continued on this front after Ecgfrith's defeat at Dunnichen Moss in 685, but Bede does refer to a treaty of peace existing between Northumbrians and Picts at the time of finishing his *Ecclesiastical History*. Nechtán himself backed the followers of Adomnán, for Bede makes Nechtán proclaim when he received Ceolfrith's letter: 'I knew before that this was the true observance of Easter', and we also gather from Bede that Nechtán had been interested in the Easter dispute for some time before he wrote to Ceolfrith since he had 'no small measure of knowledge in these matters'. Bede also shows that the initiative came from within Pictland rather than from Jarrow, and on this at least he must have known his facts since he was a mature monk at Jarrow when Nechtán's letter arrived.

The obvious origin for the Roman party within Pictland must lie with Adomnán and his Iona followers. The English bishop, Egbert, may well have continued to support Adomnán's cause among the Picts, but Egbert did not reach Iona until *c.* 712, some 24 years after Adomnán's efforts to persuade the Columban *paruchia* to acceptance began. Some at least of the dedications to Adomnán in Banff, Aberdeen, Angus and elsewhere must reflect a genuine historical association with this saint who flourished relatively late in the Dark Ages. The time when Adomnán had most opportunity to visit his Pictish *paruchia* was when he undertook his roving commission on the Easter question between 688 and 704, and some of these Pictish churches may well have been founded by Adomnán in the Roman rite or converted from Celtic ways. Adomnán had earlier received the backing of Nechtán's brother for his Law of Innocents, and he may have known Nechtán personally as well. That is why Ceolfrith's lengthy digression on Adomnán in the letter to Nechtán must be significant. Adomnán's great sanctity and learning are stressed; his conversion to Roman ways applauded; and the only hint of censure comes in his failure to force acceptance on his followers. All this would carry special weight if Nechtán is seen as a great admirer of Adomnán, whose reputation in death was now even greater than in life, for already by 727 Iona monks had translated Adomnán's relics into a portable shrine.

Nechtán's expulsion of the *familiae* of Iona across the Spine of Britain in 717 may be seen then, as a symptom of the deepening political crisis within Pictland which eventually erupted into anarchy in 726. The evidence at our disposal does not allow us to interpret this cryptic annalistic note to mean that the expulsion of 717 brought an end to Columban influence on the Pictish church and culture. On the contrary the partial acceptance by Iona of the Roman rite in 716 meant a triumph for Adomnán's party and those monks expelled from Pictland were most likely those who refused to conform as in the case of Colmán and his followers at Whitby. Adomnán's Roman party from Iona not only held its ground among the Picts but it may have gained in strength.

Adomnán died as an old man of 77 among his own divided community on Iona in 704. He had been on friendly terms with the kings of Northumbria, Pictland and Dál Riata. He was himself an aristocrat of the line of Niall of the Nine Hostages and the confidant of Irish highkings. He was, by the standards of his day, a prolific writer with wide interests and learning. He wrote with humility and with a deep spiritual sensitivity, and his primary aim both in his *Holy Places* and his *Life of Columba* was to bring men closer to the things of God. The most impressive evidence for his sanctity and learning comes from Northumbrian writers, who were admittedly pleased that he had conformed to their ways. For Bede, Adomnán 'was a good and wise man with an excellent knowledge of the scriptures'. Adomnán was not a Wilfrid who disturbed the peace of the Christian community. He did not push his differences with his own community to a bitter confrontation, although he may, as Ceolfrith said, have been at fault by not 'making it his business' to

140 *The World of Adomnán*

have 'sufficient influence' over them. But he did have remarkable powers of leadership as is demonstrated by the phenomenal support which he mustered for his Law of Innocents, and his failure to persuade Iona on Easter may be explained by Bede's observation that he was 'a man who greatly loved unity and peace'. Finally, Ceolfrith too, who actually met him and had lengthy discussions with him, found Adomnán to be 'a renowned abbot and priest of the community of Saint Columba', who 'showed wonderful prudence, humility and devotion in word and deed.' Adomnán was one of the last great holy men of the Dark Ages. He combined the fiery asceticism of Columba with the simplicity of Cuthbert and he shared too in the visionary tradition of Fursa and the scholarship of Bede.

5

Vikings: 'Warriors of the Western Sea'

In Lewis Isle with fearful blaze
The house-destroying fire plays;
To hills and rocks the people fly
Fearing all shelter but the sky.
In Uist the king deep crimson made the lightning of his glancing
blade;
The peasant lost his land and life
Who dared to bide the Norseman's strife.

The hungry battle-birds were filled
In Skye with blood of foemen killed,
And wolves on Tiree's lonely shore
Dyed red their hairy jaws in gore.
The men of Mull were tired of flight;
The Scottish foemen would not fight
And many an island-girl's wail
Was heard as through the Isles we sail

On Sanda's plain our shields they spy:
From Islay smoke rose heaven-high,
Whirling up from the flashing blaze
The king's men o'er the island raise
South of Kintyre the people fled
Scared by our swords in blood dyed red,
And our brave champion onwards goes
To meet in Man the Norsemen's foes.

Thus did Björn Cripplehand, court-poet of King Magnus
Bareleg of Norway, celebrate the triumphant expedition of his
royal master to the Scottish Isles in 1098. Although by then the
steam had gone out of the Viking Age, Christian Norsemen could
still gloat over the cruelty and violence practised in this case against

fellow Scandinavians who had been settled in the Isles for three
centuries. Björn's mocking sentiments are a chilling reminder of
the fate meted out to the exposed and relatively defenceless Gaelic
and Pictish population caught up in the first fury of heathen Viking
attacks at the close of the eighth century.

While this late eleventh-century poem is conspicuous for its
detailed topographical knowledge of the Hebrides, it is but part of a
much wider and earlier tradition of contemporary Norse poetic
comment on Viking exploits in Scotland. It echoes in more detail
for instance, the gory sentiments of the Icelandic poet, Egil Skalla-
Grímsson, who back in 950 praised King Eirík Bloodaxe of
York with the following lines:

> The destroyer of the Scots fed the wolves. Hel trod on the eagle's
> evening meal [of corpses]. The battle-cranes flew over the rows
> of the slain; the beaks of the birds of prey were not free from
> blood; the wolf tore wounds and waves of blood surged against
> the raven's beaks.

Even allowing for the clichés, skaldic poetry reflects a taste for
violence on the part of the Norse aristocracy which verged on the
psychopathic – (the poet Egil was remembered in later Icelandic
tradition for slaying old women and defenceless settlers sleeping
in their beds). When we take contemporary Norse verse alongside
what Christian and Islamic writers had to say of Viking marauders,
it is difficult to dismiss Norse atrocities as either exaggerated or part
of a bad press which was monopolized by monastic chroniclers.
Those who naively argue for the Vikings as harmless traders and
colonizers must explain the shift in ethos from the writings of
Adomnán to those of the skalds. Compare Adomnán's account of
the tender treatment of 'a crane tossed by winds through the air
with its strength exhausted' which fell half dead on to the shores
of Iona and was fed by Columba, with skaldic images of ravens
gorging on the entrails of the Hebridean slain in the following
centuries. In both cases we may only be dealing with literary
images but the images of Adomnán reflect the gentleness of a
cultivated Classical Christian civilization, while the cut-throats
and beer-vomiting heroes of the skalds belong to a world of brutal
barbarism. The impact of the Viking invasions can never be ade-
quately assessed by the mere counting of slain monks, Viking war-
ships, or – even less plausibly – Scandinavian elements in British
place-names. The burning of the monastic library on Iona for

instance, might have dealt a greater blow to western civilization than the destruction of the entire town of Nantes in a Viking raid in 843. While Iona may have been of little commercial consequence, it was a spiritual and intellectual powerhouse which helped among other things to fuel the Carolingian renaissance. Yet its exposed position and the fragility of its books and of the men who could read them, in the face of the Norseman's axe, needs no stressing.

Arguments for and against this 'well-meaning barbarian' thesis have unfortunately polarized modern scholarship on the Viking Age into those who hold only with the image of the manslayers in the blood-soaked sagas and chronicles, and those on the other hand who would rehabilitate the Northmen as well-meaning traders and farmers in search of an honest living. The subject is bedevilled by those who confuse different phases of activity in the Viking Age and who fail to recognize a separation of roles for traders, warriors and settlers within any one phase. It is not always helpful, for instance, to compare events from the late tenth and eleventh centuries with those of the early ninth. By the later period, Scottish Vikings had settled down as farmers and fishermen under the rule of earls in the Orkneys and Hebrides and they were rapidly adopting Christianity and borrowing heavily from the culture of their Gaelic neighbours. In the early ninth century, on the other hand, the Norsemen were embroiled in piratical raiding throughout the Isles at a stage when the most ruthless and irresponsible elements in their warbands were clearly encouraged to spearhead the drive towards colonization. At another level, while it is true that the roles of farmer, fisherman, warrior and trader might all blend in one individual, it is equally clear that traders and warriors were on the whole a separate class or that at the very least, trading and fighting were seen even by the Norsemen themselves as quite different activities! The Icelander, Olaf Peacock in *Laxdoela Saga*, requested Queen Gunnhild of Norway to fit him out with a ship and 60 crewmen for a voyage 'west over sea' to Ireland via the Scottish Isles. Olaf 'added that it mattered a great deal to him that the crew appear more like warriors than traders'. The implication was that warriors not only looked rather different from traders, but that in the eyes of the barbarian élite they were clearly superior. Archaeological evidence confirms that Norse longships used for war were quite different from the bulkier merchant vessels. It is therefore absurd to use evidence for peaceful Norse trading activities as a plank in the argument that Christian records of Viking military atrocities have been exaggerated. Nor is it meaningful to gauge the effects of Viking destruction in terms of size of armies. A huge Scandinavian host bought off successfully by the local population – as, for example, in eleventh-century England – might cause negligible damage compared with a handful of bloodthirsty ruffians unleashed against a hapless and unsuspecting monastic township in the ninth century.

The causes of the Viking expansion relate to conditions within Scandinavia and while clearly connected with problems of over-population, their details do not concern us here. Whatever the immediate causes of the Viking onslaught, we are sure that by the close of the eighth century the Vikings had perfected a primitive ship technology and weaponry which ensured their military superiority over their Scottish and English neighbours on the other side of the North Sea, and which made it possible for them to cross that sea with ease. Already by the Middle and Late Bronze Ages Scotland had been in close touch with Scandinavia and finds of pottery and Late Bronze Age ornaments show that the Great Glen was a favourite route for wandering merchants journeying from the Irish Sea to Scandinavia. Some of these craftsmen and merchants may, like the Vikings, have followed in the wake of warlords from the far north. Irish and Scottish folklore of the Middle Ages contained vague memories of a sinister people known as Formorians (*Formoire*) who once held the Northern Isles in their grasp and who in the prehistoric past terrorized the coasts of the Gaelic world. Whatever the realities behind these ancient tales, the bronze-smiths and pedlars of the Late Bronze Age, and their warlike masters if they followed such, cannot have been very numerous. They braved the waters of the North Sea in fragile boats which could capsize and which, if they could sail at all, were at the mercy of the winds. As soon, however, as Germanic warriors on the shores of Oslofjord had perfected a longship of the calibre of the famous example excavated at Gokstad in 1880, a new era had dawned with profound consequences for Atlantic Europe and for Scotland in particular. The longship had been slowly evolving in the fjords of southern Norway over centuries. Abundant resources of iron and timber, combined with the necessity to travel from fjord to fjord by sea, ensured that eventually the Norwegians would become masters of ship-building and navigation. By the end of the ninth century, boats had been perfected with a keel which prevented easy capsizing. Planks were adzed into shape and held together by thousands of iron rivets to provide a flexible skin of timber capable of withstanding the pounding of the open ocean; while at the same time producing a vessel of shallow draft suitable for creeping up the rivers of Britain and ferrying warriors far inland. All of these qualities were combined in a craft which could go under oars and sail, and where centuries of seamanship had devised techniques of sailing not only before the wind but also into it.

These ships were fast, efficient and graceful. Contemporary writers saw them slip through the water like huge serpents or dragons, and Scandinavian kings were not only proud to own them, but regularly commissioned whole fleets to give substance to their royal authority throughout Scandinavia. The birth of these magnificent vessels spelt the end of Scottish isolation 'on the edge of the world' as the Romans and early Christian chroniclers knew it, and over night Scotland, which for a thousand years had lain hidden on the periphery of Britain, found itself suddenly and violently exposed to the full fury of sea-borne attack from the northern ocean.

The earliest mention of Viking raiders in British annals is the record in the *Anglo-Saxon Chronicle* of the 'plunder and slaughter' carried out by heathen men on Lindisfarne in 793.[1] This raid heralded a full-scale assault on the coastal territories of Scotland. The *Annals of Ulster* – a chronicle with a keen interest in western Scotland – takes up the story in 794 when it glumly records 'the devastation of all the islands of Britain by gentiles'. The annalist clearly had the Scottish Isles in mind and the Northern Isles in particular, since in the following year (795) he noted the wasting and pillaging of Skye by the same gentiles who came as far south as Rathlin off the Antrim coast on that expedition. Some even ventured further south and west into the Atlantic to attack monasteries on Inismurray and that exiled Lindisfarne community of Inisbofin off the Connaught coast of Ireland. By 796 the Northmen were making inroads on the Irish mainland: the Viking Age had dawned.

These records of the earliest attacks strongly suggest that the Norwegians did not gradually infiltrate the Northern Isles as farmers and fishermen and then suddenly turn nasty against their neighbours. Had there been a sizeable Norse population on Orkney, for instance, in the decades prior to the attacks of 794, Irish annalists

[1] An earlier mention of a Norse landing in Wessex in 789 is not, as it stands, a contemporary record.

would have taken note of such a remarkable occurrence. The pattern of the earliest raids as recorded by Irish and Anglo-Saxon writers suggests, too, that we may be dealing with massive military expeditions which were coordinated with the characteristic speed and ruthlessness of the later Viking period. The attack on Lindisfarne in 793 was probably mounted by a splinter group from the expedition which harried the Isles in 794 and which, incidentally, ravaged Iona in 795. All this suggests that the Viking Age opened in Scotland, as it did in Ireland and England, with a violent piratical phase as a prelude to more determined and successful attempts at colonization. There is no evidence to support a hypothesis for gradual infiltration or for settlement prior to 790. No doubt there had been earlier trade between the folk of the Isles and the Scandinavians, but in 793 the first Viking war party sailed against northern Britain and all the evidence suggests that the Scottish Isles bore the full brunt of the fury of these invaders who were instantly conspicuous to Scots, English and Irish alike, for their brutality and heathenism.

We have no adequate Scottish records from this period of crisis and invasion, but the fate of Iona, due to its prestige and importance, was followed carefully by Irish chroniclers. We do know that Norse piracy in the Western Isles was relentless and sustained during the first quarter of the ninth century. Norse raiding parties were again making inroads into Scotland in 798 and the Hebrides were also plundered in that year. Clearly, the days of monasteries such as Eigg, Applecross and countless other communities throughout the north and west were now numbered. Iona, which for centuries had been the cultural and religious capital of northern Britain, was constantly exposed to Viking marauders. Its position on the western seaways and near the mouth of the Firth of Lorn, which gave it such a commanding position in the days of Columba or Adomnán, now spelt its doom at the hands of sea-borne raiders. It had much to offer the heathen freebooter. It was a monastery enriched for centuries by Scottish, Pictish, northern British, Irish and Anglo-Saxon kings. The Vikings returned again and again to centres such as this, which in western Christian eyes were sanctuaries where it was sacrilege to spoil, but which to the Vikings were shop windows crammed with the loot of centuries, and occupied by unarmed monks who worshipped the 'White Christ'. To the Northmen, Christ was a god who preached everything their warlord Odin despised: peace, humility and suffering as opposed to war, cunning and brutality. The Northmen returned to Iona in 802 and again in 806, when 68 members of the community, monks and laymen, were butchered. This blow convinced the abbot, Cellach, that Iona would have to be temporarily abandoned, and in the following year he commenced the building of a new monastery for his community at Kells in Co. Meath in the kingdom of Brega in eastern Ireland.

Iona was not completely abandoned in 807. It struggled on with a token community of zealous monks willing to face martyrdom at the hands of the heathen whose ships now infested the surrounding waters. The monastery retained its position as the symbolic centre of Columba's community and succeeding abbots of Kells continued to be styled abbots of Iona. Cellach, who retreated with his monks to Kells in 807, resigned his abbacy in 814 and returned to die on Iona in the following year. His successor, Diarmait, travelled in Scotland in 818, and was there again from 829 until 831 when he carried with him the shrine of Columba. The migration of the Iona community to Kells, and the later abandonment of Lindisfarne, show that there could be no compromise between Christ and Odin during that first confrontation between Northmen and Christians in northern Britain. Similar monastic migrations took place in ninth-century Francia as in the case of Noirmoutier and for a time also at Tours. The account of the martyrdom of Blathmac on Iona in 825 affords us a glimpse into those terrifying times. A detailed account of his death was written up by Walafrid Strabo, abbot of Reichenau in southern Germany (838-849). Blathmac was an Irish warrior and aristocrat turned monk, who settled on Iona in a deliberate attempt to seek martyrdom from the Vikings. The Carolingian poem describing what followed is full of conventional statements about the Blathmac's sanctity, his courage and prophetic vision. According to Walafrid, Blathmac had foreknowledge of a Viking attack and advised those monks who lacked courage to take to their heels 'by a footpath through regions known to them'. The Vikings struck at dawn and slaughtered all Blathmac's followers who had chosen to stand by him. Blathmac was spared on condition he revealed the whereabouts of Columba's shrine and on refusing to divulge this information 'the pious sacrifice was torn from limb to limb' and the Northmen began to dig feverishly in their greed for buried monastic loot. There is much in this account which is sustained from records of Viking atrocities elsewhere. The mutilation of Blathmac may well have marked out his martyrdom for special attention by Christian annalists in Ulster and even in Reichenau. Similar brutal treatment was meted out to King Edmund of East Anglia by the Great Army of Danes in November 869 which had all the hallmarks of a ritual Norse killing. Blood-eagling, which involved tearing the victim's rib cage apart in a rite of Odin sacrifice, was practised throughout Scandinavia and indeed, according to *Orkneyinga Saga* that butchery was practised in Orkney by Earl Turf Einarr in the 870s. The torturing of Blathmac to make him reveal the hiding-place of monastic treasure, reminds us of similar tales told in the fourteenth-century account of Norse looting in Crowland Abbey in the East Anglian fens by Ivar's Danes in 868. Earlier and more reliable accounts of the torturing of monks at St Bertin in 860 come from Frankish sources. Several of Walafrid. Strabo's statements shed valuable light on conditions in western Scotland at that time. We are told, for instance, that because Danish warbands landed there so frequently Blathmac chose Iona as a likely place for martyrdom (perhaps as early as 818). Walafrid's evidence for the survival of a community, however small, on the island during the worst years of Viking piracy helps to explain the ultimate survival and re-emergence of Iona as a centre for Norse as well as Celtic Christianity in the tenth century.

It was inevitable that Norse settlers would soon accompany the freebooters and whole households from Scandinavia must have been settling down to fish and farm in the Isles by the end of the first quarter of the ninth century. In the Northern Isles at least, the dominant Scandinavian flavour of this colony was to endure even in political form until the fifteenth century, while a Scandinavian dialect endured there into the eighteenth. It was the coming of these settlers which transformed the culture of northern and western Scotland to the extent that this region became an integral part of the Old Norse world, so much so that places such as Islay Sound (*Ila Sund*), or Pentland Firth (*Péttlandsfjördr*), became household words not only in the talk of hardened Viking seamen but in fireside tales throughout the farms of Scandinavia and Iceland. Major islands and peninsulas which had enjoyed Celtic names for perhaps more than a millenium were now changed irrevocably by the language of the colonists. The Orkneys, previously known as *Inse Orc* ('Boar Islands'), were transformed into *Orkneyjar*; the Hebrides once known as *Domon* became the *Sudreyjar* ('Southern Isles', hence Sodor). Indeed, the Hebrides had become so heavily colonized by Norsemen that Gaelic speakers coined a new name for them in their own tongue – *Inse Gall*, 'Islands of the Foreigners'; while the northern Pictish region of *Cait* was transformed into *Katanes* ('Cat Headland', now Caithness).

This renaming of important places on the map of northern Britain was but the tip of an iceberg: countless farms, streams, fields and hillocks were undergoing a similar transformation in the speech of invading farmers and their families who were settling into remote corners of the north and west. Norse placenames with the second element in *stadir* ('farmhouse, farm') which date from the earliest phase of Norse colonization in the Isles are still most abundant on Shetland, Orkney, Lewis and northern Skye. Nicolaisen would see the distribution of *stadir* names as representing the earliest phase of colonization prior to say, 850; while the similar but denser distribution of names with the *setr* ('dwelling') element are dated to the period 880-900 and represent an intensification and expansion of Norse settlement. The distribution of these names also shows evidence for dense Norse settlement in eastern Caithness where some 56 instances of *setr* occur. A further chronological stage in the Norse colonization of Scotland is seen in the distribution of *bólstadr* ('farm, outlying farm') names which likewise cover the Northern Isles, Caithness, Lewis and Skye, but which also demonstrate a considerable Norse expansion southwards through eastern Caithness and Sutherland to the Moray Firth and southwest over the old Columban *paruchia* on Coll, Tiree, Mull, and on to southern Islay. The distribution of this place-name element, according to Nicolaisen, '*is* the map of Norse settlement in the Northern and Western Isles and on the adjacent mainland, when such settlement was at its most extensive and Norse power at its height.' On the other hand, the distribution of Norse *dalr* ('valley') is more widespread than any of the elements discussed above. It is densest on Shetland and Orkney as well as on Skye and the Outer Hebrides, but it also covers Caithness and all the coastal region north of the Great Glen. Where the distribution of this element differs significantly from *setr* and *Bólstadir* names is that it is found also in old Dál Riata territory in the extreme south-west in Jura, Arran, Bute and Kintyre. This distribution is seen by place-names experts as representing Norse 'spheres of influence' rather than actual settlement. But how strong does political pressure have to be for a people to abandon the age-old names of their native glens in favour of alien Norse forms? Places do not change their names when they fall under a new sphere of political influence. At least some of the new dominant military class must have actually settled in the valleys that they named. Place-name evidence for the extent of Norse conquests in northern and western Scotland is confirmed by statements in medieval Scandinavian sources. The Northern Isles, Hebrides and Caithness (which then included east Sutherland as far as the Oykel) were regarded as being wholly Scandinavian lands. Sources such as *Njáls Saga* and *Laxdoela Saga* make even greater but vaguer claims for the extent of Norse domination. *Njáls Saga* claims that in the late tenth century Earl Sigurd the Stout of Orkney held 'Ross, Moray, Sutherland and the Dales' as well as Caithness on the Scottish mainland, and while the saga as it stands dates from the late thirteenth century, the compilation does include earlier material from the Scandinavian colonies of Dublin and the Scottish Isles. The 'Dales' (*dali*) listed as part of Sigurd's Scottish realm cannot be identified with certainty, but the density of the *dalr* place-name element all along the western coast of Scotland to the Mull of Kintrye must surely be relevant to this discussion. If we accept that the Norse colony definitely included Islay, it is difficult not to conclude that the exposed lands on neighbouring Kintyre and Arran had fallen under Norse domination by the tenth century at least. South-western Argyll must have been in a regular tributary position to Norsemen of the Hebrides and Orkney by this time. Witness the account in *Njáls Saga*, for instance, of how in the 980s the sons of Njál joined in an expedition led by Kari, the bodyguard of the Earl of Orkney, in which they plundered the Hebrides, Kintyre and *Bretland* – in this context almost certainly Strathclyde rather than Wales proper. Earlier in the saga we are introduced to this same Kari sailing through the Minch on a mission for his master, Sigurd of Orkney, which involved collecting tribute from Earl Gilli of the Hebrides.

By the middle of the ninth century, the Norwegian conquest and occupation of the Isles and the north-west had become an accomplished fact. This rapid extension of Scandinavian influence to an area of great strategic importance along the Atlantic trade routes to the Carolingian Empire and further south to Islamic Spain attracted the attention not only of freebooters but also of the kings of Vestfold in southern Norway. As the middle of the ninth century approached, two major developments occurred in the Norwegian colonies in the British Isles. Firstly, a number of 'royal fleets' sailed from Norway and Denmark in a successful attempt to establish trading strongholds on the hostile western shores of the Irish Sea at

Dublin and elsewhere, and secondly, this trading investment had to be safeguarded by bringing the Scottish Isles into a closer relationship with kings of the Scandinavian homelands. This new phase of activity opened as early as 832 when the first of the great expeditions, put at 120 ships by contemporary Irish sources, attacked the northern and eastern kingdoms of Ireland. This host was probably led by the notorious Northman, *Turges*, who appears in contemporary Irish sources soon after this time, and who was a member of a Norwegian royal house, probably from Vestfold. From 832 until Turges was captured and drowned by the Irish in 845, Ireland experienced an orgy of Viking savagery which was aimed at the setting up of a new Norse colony there. Shortly before the drowning of Turges, his armies had established their first permanent war-camp and trading station at Dublin in 841 which was soon to grow and dominate the trading life of the Irish Sea. Eight years after the foundation of Dublin, 140 ships 'of the people of the king of the Foreigners' came to subdue those Vikings who were already in Ireland, so that 'they disturbed all Ireland afterwards'. This first hint of unrest among the Viking colonists of the west suggests that powerful kings in Scandinavia were not content to let the rich pickings from Norse trading centres slip out of their grasp. They were interested in a slice of the profits from Dublin and the Isles, and it was important for them to establish rulers along the Atlantic trade routes who would cooperate with kings in the Scandinavian homelands. In 851, only 10 years after its foundation, Dublin and other Norwegian strongholds in Ireland were attacked and looted by Danish Vikings. In the following year these Danes, possibly led by Ragnar Lodbrok and his son, Ivar, inflicted a crushing defeat on the old Norwegian settlers who made a last stand against the invading Danes with no less than 160 ships in a battle at Strangford Lough. This Danish victory in the North Channel meant that not only Dublin but certainly the Western Isles would now fall unchallenged into Danish hands unless steps were taken in Norway to check this Danish advance into what Northmen called 'the Western Sea'. We know that from this time onwards Ivar the Boneless, a reputed son of Ragnar Lodbrok, made himself king of Dublin and that he was soon planning the most spectacular military achievement of his career, namely the Danish conquest of northern and eastern England. The twelfth-century Danish historian Saxo Grammaticus tells how Ragnar and his sons had earlier launched several Danish expeditions against the Northern and

Western Isles of Scotland and how on one of these campaigns they ravaged the Orkneys and invaded the Scottish mainland, slaying a king there called Murial. Ragnar's men also sailed against the Hebrides and the Old Norse poem, *Krákumál*, tells how they were repulsed by Herthíofur, its Norse defender, and how on this expedition Ragnar lost one of his sons, Rögnvaldur. The Danish fleet then passed south through Islay Sound and on into the Irish Sea, where Irish annalists take up the story with their account of Danish attacks on the Norwegians of Dublin in 851-2. The poem *Krákumál*, which pretends to be the 'Lay of Kráka', one of Ragnar Lothbrok's many queens, was composed in the Scottish Isles in the twelfth-century but it can be shown to be based on earlier traditions from the Viking Age. Yet another poem, *Háttalykill*, survives from twelfth-century Scandinavian Orkney which also testifies to traditions then circulating there to the effect that the Danish dynasty of Ragnar Lothbrok had a special interest in the Isles. *Háttalykill* is a catalogue of Scandinavian heroes from the Volsungs to Cnut the Great of Denmark, and it gives prominent notice to Ragnar and his sons. It was composed by Earl Rögnvaldur of Orkney and by the Icelandic poet, Hallur Thórarinsson. To this day there survives a twelfth-century runic inscription in the great prehistoric tumulus at Maes Howe on Mainland Orkney which commemorates the memory of Lothbrok and his sons – 'never were there men of such high deeds' it avers.

The kings of Vestfold in southern Norway had to act fast if their people who had settled down to farm in Scotland were not to fall a prey to Danish Vikings, and if Norway were not to have its trade-route with Dublin cut. Several Icelandic sources including Snorri Sturluson's *History of the Kings of Norway* (*Heimskringla*) refer to this crisis involving a struggle between Danes and Norwegians for control of the Isles in the middle of the ninth century. We are told that the Norwegian king, Harald Finehair, sailed west one summer to punish those Vikings who 'harried Norway during the summer, but spent the winter in Shetland or the Orkneys'. This expedition was also believed to have cleared the Hebrides and the Isle of Man of Viking marauders. It is now no longer possible to attribute this expedition to Harald Finehair. The Vestfold king who cleared the Isles of Danish marauders, who set up the earldom of Orkney, and who established order in the Hebrides in the time there of Ketil Flatnose, was almost certainly Olaf of Vestfold. We know from contemporary Irish chronicles that Olaf led just such an expedition which reached Ireland in 853 with the specific intention of subduing the foreigners of Dublin and elsewhere. We also know from Irish chronicles that Olaf, who ruled from Dublin between 853 and 871, also campaigned widely in Scotland and the Icelandic *Book of Settlement* (*Landnámabók*) vouches for Olaf the White's rule at Dublin, for his Vestfold royal origin, and for his Scottish conquests. This expedition of the mid-ninth century resulted in the establishment of the earldom of Orkney which was placed in a tributary position to the kings of Vestfold and which was vested all through the Viking Age in the descendants of the first Earl or *jarl* – (the English title is borrowed from the Norse) – Rögnvaldur of Moer in western Norway. Soon after this we are told in *Heimskringla* that both Danish and Norwegian marauders once more infested the region. Two Danish freebooters emerged from the anarchy that followed and they settled down in the Isles preying on Norwegian farmers and on the shipping which plied the Atlantic route and which needed the Isles as vital bases for taking on water and supplies:

> Both in harvest, winter and spring, the Vikings cruised about the Isles, plundering the headlands and committing depredations on the coast.

In summer on the other hand, these Danish Vikings were harrying the coasts of Norway. The older Norwegian colonists in Scotland were by now turning from plunder to the plough, but the Danes or 'New Foreigners' who began their migration a whole half-century after the first Norwegian onslaught, were still hungry for loot. Not even Viking anarchy could go on forever, and Einar, the youngest son of Earl Rögnvaldur eventually took over Orkney *c.* AD 895 and cleared the Isles of freebooters. This illegitimate son of Rögnvaldur may be regarded as the first historical earl of Orkney, being the father of Thorfin Skull-cleaver and great-grandfather of Earl Sigurd the Stout who fell fighting under his raven banner at Clontarf on Good Friday 1014.

Heimskringla gives us a thumb-nail sketch of Earl Einar. He was despised by his father as the son of a slave-girl and descended from 'born slaves': 'he was ugly, and blind of an eye, yet sharp-sighted nevertheless', and was remembered in Norse tradition as 'a mighty man'! Not only did he break the Viking hold on the Isles, but he also withstood an invasion by Hálfdan Highleg, son of Harald Finehair of Norway, who wished to establish himself as a king over Orkney. Hálfdan's fate was not pleasant: after his defeat in battle he fled from Mainland across to North Ronaldsay. Einar had old scores to settle with this royal invader who had burnt his father Rögnvaldur in his own house along with 60 men back in Norway. *Heimskringla* tells the tale of Hálfdan's end with its eye fixed clearly on the Orkney landscape and with all the horrific detail that surrounded the rituals of Odin:

> Einar and his men lay all night without tents, and when it was dawn they searched the whole island and killed every man they could lay hold of.
> Then Einar said, 'What is that I see upon the Isle of Ronaldsay? Is it a man or a bird? Sometimes it raises itself up and sometimes lies down again.'
> They went to it and found it was Hálfdan Highleg, and took him prisoner.
> Afterwards Earl Einar went up to Hálfdan and cut a spread eagle upon his back, by striking his sword through his back into his belly, dividing his ribs from the backbone down to his loins, and tearing out his lungs.

Hálfdan was, according to *Orkneyinga Saga*, offered to Odin as a sacrifice for victory, and with this bloody rite, Einar established his credentials as ruler of the Northern Isles. He was clearly something more than a blood-thirsty butcher, since tradition also held that he had sufficient diplomacy to come to terms with Harald Finehair by paying the king a fine for the slaughter of his son. He was also remembered for taking away the udal rights or the independent tenure of the Orkney and Shetland farmers which were restored under the rule of his great-grandson Sigurd the Stout. *Orkneyinga Saga* explains Torf Einar's nickname by claiming he was the first man to dig peat (*torf*) for fuel in the treeless environment of the Northern Isles. Peat had provided fuel in this region from prehistoric times, but Einar's nickname is probably genuine. *Orkneyinga Saga* states that he organized peat cutting as far south as Tarbat Ness in Easter Ross, confirming those numerous other Norse traditions which put the frontier between the Orkney earls and the Scots at least as far south as the Oykel if not south of the Moray Firth.

Those royal expeditions which brought some semblance of order to the Northern Isles in the middle of the ninth century also affected the Hebrides to the south. Several of the Icelandic Family Sagas of the thirteenth century, and also *Heimskringla* and the earlier Icelandic *Book of Settlement* contain deeply rooted traditions which centre on Ketil Flatnose, a Norwegian chieftain who ruled over the Hebrides in the Viking Age. Icelandic sources give remarkable detail on Ketil and his family and there are several reasons why these traditions were preserved. The first is that members of Ketil's numerous kin later left the Hebrides to settle permanently in Iceland, and these aristocratic emigrants had come under strong Christian Celtic influence while in the Hebrides and so stood apart from other leaders of the Icelandic settlement who remained pagan until AD 1000. Ketil's kin provided leadership to an entire migration of Gaelicized settlers from the Hebrides to Iceland, and it may well be that aristocratic Gaelic obsession with genealogy combined with the Icelandic preoccupation with family history to perpetuate the memory of this particular family in sagas such as *Laxdoela* and *Eyrbyggja Saga*. These Icelandic traditions of a later age, in spite of their impressive detail – much of which may well be accurate – follow a well established pattern in those sources by dating the exploits of Ketil and his family to the reign of Harald Finehair. The reign of Harald, who flourished in the early tenth century, saw a determined attempt to suppress tribal kingship and tribal loyalties in Norway and to unify the realm under a strong central kingship centring on Harald's dynasty at Vestfold. This period was seen later as a watershed in Scandinavian history and later Icelandic sources liked to blame Harald for driving aristocratic Norse rulers abroad in search of a new life. Consequently, in the oral tradition of Scandinavia, the exploits of sea kings who flourished in the period prior to Harald's reign were either completely forgotten or tended, as in the case of Ketil Flatnose, to be taken out of their true context and forced into a cycle of stories centring on Harald's reign. It is the astonishing amount of detail, however, which Icelandic sources preserved on Ketil's family which allows us to check that information against contemporary chronicles in the British Isles. It allows us to vouch for its authenticity, but it also enables us to date Ketil's rule in the Hebrides not to the reign of Harald as later Icelandic historians believed, but to the reign of that same king, Olaf, who brought order to the Orkney and Dublin colonies in the middle of the ninth century.

Ketil is associated in Icelandic tradition with that great Norwegian expedition of the 850s designed to suppress Danish interests in the Western Sea and wrongly believed by Icelanders to have been led by Harald Finehair. This expedition we know from Irish sources was led by Olaf who ruled over western waters from Dublin from 853 until 871. *Eyrbyggja Saga* claims that Ketil led a Norwegian expedition in his own right but with a mandate from the king of Vestfold to drive the Vikings out of the Scottish Isles. Ketil is said to have reluctantly undertaken the expedition; to have subdued the Isles; and without Harald's consent, to have set himself up as ruler of the Hebrides. Harald retaliated by confiscating Ketil's estates in Norway and later by outlawing Ketil's son, Björn, who in his turn was forced to follow his father and sisters to the Hebrides. Other Icelandic accounts of Ketil's migration do not agree with *Eyrbyggja Saga* in every detail, but all these accounts have certain crucial elements in common. They agree that Ketil participated in some way in the expedition of the Vestfold king to the western colonies and that Ketil established himself as ruler of the Hebrides. They also agree that Ketil quarrelled with his Norwegian master whom we can now identify, not with Harald Finehair but with Olaf of Dublin. For not only do we know from Irish chronicles that it was Olaf who led the Norwegian expedition of 853, but Icelandic accounts are adamant that Ketil's daughter, Aud the Deep-Minded, was the queen of that same Olaf the White, king of Dublin. More remarkably, Icelandic tradition is insistent that Ketil Flatnose belonged to the same generation as the Irish king, Cerball of Ossory, and that several of the children and grandchildren of these leaders had intermarried. We are certain that Cerball died in AD 888, which again confirms that Olaf the White of Dublin and not Harald Finehair was the overlord of the Hebrides when Ketil ruled there, and if there could be any more doubt about the matter, contemporary Irish sources show Cerball of Ossory as the ally of Olaf of Dublin. All of this evidence leads us to believe that Ketil's quarrel was not with Harald Finehair, but with Olaf the White, a fact which may be reflected in Icelandic evidence which shows that by the time Olaf reached Dublin and by the time Ketil had become master of the Hebrides, Olaf had put aside Ketil's daughter Aud, who had by then returned to her father's household in the Hebrides. Irish sources on the other hand show that Olaf of Dublin chose two other Celtic queens during his stay there; the first was a daughter of the Irish highking, Áed Findliath, and the second was almost certainly the daughter of Kenneth mac Alpin, king of Scots.

Irish evidence too, supports traditions of hostility between Olaf of Dublin and Ketil of Hebrides. That at least is one way of interpreting the account in the *Annals* of *Ulster* under the year 857 when we are told that Olaf defeated Ketil the Fair and his *Gall-Gaedhil* or

'Scandinavian Gaels' who were rampaging in Munster. These *Gall-Gaedhil* were regarded by Celtic writers as a renegade band of mixed Norse and Gaelic blood who perpetrated even greater crimes against Christian communities than the Vikings proper. The *Gall-Gaedhil*, who had emerged as a mixed ethnic group already by the middle of the ninth century, could only have come into being in the older Viking colonies of Scotland and in those areas of the Scottish colony where Norse influence was dominant but not exclusive. The total subjugation of Shetland and Orkney and the survival of Norse speech there into modern times suggests that Norse culture saturated those islands to a degree that would preclude any significant cultural mix at aristocratic and military level. Indeed, we can safely assume that the important Pictish and other Celtic landowners either fled south into the Scottish mainland or were annihilated. Ireland on the other hand, although it is the first place which yields evidence for *Gall-Gaedhil* armies on a rampage, was a very unlikely setting for the home of such a people as early as 850. The obvious homeland of the *Gall-Gaedhil* must have been the Hebrides and south-west Scotland, where from place-name and linguistic evidence, Norse influence was initially strong but eventually underwent considerable Gaelicization. The Gaelic language, for instance seems to have re-emerged in the Hebrides by the eleventh century if not earlier. *Orkneyinga Saga* refers to *Gaddgedlar*, the Norse form of *Gall-Gaedhil* in the context of Galloway, which does indeed take its name from that people. The Irish evidence is in no way at variance with this picture of the Norwegian Ketil leading a renegade band of Norse and Scottish freebooters who were a menace to Scots and Irish alike and who were a threat also to Olaf of Dublin whose ambitions centred on bringing all the western colonies under the tight supervision of Dublin, and ultimately, perhaps, of Norway. That contemporary Irish source which names Ketil as leader of the *Gall-Gaedhil* in 857 implies he must have been a prominent Norseman either from Galloway or the Hebrides at precisely the same time as Ketil Flatnose ruled the Hebrides according to Norse sources. In this confrontation with Olaf of Dublin, we see that same Norwegian king who came to Ireland to bring the Vikings there under his rule in 853 now trying to rid it of marauding Norse freebooters from Scotland. This is precisely the picture which Norse sources paint of the Norwegian royal fleet which sailed into the Western Sea in the ninth century but wrongly attributed there to the leadership of Harald Finehair. Icelandic sources suggest that

while Ketil first cooperated with the Norwegian king, he later quarrelled with him and ruled the Hebrides in defiance of him. Finally,
Laxdoela Saga relates that from his Scottish base Ketil Flatnose
claimed 'the lands round about were known to him, for in his youth
he had harried there far and wide.'

Something went badly wrong with the Hebridean leadership in
the period from 866 to 880 and the evidence for this comes yet again
from Icelandic sources and from reliable chronicles relating to Ireland and Scotland at this time. The defeat of Ketil and his *Gall-
Gaedhil* in 857 may have signalled the end of his brief sway over the
Hebrides. As soon as Olaf had consolidated his position in Dublin,
he and his fellow king there, Ivar, began to turn their attentions to
Britain. Ivar prepared for the invasion of England by the Great
Army in 865, while in 866 Olaf launched a campaign in Scotland.
In that year the *Annals of Ulster* inform us that Olaf led a combined
hosting of Irish and Scottish Vikings against *Fortriu* or Pictland
'when they plundered all the territories of the Picts and took their
hostages'. There is reason to believe that Olaf remained in Scotland
from 866 until 869 during which time he lived off tribute from the
Picts. He is noticeably absent from Irish chronicles in 867 when a
fortress which had been built by him at Clondalkin near Dublin was
stormed by the Irish, and he was absent again in 868 when the
highking Áed Findliath won an important battle over Irish
Norsemen in Co. Meath. In 869, however, Olaf's army was back in
business in Ireland when it fell upon Armagh, probably on St
Patrick's Day (17 March), as is stated in the *Scottish Chronicle* (Version A) and this raid was most likely directed from Scotland. Olaf
was back in south-west Scotland during the period 870-1 when he
laid siege to the British fortress of Dumbarton, after which he
returned with his booty and slaves to Dublin in 871. All this shows
that the career of the Norwegian Olaf had a much more important
bearing on Scottish history than has formerly been supposed and
that the claim of *Eyrbyggja Saga* that Olaf the White of Dublin was
'the greatest warrior-king of the Western Sea' must be taken seriously. Such a claim implies that Olaf was much more than king of
Dublin, and that he was also a dominant figure in the Northern and
Western Isles.

This remarkable king disappears mysteriously from Irish and
Scottish chronicles in 871 and conflicting guesses were made by
medieval writers as to what his fate may have been. The Icelandic
Book of Settlement (*Landnámabók*) claimed Olaf the White died

fighting in Ireland, but that was a guess inspired by the known fact that he ruled from Dublin. The *Scottish Chronicle* states that Olaf was slain while raiding in Scotland in 865 and that he was killed by King Constantine, but that particular passage is very corrupt, and besides, we know that Olaf was alive and well in Ireland in 869 and on the Clyde in 870-1. In spite of its garbled nature, however, this Scottish record is important in that it supports Irish evidence of Olaf's prolonged stay in Scotland and for his raids on the Scottish mainland. No contemporary Irish chronicle mentions Olaf's death in Ireland, which strongly suggests that he died elsewhere, while a later Irish source claims he eventually abandoned his Dublin throne to assist his father, Guthfrith, in a civil war in Norway. If this source is correct, then Olaf of Dublin was the same king as Olaf Guthfrithsson who later ruled over Vestfold and who was eventually laid to rest in the Gokstad ship. That magnificent vessel clearly suggests that Olaf of Vestfold was a great sea-king which fits in turn with Old Norse verses claiming that this Olaf also 'ruled far and wide over the Western Sea'. This claim is later echoed by *Landnámabók*, which states that Olaf the White of Dublin was indeed of the house of Vestfold (albeit wrongly placed in that genealogy) and that he 'harried in the Western Seas' (*vestrvíking*), a phrase which recalls not only the early skaldic verse on Olaf of Gokstad and Vestfold but also the claim in *Eyrbyggja Saga* that Olaf the White of Dublin was 'the greatest warrior-king of the Western Sea'.

Old Norse sources mention two Olafs belonging to the ninth-century house of Vestfold. The first of these, Olaf the White, because of his connections with Dublin and with Ketil Flatnose, must be identified with Olaf king of Dublin as described in early Irish and Scottish chronicles (853-871). We are also told in *Heimskringla* of Olaf Gudrödarson (or Guthfrithsson) of Vestfold who according to the near-contemporary skaldic verse of Thjódólfur, harried in the Western Sea (*Vestmarr*); was buried in a ship at Geirstadir; and on good archaeological evidence can be identified with the king buried in the Gokstad ship. Both these Olafs were believed in Scandinavian sources to have ruled over the Western Sea which stretched from Mizen Head in south-west Ireland to furthest Shetland, and to have flourished at precisely the same time in the third quarter of the ninth century. It is possible that there was originally only one such king, Olaf Guthfrithsson of Vestfold, who in his earlier days ruled from Dublin and raided in

Scotland and who later in 871 returned to claim his Vestfold kingdom. Traditions relating to the Norwegian and colonial phases of
this king's career may have become separated in Hebridean and
Norwegian accounts, so that eventually Icelandic historians concluded there had been two different Olafs in question. The Irish
Three Fragments of Annals, while not actually proving such a theory,
do support the case for regarding Olaf Guthfrithsson of Vestfold as
being the same as Olaf the White of Dublin and the Scottish Isles.
The *Fragments* claim that Olaf of Dublin ended his reign there when
c. 871 he returned to Norway to support his father Guthfrith in a
struggle for a kingdom. This passage, then, would identify Olaf
of Dublin, *alias* Olaf the White of *Landnámabók*, with Olaf
Guthfrithsson of Norway.

Olaf's domination of the Western Sea must have placed Ketil
Flatnose and his kin in a very vulnerable position if as is claimed by
Scandinavian tradition, Ketil had quarrelled with Olaf over the
lordship of the Hebrides, and if Olaf's estranged queen had
returned to brood in the Western Isles at the court of her father,
Ketil. The campaigns which Olaf launched in Scotland in the third
quarter of the ninth century may have spelt the end of Ketil's hold
over the Hebrides, particularly when the *Annals of Ulster* inform us
that Olaf led not only his Dubliners into Scotland but that he led
'the Foreigners of Alba' as well. Irish and Scottish chronicles
relating to the tenth century and later are ominously silent on the
fate of Ketil's descendants. We find the Hebrides or *Inse Gall* then
ruled by Norse kings, and in so far as we can guess at their origins,
the later Hebridean house seems to descend not from Ketil Flatnose, but from the royal line of Ivar of Dublin. The house of Ketil
had disappeared into thin air as far as sources from within the
British Isles are concerned. Icelandic tradition does indeed high-
light the dilemma in which Ketil's kin found itself in the 870s and
880s, and while the compilers of those traditions had only a faint
understanding of the causes of the crisis, nevertheless a crisis as
such left its mark on the record.

Briefly, this tradition states that Ketil Flatnose died in the
Scottish Isles and the collapse of his family's fortunes was complete
with the slaying of Ketil's grandson, Thorstein the Red, who was
the royal son of Aud the Deep-Minded and Olaf of Dublin. While
Ketil had mastered the Hebrides, Thorstein harried in northern
Scotland along with Earl Sigurd the Powerful of Orkney where he
carved out a kingdom for himself covering the whole of Caithness

and parts of Moray, and Ross and, less probably, parts of Argyll. *Landnámabók* and *Laxdoela Saga* claim that Thorstein made himself king over half of Scotland, while *Heimskringla* more modestly puts the boundary of his realm at *Ekkjalsbakke* or Strath Oykel, west of the Dornoch Firth in south Sutherland. It was also on the banks of the Oykel, according to *Orkneyinga Saga*, that Sigurd the Powerful of Orkney was buried in a mound after dying from a wound received in a skirmish with the Scots. Thorstein dominated eastern Sutherland and all of Caithness and perhaps the southern shores of the Moray Firth, but his overlordship further south in Ross and Moray collapsed when he was slain by the Scots, and his family fortunes took a turn for the worse even in the securely Norse-held region of Caithness. Thorstein's mother, Aud, was in Caithness when news of her son's death reached her. 'She felt', according to *Laxdoela Saga*, 'she did not have much chance of recovering her position there, now that her father [Ketil Flatnose] too was dead'. She commissioned a ship to be built secretly in the woods, and assembling her entire kin, her slaves and some of her family friends, she led an expedition via Orkney and the Faroes to find a new life in Iceland in her old age.

It is no longer possible to dismiss these tales of Aud and her father Ketil as unverifiable oral traditions which circulated in twelfth-century Iceland, or even worse as mere figments of a saga writer's imagination. One thing is certain: this Scottish tradition in Icelandic oral history is of far greater antiquity than the thirteenth-century saga age, and it was so strong that it survived for centuries in spite of being poorly understood and indeed unfashionable for the Icelanders themselves. Why, for instance did the compilers of both *Laxdoela* and *Eyrbyggja Sagas* – two of the greatest of the Family Sagas – feel obliged to begin by recounting the story of Ketil Flatnose's voyage and settlement in the Scottish Isles? It was as though the saga writers were aware they were going back to the well-springs of the Icelandic past – to the beginning of things which centred not, as they otherwise wished to believe, on Norway but on a group of stubborn Vikings settled in the Hebrides in the 860s and 70s. Both sagas open in a ritual fashion with this Hebridean origin of the great families of the western fjords of Iceland: it is a solemn beginning, clearly as well known to its Icelandic audience as the *Book of Genesis* was to the Hebrews:

There was a man called Ketil Flatnose, the son of Björn Rough-Foot. He was a powerful chieftain in Norway and high born. . . . '

The names of Ketil's children and their marriages are set out and all this is tied in with the voyage to the Scottish Isles and the relationship with Olaf of Dublin and Cerball of Ossory. Most of the genealogical details derive from a manuscript tradition older than the saga age and are to be found in earlier works such as *Landnámabók* and in the Ari Thorgilsson's early twelfth-century *Íslendingabók* (*Book of the Icelanders*). The genealogies upon which the introduction to these sagas are constructed are complex, yet chronologically consistent. Such material was by its nature easy to condense and easy to transmit orally from one generation to another especially if reinforced by geographical detail. Ketil's daughter, Thórunn Hyrna, was married to Helgi the Lean, a Norse grandson of Cerball of Ossory, while Cerball's granddaughter, Thurídur, was in turn married to the Scottish Viking, Thorstein the Red, Ketil's grandson. Helgi the Lean was either born or fostered in the Hebrides. This would account for his marriage to Thórunn, and both marriages are explained, too, by contemporary evidence from Irish chronicles for Cerball's alliance with Olaf of Dublin in the 850s. But it is the Hebrides and not the more powerful Dublin kingdom which is at the centre of what we can describe as the earliest Icelandic tradition. Thorstein the Red derived his royal status and lineage from Olaf the White of Dublin, but it was as the son of Aud the Deep-Minded from the Hebrides that he was remembered in Iceland. His son, Olaf Feilan, sailed off with Aud to settle in Laxárdal and this Olaf became the progenitor of a great Icelandic family. Aud's sister, Jórunn, was the mother of Ketil the Fool who also came out to Iceland from the Hebrides. Björn the Easterling is named as the last of Ketil's sons to reach the Hebrides from Norway some time after his father had died, but he chose not to settle there and went off at once to Iceland. Yet even Björn was taken by Icelandic writers to the Hebrides before he finally embarked on his Icelandic voyage, and like so many of his kin it is also possible to detect from Icelandic sources that he had been in touch with Celtic cultural influence. Björn's fosterfather is named as Earl Kjallakur of Jamtaland in Norway. But *Kjallakur* is derived from the Gaelic *Cellach* and was a name more suited to a Hebridean Christian Norseman than to a true Norwegian. For this is one of the most remarkable qualities about the information supplied by later Icelandic writers on the Hebridean tradition: not only is that information chronologically consistent in spite of its complexity, but Gaelic linguistic and Christian influence which could never have been invented by twelfth-century Icelanders is evident throughout.

Björn's brother, Helgi, had the Old Icelandic nickname *Bjólan* which derives from the Gaelic, *Beolán* ('little mouth'), while the Icelandic settler Olaf, son of the Scoto-Norse king, Thorstein the Red, had the nickname *Feilan* coming from the Gaelic *Fáelán* ('little wolf'). Several other names among these Hebridean and Hiberno-Norse settlers – such as Kjartan and Melkorka, to name but two others – have a Gaelic origin. There is evidence, too, for the adoption of Christianity by some of Ketil's family which tallies with their Hebridean background. Aud the Deep-Minded was remembered for her wish to be buried in the sand on an Icelandic beach because she did not wish to lie in unconsecrated ground, and in life she was alleged to have set up crosses at Hólar. Aud's brother-in-law, Helgi the Lean, was a Christian from the Hebrides who settled at Kristnes (Christ Headland) in Eyjafjórdur in northern Iceland. But Helgi, we are told in *Landnámabók*, hedged his religious bets and continued to worship Thor in moments of crisis. Such an attitude is what we should expect from those *Gall-Gaedhil* who, according to Irish writers were a mixture of pagan and Christian, of Norse and Gaelic origin. The National Museum of Iceland contains an impressive collection of somewhat debased penannular brooches and pins of undoubted Celtic provenance from the ninth and tenth centuries which would fit well in the context of the Hebridean *Gall-Gaedhil*. Professor Gwyn Jones has drawn the parallel with a boat burial discovered in Patreksfjórdur in northwestern Iceland in 1964. This tenth-century find contained a mixture of Christian and pagan cult objects with clear connections with south-west Scotland and Cumbria and reflecting a material cultural admixture of precisely the sort vouched for in Icelandic accounts of the Hebridean migration. Indeed Patreksfjördur was claimed by the compiler of *Landnámabók* to take its name, not from the better-known Irish saint but from an early tenth-century Hebridean bishop. This bishop Patrick was regarded as the fosterfather of Orlygur Hrappsson, the nephew of Ketil Flatnose who had come out to Iceland from the Hebrides and named the fjord where he landed after the Scottish prelate.

The catalogue of Scottish settlers is well known to Icelandic historians and has for years formed the centre of a debate as to the ethnic origins of the Icelandic people. The role of these Scottish settlers has been played down on the grounds that they were not numerous and that neither their Christianity nor their Celtic influence endured for long. All this may be true: Christianity among some early settlers such as Helgi the Lean was not strong, and while the

Christian Svartkel from Caithness (who settled at Eyrr in Havalfjördur) left a grandson who still prayed rather vaguely before a cross, other Icelandic accounts show that the new faith from Scotland died out completely in some parts and had to be reintroduced from Norway at the turn of the millenium. Even the children of Aud the Deep-Minded seem to have reverted to heathen ways. According to *Landnámabók* her descendants worshipped the very hills where she once prayed as a Christian, and when Kjartan Olafsson, fifth in descent from Aud, converted to Norwegian Christianity, there was still no church in Laxardál when he was slain there in the early eleventh century. It is equally true that the Scottish element among the settlers was numerically low, perhaps accounting for one seventh of the *landsmenn* or leading settlers mentioned in *Landnámabók*. Nor should we even argue that these people, strictly speaking, were Pictish or Scottish.[2] It is clear from Icelandic sources that the Hebridean leaders were Norsemen in speech and culture. They were only Scottish in so far as they had previously been settled in the Hebrides and come under Scottish cultural influence there, as well as taking with them to Iceland a number of Scottish and Irish slaves. The Icelanders are today a thoroughly Scandinavian people and the majority of the early settlers probably came from southern and western Norway. On the other hand, it is not always helpful to argue from a statistical standpoint when dealing with a problem which is concerned not with numbers but with an aristocratic and culturally superior élite whose influence on Icelandic society may have far outweighed its numerical strength. As for the exclusively Scandinavian character of modern Iceland, we must remember that the political evolution of northern Europe since the later Middle Ages has drawn Iceland more and more tightly into the Scandinavian world and away from that Scottish dimension which was undoubtedly present in the first four centuries of its history. For just as the Scottish Isles have shed their Scandinavian characteristics in the modern age, so too Iceland has lost its Gaelic cultural ties with Scotland. What we do not yet understand is why a small bunch of Celticized Vikings from Scotland dwarfed the apparently more prestigious Norwegian dimension in the historiography of medieval Iceland.

We can begin to solve this problem by asking a more

---

[2] The word Scottish occurs in Icelandic Family Sagas as an umbrella term for all the inhabitants of modern Scotland.

fundamental question, namely why a colony of Hebridean and Scottish Norsemen decided to migrate to Iceland in the first place. Why did these Vikings risk a long and perilous ocean voyage in preference to staying on in a colony where they had earlier chosen to settle and even to rule? The safe explanation offered as a solution to this problem is that by 902, Ireland was closed to Northmen and a build-up of colonists on the Scottish Isles forced a secondary migration to Iceland. This is neither accurate nor convincing. Dublin was not irrevocably closed to Vikings after 902, and besides, Norsemen were finding rich farmland to settle at this time all over north-west England. In any case the migration of Ketil's family from the Hebrides can be dated to the last quarter of the ninth century rather than to the tenth. As for the idea of a secondary migration, that is undoubtedly correct, but it fails to explain why men of family and substance chose to join the Hebridean migrants rather than consolidate their hold on the Western Isles of Scotland. Twelfth- and thirteenth-century Icelandic writers believed that their country had been colonized by Norwegians of noble birth who had been persecuted in Norway by the ambitious king Harald Finehair. There may also be some truth in that, but the ambitions of Harold and his sons for centralized kingship drove out their enemies in the tenth century and not the ninth. If we are to seek for a Norwegian king who made his realm too hot for Vikings chieftains to settle in, then we must choose Olaf the White of Dublin, that warrior who harried far and wide over the Western Sea in his bid to bring order to the Norse colonies in Scotland and to keep his trade routes open to Oslofjord. The problem that dogged medieval Icelandic historiography was an understandable desire to avoid the charge that the country had been founded and settled by a bunch of unruly Scottish Vikings. Yet the Hebridean tradition was so strong and Icelandic obsession with genealogy so great, that a way had to be found to accommodate the Hebrideans into a more desirable but less historical Norwegian scheme of things. Thus, while the detailed and complex genealogies of Scottish Vikings were preserved in *Landnámabók* and elsewhere, no opportunity was lost to stress that such Icelanders were really Norwegian magnates rather than Hebridean trouble-makers. By the time the Family Sagas took final shape in the thirteenth century, the Hebridean tradition was still strong. We read of prestigious voyages by Icelandic heroes to their relatives in the Scottish Isles and Ireland. More convincingly, the sagas abound in incidental references to trading ships plying between Iceland and Orkney, Caithness, the Hebrides and Dublin. It is even possible to glimpse cargoes of timber, corn, and other essential supplies as well as luxury goods, going north while presumably slaves and Icelandic raw materials were shipped south. As late as the first quarter of the thirteenth century the compiler of *Laxdoela Saga* could describe the eleventh-century settlers of the western dales of Iceland as using characteristic 'Scottish saddles' (*skozkum södli*) and there are even hints that the physical appearance of these westerners (red hair, and dark hair and swarthy complexion) bespoke their Scottish Celtic origin. On the other hand, saga compilers were always anxious to stress that early Icelandic heroes could win acceptance in Norway, which was clearly regarded as the cultural homeland of the Icelandic people. Thus, in *Laxdoela Saga*, although the Hebridean and Irish ancestry of its heroes Höskuldur, his son Olaf, and grandson Kjartan Olafsson, form a central theme in the saga, nevertheless the compiler sent these heroes off on triumphant voyages to the Norwegian court to underline their acceptability in Scandinavia as a whole. The Icelanders were proud of the royal blood in their leading families, but embarrassed that it was Hebridean Viking stock, however distinguished. This attitude helps to explain why Icelandic historians exaggerated Harald Finehair's role as a tyrannical king who goaded his freedom-loving chieftains into seeking a new life in Iceland. The reality may have been quite different. Olaf the White of Dublin and later kings of Vestfold were anxious to bring the Scottish Isles into a regular tributary position and to curb the depredations of ruthless pirates who terrorized the farmers of the Isles and made trading voyages unsafe. It was the eventual defeat of these Hebridean pirates by Olaf and his successors which forced them to follow the route of the *papar* or Celtic monks to Iceland.

This Scandinavian migration from the Hebrides to Iceland reminds us of the remarkable fact that Iceland was discovered in the first instance not by Vikings but by Celtic monks who came from precisely that area whence Ketil's dynasty fled in the late ninth century. One of the few certainties regarding the early history of Iceland is that the land was first discovered and regularly visited by those monks, and that they had reached it from the Scottish Isles. Already when Adomnán was writing in the late seventh century, he could describe voyages in curraghs under sail into the North Atlantic from Iona. Several of these were led by Cormac Ua

Liatháin who according to Adomnán and the *Life of Comgall* of Bangor, explored Orkney and other northern Isles. Adomnán also tells how Cormac on his third expedition, sailed for 14 days into the northern ocean: 'Such a voyage appeared to be beyond the range of human exploration, and one from which there could be no return'. Yet Cormac did return, although he apparently failed to find land in the Arctic. The navigator *par excellence* in Irish hagiographical tradition was Brendan of Clonfert in western Ireland and there is a genuine historical basis to the elaborate traditions surrounding his wanderings in the North Atlantic. Far from sailing west into the uncharted ocean off Connaught, Brendan sailed north and east along the coast of western Scotland. Adomnán records a visit by Brendan to Columba when that saint was on Hinba, and significantly he informs us that Brendan was accompanied by Cormac Ua Liatháin, that intrepid explorer of the northern ocean. Later hagiographical traditions surrounding Brendan are consistent with a series of voyages through the Northern Isles, to the Faroes and Iceland, and such voyages in turn are consistent with a monastic base in western Scotland. Evidence for this is supported not only by Adomnán but by the *Vita Prima* of Brendan which claims that the saint founded a monastery on Tiree and another at *Ailech*, convincingly identified by W.J. Watson with the Garvellachs in the Firth of Lorn. Adomnán also tells us of a certain Aidan mac Fergno who once visited Columba on Iona. This man had been a disciple of Brendan of Clonfert for 12 years and was no doubt based in one of Brendan's Scottish houses. But as time passed, the prestige of Iona soon outshone all other foundations in western Scotland, and it was Iona rather than Tiree or elsewhere that provided the major base camp for wandering ascetics and explorers seeking a 'desert' in the northern ocean. The experience gained by those mariners who were fortunate enough to return, and the tales which they told, must have been of interest to the Iona community, renowned as it was for its writers and its learning. Adomnán provides proof of that interest at the close of the seventh century, for these remarkable voyages survived the first burst of ascetic fervour in the Age of Saints and continued right up to the Viking era.

The Irish monk, Dicuil, who wrote his *World Geography* at the Carolingian Court in 825 actually met a holy man who had visited the Faroes which were reached after two days sail 'from the northernmost British Isles'. Irish hermits had been going there for roughly a century from *c*. 725. Dicuil also described the island of

Thule which we can unhesitatingly identify with Iceland. Clerics who had stayed on Thule from February to August, in about 795 (30 years before Dicuil wrote) had spoken personally to him of their experiences. He talks, too, of Norse pirates who had driven the anchorites away from these lonely islands; of the sheep and seafowl which abounded in the Faroes; of daylight hours in Iceland; and he was even aware of the pack-ice which lay one day's sail to the north of Iceland in the Arctic Ocean. Dicuil's varied and first-hand knowledge of several men who had explored the Northern Isles, the Faroes, Iceland, and beyond, strongly suggests that he once served as a monk (some 30 years before) in a house which provided a base in Scotland for these travellers. It must have been a monastery which had a fine library and good teachers to produce a man of Dicuil's ability as a grammarian, astronomer, and geographer. Iona is the obvious candidate for such a house, and Dicuil was almost certainly a monk there. He gives the name of his Irish teacher as one Suibhne, stating that he was present when this Suibhne received a monk who had visited the Holy Land before 767. Suibhne was a common name for Irish ecclesiastics, but the fact that Abbot Suibhne ruled Iona from 766 to 772 would appear to clinch the identification of Iona as Dicuil's monastic home. It was here he quite naturally acquired his interest in such diverse pursuits as calculating the date of Easter and exploration of the northern ocean. We know that he had already settled into the Carolingian court circle by 814, so we may assume that he had fled from Iona after one of those violent Norse attacks in 795, 802 or – most likely – 806.

Dicuil's claims of a confrontation between anchorites and Vikings in Iceland are substantiated in the later writings of Icelandic historians. Ari Thorgilsson vouches for the presence of Christian *papar* or priests who were living in Iceland when the Northmen arrived there and who abandoned that land to the heathen newcomers, leaving behind their 'Irish books, bells and croziers'. The list of these monastic items is suspiciously alliterative in Ari's account (*boekr, bjöllur ok bagla*) yet we know from early manuscript sources and from early Christian sculpture, that the book, bell and crozier were symbols of the Celtic abbot's office. The very word Ari uses for crozier (*bagall*) may derive from the Old Irish *bachall* ('staff'), and the Old Icelandic name, *papar*, derives from Old Irish *papa* or *pobba* meaning 'father'. The case for the earliest discovery of the Faroes and Iceland by Scottish and Irish *papar* sailing from the Scottish Isles in the seventh and eighth centuries is unshakeable. They have left a trail of place-names coined in the speech of the Northmen who later followed in their tracks, which stretches from Papadil on Rhum, Pabbay (Pabay) off Barra and Skye, and in the Sound of Harris in the Outer Hebrides through Paplay, Papa Stronsay, and Papa Westray in the Orkneys, past Papa and Papa Stour and the various Papils in Shetland, and so on to Iceland. That list is by no means exhaustive, and at the end of the trail we have Papey, 'Island of the *papar*' off south-east Iceland, and Pappabýli ('Home of the *papar*'). This is a route which leads essentially from Iona in the 'Western Sea' to southern Iceland: it presents us not only with the sea-route travelled, according to Dicuil, for 100 years before the Vikings came, but with a list of monastic settlements – the more northerly no doubt seasonal – which provided staging posts for the intrepid *papar*. In the light of this evidence is it reasonable to suppose that the Norsemen ever discovered Iceland when they found such a well travelled route already in use when they reached the Scottish Isles?

Medieval Icelandic writers were not agreed on which of their own Norse ancestors first visited Iceland. While none of the Icelandic accounts can be accepted in all its details, nevertheless many of these traditions point not to Norway but to the Scottish Isles as the immediate starting point of the earliest Norse voyages of discovery and colonization in the North Atlantic. According to *Faereyinga Saga*, the first Norse settler on the Faroes was Grímur Kamban who was alleged to hail from Norway, but the second element in his name is Gaelic and points to an origin among the Hebridean *Gall-Gaedhil*. The Norseman who has the best claim to first sighting Iceland is the Swede, Gardar Svavarsson, who, as we are told in *Hauksbók*, set out on a voyage from Scandinavia to claim his wife's paternal inheritance in the Hebrides. He sailed through the Pentland Firth, but was blown off course and out into the Atlantic where he eventually made a landfall near the Horn at the southeastern tip of Iceland. This mariner may indeed have been a Swede, but his Hebridean contacts, his voyage from the Pentland Firth and his landing in the vicinity of Lón and Papey shows that he was believed to have followed closely along the old route of the Scottish *papar*. A Norwegian called Naddodd is claimed in *Landnámabók* to have been blown off course from Norway to the Faroes and to have paid a brief and uneventful early visit to Iceland. The man who led the first colonizing expedition, albeit an abortive one, was claimed to be Flóki Vilgerdarson who was remembered for giving Iceland its uncomplimentary name. Flóki not only took livestock on this voyage intending to settle, but he sailed via Shetland and thus along the route of the *papar* to the Horn of Iceland. Although alleged to be a Norwegian, *Landnámabók* offers significant detail on place-names associated by apocryphal tradition with Flóki and his daughter in the Shetlands. More remarkably, we are told in *Landnámabók* that he had on board his ship a Hebridean named Faxi who is alleged to have given his name to Faxaflói the greatest bay in western Iceland, and it was this Hebridean who was believed to have made the first comment on the nature of Iceland.

The founding father of the Icelandic colony was Ingólfur Arnarson who with his foster-brother Hjörleifur landed with the first successful colonizing party in about 874. Later Icelandic tradition liked to think of Ingólfur and Hjörleifur as two Norwegians leading a distinguished Norwegian band to Iceland, but even this story has a strong Celtic dimension as related in *Landnámabók*. Hjörleifur's nickname ('Sword Leif') was believed to have arisen from his seizing a sword while raiding a souterrain or underground chamber in Ireland. The infant Icelandic colony came close to disaster when Hjörleifur and his men were slain by his rebellious Irish slaves who seized the women and goods of his party. The leader of the slaves is given a genuine Irish name, Dufthakr (Old Irish *Dubthach*), and we are also told of an Irish concoction of flour and butter called *minnthak* which the Irish used when drinking-water ran out on the initial voyage. All this is consistent with Hjörleifur's having gone to Iceland after a previous stay in the Western Sea (*vestrhaf*). In narrating this episode the compiler of *Landnámabók* availed of the opportunity to explain that the Vestmannaeyjar ('Islands of the Westmen') were called after Hjörleifur's slaves. But the word *vestmenn* clearly meant something other than 'Irishmen' – Icelanders had a specific word for them (*Írar*). *Vestmenn* meant simply 'Men from the West' or the *Vestvíking* – from that same Western Sea where Olaf the White held sway at precisely the time Iceland was colonized by Vikings. The *Vestmenn*, then, had come to Iceland from Scotland and Ireland. In a similar way the Dublin Norsemen called themselves *Ostmen* or 'Men from the East' because they had come from the Scandinavian east to settle in the *vestvíking* at Dublin. *Vestmenn* was, after all, a Norse name, intended for Norsemen and Celts alike who had come from the West. The very fact that such a name was coined at all in early Iceland and that it left its enduring mark on the important and fertile Vestmannaeyjar, shows how significant the Vestmenn originally were. Under that banner we can include all those Hebrideans who migrated under the leadership of Ketil Flatnose's kin along the older route of the *papar*, and along that route we find the name *Vestmann hafn* in the Faroes. It is not surprising then to find that as soon as *Landnámabók* has disposed of the earliest explorers from the west, and of Ingólfur's settlement, it immediately turns to the migration of Ketil Flatnose's kin from the Hebrides to Iceland. It was this early tradition that in turn provided the starting point for *Laxdoela Saga* and *Eyrbyggja Saga*.

The fact that early Icelandic tradition shows that the first explorers and settlers in Iceland were intimately connected with the Western Sea and with those *Vestmenn* who lived there, strongly suggests that it was the *papar* who willingly or unwillingly led the Vikings to the Faroes and Iceland. In the Hebrides in particular the indigenous Celtic population was not annihilated nor was the Christian faith completely destroyed. On the Icelandic side we have detailed information from the twelfth century which suggests that Hebridean Norse settlers had adopted Celtic Christianity during their stay in Scotland. That particular brand of Christianity was controlled and dominated by Iona, and whatever harsh fate befell the monasteries in the Northern Isles, we have contemporary evidence from Irish chronicles to show that Iona struggled on with a token community even during the most barbarous phase of the Viking onslaught in the early ninth century. We shall see that Iona was revitalized as a centre of Norse Christianity in the later tenth century, when even the half-pagan kings of Norse Dublin resorted to it as a place of pilgrimage. According to *Landnámabók*, the late ninth-century Icelandic settler Orlygur Hrappsson, the nephew of Ketil Flatnose, had not only been fostered by a Hebridean bishop, but he had taken the cult of Columba with him to western Iceland. Orlygur settled at Esjuberg whose great mountain dominates the skyline of Ingólfur's settlement at nearby Reykjavík. At Esjuberg, Orlygur kept his promise to bishop Patrick and built his church in honour of Columba with some timber taken from the Hebrides for that purpose, and this church housed an iron bell, a plenarium, and consecrated earth which the Hebridean bishop had entrusted to the migrating Orlygur. He and his kinsmen 'put their faith in *Kolumkilli*'. Orlygur's nearest neighbour to the north, incidentally, was his Hebridean cousin, Helgi Bjólan, and beyond him lived Svartkel, that Christian settler from Caithness. We must conclude from these Icelandic traditions that Hebridean settlers had been in favourable contact with Iona Christianity and had taken the cult of Columba with them to Iceland as early as the 880s. Björn the Easterling, a son of Ketil Flatnose, is said to have sailed from the Hebrides some 10 years after Ingólfur had founded the Icelandic colony. That would put Björn's voyage somewhere about 884. Björn's nephew, Ketil the Fool, was not only a Hebridean Norse Christian and a grandson of Ketil Flatnose, but according to *Landnámabók* he chose to settle at Kirkjuboer in Sída in the *papar* country of the south-east. The compiler of *Landnámabók* clearly saw a connection between the coming of this Hebridean to Iceland and previous activities of the Scottish *papar*. Ketil, we are told, settled on land previously occupied by *papar* and to underwrite the continuity of Scottish Christian settlement there we are told that no heathen could ever live on that hallowed ground. This might suggest that unlike the descendants of many other Hebrideans, the posterity of Ketil the Foolish retained their Christianity into the eleventh century. That would indeed seem to be so, for according to *Njáls Saga*, when Thangbrand, the missionary who evangelized the heathen Icelanders in *c.* AD 1000, visited Surt, the great-grandson of Ketil, at Kirkjuboer he found that 'all these men had already become Christians'.

For too long we have treated the Columban phase of Scottish Christianity in isolation from the later Scandinavian period, and equally, Scandinavian historians have tended to treat the discovery of Iceland by the *papar* as an event which had no bearing on later Scandinavian history, treating voyages of the celibate *papar* as a sort of demographic cul-de-sac. This approach shows a remarkable lack of economy – involving as it does the idea that Iceland was discovered twice within a century – but it also fails to appreciate the profound impact which Iona had on Scandinavian civilization as soon as the Vikings came into sustained contact with it. However vulnerable to attack Iona itself may have been as an island monastery, it was inconceivable that the Northmen in conquering Iona's sprawling *paruchia* in the North Atlantic could obliterate two centuries of one of the most powerful civilizing forces in Europe. It was inevitable that barbarian Vikings, with their primitive beliefs in outmoded gods and with their lack of writing and book learning, would be greatly influenced by the higher Christian civilization which they encountered at such close quarters in the Scottish Isles. As the earliest Norse settlers turned to fishing and farming in the Isles, they came into sustained contact with Hebridean Christianity and its clergy. They learnt among other things of voyages into the northern ocean by way of Shetland and the Faroes to Iceland and beyond. We have seen how the compiler of *Landnámabók* told of a Hebridean mariner on the ship of the first colonizing voyage to Iceland. That was the compiler's way of telling us something of how Flóki found Iceland in the first place. Similarly, in *Groenlendinga Saga* we are told that Leif Eiríksson took with him on his voyage of discovery to North America, a certain Tyrkir from Southern Europe, a detail which prepares us for the identification of the vines and grapes by Tyrkir when Leif's men reach Vinland. The ancient Celtic sea-way of the *papar* may not have ended at Iceland. Dicuil, we recall, had spoken to men who had explored the Arctic Ocean beyond Iceland. When Eirík the Red sailed on his colonizing expedition to Greenland at the end of the tenth century we are told there was a Hebridean Christian on the ship of Herjólfur, a prominent settler in Greenland who hailed from the Reykjanes area of Iceland. This Hebridean was remembered for a poem he composed to his Christian God begging for a safe passage through such treacherous seas as those off Cape Farewell in southern Greenland. That poem, *Hafgerdingadrápa* or 'The Lay of the Towering Waves', survives in one verse:

> I pray the blameless monk-prover
> Our Father, my journey to further
> Heaven's Lord may he bless and let hover
> His hawk-perching hand over my head.

The reference to God as the 'monk prover' (*munka reyni*) is a peculiarly Celtic way of viewing the Creator and reflects the attitude of a monastic church alien to later medieval Scandinavia and Europe generally, but completely at home in a Hebridean or Iona context. The presence of a Hebridean Christian on the Greenland voyage reminds us, too, that Leif Eiríksson, the Greenlander whose name is so firmly associated with voyages to Vinland and other areas of North America, had spent a whole summer in the Hebrides before his expedition to the New World. The more we study Old Icelandic records the more we appear to be faced with a long line of apparent historical accidents which require an explanation. We learn for instance in the Icelandic annals of a bishop Eirík of

Greenland who sailed off in search of Vinland in 1121. Is it yet another coincidence that according to *Landnámabók* this bishop was fifth in descent from the Hebridean, Orlygur Hrappsson, who took with him the cult of Columba to Western Iceland? It may well be that the legacy of Iona and knowledge of the North Atlantic that was accumulated there led the Northmen not only to the shores of Iceland but to Greenland and a new world beyond.

6

'He Shall Preside over Alba as one Lord': The Birth of Medieval Scotland

The ninth century began with the Dark Age order of things virtually unchanged since the days of Columba – with Dál Riata Scots still perching precariously in the south-west; with Picts dominating the north and east, and with British and Anglian territories south of the Forth–Clyde line still outside the ambit of what we might call Scotland proper. By the end of the tenth century, the Scots had pushed eastwards across the Spine of Britain and assumed the leadership of the Picts; the frontier had been pushed across Lothian to the Tweed, and the Strathclyde Britons had been incorporated into Scottish territory giving access to the Solway. This growth of Scottish royal power and its consequent territorial gains was balanced by the complete loss of the Northern and Western Isles, as well as Caithness, to the Norsemen. We must take into account, too, the establishment of a hostile Scottish dynasty in Moray, north of the Mearns, together with the emergence of a mixed Gaelic-Norse dynasty in Galloway. The Scottish Isles and Galloway were areas of great importance from the ninth to the twelfth centuries, but with the eventual decline of Scandinavian sea power they were destined to revert to a peripheral zone which was essentially Scottish and which might easily be dominated by a strong monarchy based in the richer Lowlands. It was just such a monarchy which emerged south of the Mounth in the ninth century and which achieved the much more crucial and difficult annexation of northern English territory south of the Forth in the following century. By 1018, Scotland, with its frontier moved southward to the Tweed and Solway, had taken a recognizable and viable shape which would enable it to take its place among the national monarchies of Europe. It may seem easy to describe in broad outline the momentous changes which came to northern Britain in these centuries. It is more difficult to explain how these changes came

175

about. The annals of Iona, which had hitherto provided much contemporary information on Scotland, cease soon after 740. The collapse of Northumbria under a Danish assault in 866, which was preceded by a century of decline, has meant that northern English sources are extremely fragmentary and have little to say on Scottish affairs for the ninth and tenth centuries. With Scotland surrounded by Scandinavian invaders, and with its own ancient dynasties in turmoil, it is not surprising that sources from within the Picto-Scottish world are also contradictory and fragmentary. There are few certainties to guide us, but we can learn much by way of inference from even the most fragmentary material in the chronicles and genealogies which survive.

By the middle of the ninth century, the Scandinavians had achieved a political and economic stranglehold on the British Isles and the northern orientation of this Scandinavian power obviously had a profound effect on Scotland. Not only did Scotland lose its western seaboard and islands to the invaders, including its cultural heartland based on Iona, but Norse domination of the seas isolated and monitored all contacts between Scottish Dál Riata and its Irish homeland. As time went on, Norse hostility may have mellowed, but violence gave way to the establishment of a settled Scandinavian cultural zone which drove a wedge between Ulster and its colony on the other side of the North Channel. This, together with the shift in Dál Riata power eastwards into Perth and Fife, a phenomenon related to the Norse invasions, must have promoted a growing 'Scottish' self-awareness in the Cenél Gabhráin dynasty and a significant decline in the Irish dimension. Scandinavian colonization was not confined to western Scotland. The Norwegian settlement there was followed in the second half of the ninth century by the establishment of a Danish sphere of influence stretching from York across the Pennines and the Irish Sea to Dublin. This new zone, which was united under a formidable Scandinavian dynasty, upset all previous political relationships in northern Britain and Ireland. The conquest of Anglian Northumbria by a strong Danish warband which was openly hostile to the English kings of Wessex, created an entirely new situation for the emerging Scottish house of Kenneth mac Alpin (Cináed mac Alpín). Instantly, it found itself cut off from the mainstream of English influences on its southern flank, just as its Irish contacts had been violently severed in the west. Kenneth's dynasty found itself hemmed into the south-eastern corner covered today by Fife, Perth and Angus, and cut off from most of its former contacts in Britain. Paradoxically, at that very point in time, the embattled kingdom of Scotia found itself in the mainstream of international contacts made possible by its proximity to a Viking empire which controlled the coastal waters of western Europe. It is against this backdrop of major changes in the political map of northern Britain that we must study how the dynasty of Kenneth mac Alpin came to power and replaced the old Pictish kingdoms of the south-east.

Kenneth mac Alpin's conquest or annexation of southern Pictland in the years between 840 and his death in 858 is no longer viewed as a revolutionary development in medieval Scottish history. He was not the first king of Dál Riata origin to rule the Picts, nor was he the first king to rule both Picts and Scots. No less than three of his recent Dál Riata predecessors had ruled both peoples even if it is not certain that they held (in Dr Marjorie Anderson's words) 'both kingships simultaneously, by hereditary right in both kingdoms according to their different systems'. Already by the early eighth century Pictish kings such as Ciniod son of Derile and Óengus son of Fergus were sporting Gaelic names and probably had Scottish blood. By the late eighth century Pictish rulers not only had royal fathers from Dál Riata, but they ruled the kingdoms of the Picts and Scots simultaneously. This has been seen by supporters of the matrilinear theory as a merging of Scottish and Pictish dynasties facilitated by Pictish laws of inheritance and royal succession. Even if that were true, we would still have to explain why one candidate was chosen as king by both peoples when there were presumably several competent rivals even within one kin group able and willing to rule each nation in independence of the other. When we reach the ninth century, we find that Constantine son of Fergus (d. 820), of the Cenél Gabhráin line in Dál Riata, ruled as king of that dynasty; but he also appears as Castantin son of Uurguist, king of the Picts, in Pictish king lists. His brother and successor in the kingship of Dál Riata was Óengus II (d. 834), whom we meet in Pictish king lists as Unuist son of Uurguist. Constantine left a son, Drest, who ruled only as king of the Picts (834-837), but Óengus's son and successor was Eóganán, *alias* Uuen, who reigned as king of both Picts and Scots, and who died in 839.

Clearly, there must have been a compelling political and military explanation for this blending of the kingships of Pict and Scot. Skene read the signs as evidence for a Pictish takeover of the Scots

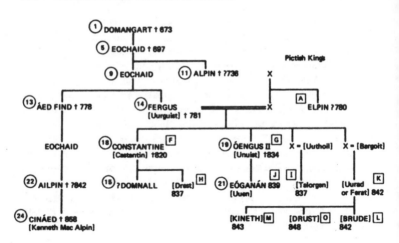

3 Kings of Dál Riata

which he saw as a sequel to the triumph of the Pictish king, Óengus I, over Dál Riata in 741. It seems reasonable to follow Dr Anderson and others in rejecting this thesis on several counts. It is inconceivable if the Picts were the dominant military faction in the century after 740 that the Scots could suddenly emerge under Kenneth mac Alpin precisely at the end of that period in such a strong position as to impose their Gaelic language and institutions on the Picts. Dál Riata ascendancy was much more likely to have evolved as a gradual process of infiltration of the Pictish east, which must have escalated under pressure from Vikings in the Hebrides and Argyll in the early ninth century (See Table 3). We have seen that as far back as 717 it was increasing Scottish influence on Pictland as much as any liturgical considerations that may have prompted Nechtan to expel the Columban clergy from Pictland. As for the ascendancy of the Pictish king Óengus I over Dál Riata after 741, the *Annals of Ulster* virtually state that Óengus was deprived of that overlordship in 750 most likely by the intervention of Teudubr, king of Strathclyde. By 768 we find the Dál Riata king, Áed Find, invading Fortriu and fighting against the Pictish ruler, Ciniod (Kenneth), which is not suggestive of a weak Scottish kingdom. Besides, Áed Find was remembered as a powerful Dál Riata king from whom the house of Kenneth mac Alpin later liked to claim descent and whose laws were imposed on Scot and Pict alike by Kenneth's brother, Donald I (d. 862). Skene may well have been wrong in seeing a Pictish takeover of the Scots, but he was basically correct in viewing the situation in terms of conquest and overlordship rather than a mere blending of genealogies by that sleight of matrilinear succession. There does indeed seem to have been a takeover process at work perhaps as early as the late eighth century, but it was the Scots who were taking over Pictish kingship and not the other way round. We have seen how Strathclyde and earlier Scottish kings had assumed the overlordship of the Picts in the past. In that sense there was nothing new about the reigns of Constantine and Óengus II in the period 811-834, but whereas earlier Strathclyde kings had intruded their kinsmen as satellites into the Pictish overlordship, in the case of Constantine and Óengus they ruled both kingdoms simultaneously. This obviously reflects an attempt by either Pict or Scot to unite both kingdoms under one rule.

We get the decided impression that Óengus II and his son Eóganán, for instance, were Scots first and foremost. Their names are thoroughly Scottish Gaelic rather than Pictish and by male descent from Fergus they appear to be in the direct line of Cenél Gabhráin. Indeed, the details of their Gaelic descent is clearer than that of their alleged kinsman, Kenneth mac Alpin. As the sons of Scots kings elected to a Dál Riata kingship, it is inconceivable that they could have been reared or fostered away from a Gaelic court – assuming for the sake of argument that the Pictish court provided that exotic non-Indo-European ambience vouched for by some scholars. Yet the evidence which survives suggests that these rulers based themselves in Fortriu in modern Perthshire rather than in ancient western centres such as Dunadd. It seems clear that by the early ninth century at least kings such as Constantine and Óengus were ruling both the Picts and Scots from Forteviot near where the Water of May joins the Earn. This might be used as an argument for a Pictish take-over of the Scots, but if we regard the dynasty of Óengus II as being essentially Scottish then we have to conclude that Dál Riata had already pushed east into Pictland a generation before the time of Kenneth mac Alpin, and this hypothesis has the merit of making the major migration of the Scots dynasty coincide with the period of most intense Norse raiding on the Dál Riata homeland in Argyll. We shall see how Constantine (d. 820) was connected with the church of Dunkeld, while his brother Óengus was associated with St Andrews and both kings are described in the *Annals of Ulster* not as kings of Dál Riata as we might expect, but as kings of Fortriu – that territory which lay east of the Spine of Britain. Óengus's son, Eóganán, was slain in a battle between the Norsemen and 'the men of Fortriu' in 839, while the legend of St Andrew informs us that this Eóganán and his brothers were based at Forteviot during the reign of their father, Óengus. According to this legend, the sons of Óengus (Eóganán, Nechtan and Finguine) were at Forteviot sometime before 834 when their father was away on an expedition in Argyll. The St Andrew's legend does not provide reliable early information, but for what it is worth, this tradition seems to suggest that already by the second quarter of the ninth century, Dál Riata kings had moved to Forteviot, and Argyll had been relegated to the status of a dangerous frontier region, which by then it must have undoubtedly become.

In 839, five years after the death of Óengus, his dynasty suffered a major catastrophe which somehow helped Kenneth mac Alpin to succeed to the Scottish kingship. In that year the men of Fortriu were slaughtered 'beyond counting' in a battle against 'gentiles' or heathen Vikings. Among the dead were two sons of Óengus, Eóganán or Uuen, king of the Picts and Scots, and Bran. This decimation of Picts and of the Dál Riata line of the house of Fergus at the hands of the Vikings left the way open, if we are to believe the Latin king-lists, for one Alpín to take the Dál Riata kingship in 839. We cannot be certain of Alpín's origins or that he really was accepted as king of the Dál Riata. There is no mention of him in the *Annals of Ulster* which recorded the deaths of so many of his predecessors and successors. The only thing we are reasonably certain of is that he was the father of Kenneth who seized power among the Scots in about 840. Alpín's historicity, then, derives from his parenthood of a more illustrious son. The *Scottish Chronicle* gives Kenneth a reign of 18 years over Dál Riata. Since he died in 858, he would then have come to power in 840, very soon after the Viking victory over the Picts and Scots in the previous year. This makes a good deal of sense and casts doubt over the three-year reign accorded Kenneth's father, Alpín, in the Dál Riata king-list. The only alleged historical information on the reign of Alpín is offered in the Latin king-lists of the Picts and Scots (the X version) and a single item mentioned in the *Chronicle of Huntingdon*. But these sources say little to reassure us. Alpín's reign was probably invented to lend respectability to Kenneth. It seems strange if Alpín really had preceded his son in the kingship, that, as Dr Marjorie Anderson noted, it was Kenneth and not his father who was seen in Scottish sources as the founder of a new era. It was only *after* Alpín's death that 'the *regnum* of the Scots was transferred to the *regnum* of the Picts', according to a comment in the Latin regnal lists, or as the *Chronicle of Huntingdon* saw it: 'he [Kenneth] was the first of the Scots to obtain the monarchy of the whole of Albania which is now called Scotia and he first reigned in it over the Scots.' Clearly, neither of these statements is correct, since there is evidence to show that the Dál Riata house of Fergus son of Eochaid (d. 781) had established itself in the east a generation before Kenneth's time and that it had certainly ruled over Picts *and* Scots. What then was so unique about Kenneth mac Alpin? The answer seems to lie in the fact that he founded a new dynasty at a most critical period in the evolution of the Scottish nation, whose sustained success over many centuries gave added posthumous glory to Kenneth. He most probably fought his way to power at the expense both of the Picts and the house of Fergus son of Eochaid of Dál Riata, and like many successful Dark Age warlords, his own origins were quite obscure.

Kenneth's mother may have been of the Pictish royal house, and various attempts have been made by Boece, Innes, and several recent historians to make Alpín descend through his mother from the Picto-Scottish house of Fergus son of Eochaid. These efforts to tie the early ninth-century kings of Pictland into the genealogy of Dál Riata by way of 'the matrilineage of Fortriu' are at best, on Dr Anderson's own admission,' plausible but unconfirmed hypotheses'. According to the twelfth-century genealogy of Kenneth, he was the great-grandson of Áed Find, a Dál Riata king of the main line of Cenél Gabhráin who died in 778. Skene viewed much of the Dál Riata genealogies before the time of Kenneth as a twelfth-century invention. That was an extreme view inspired by the notion of a Pictish supremacy over Dál Riata in the century before 840. We do not have to entertain all of Skene's doubts to have our own reservations about Kenneth's claim to belong to the main Dál Riata line. His alleged descent from Áed Find, through his father Alpín and his grandfather, Eochaid, is suspicious on several counts. If Alpín's reign was a fiction, then according to this genealogy, none of Kenneth's immediate ancestors had been kings of Dál Riata since the time of his great-grandfather. That would not make him ineligible to succeed as far as Gaelic laws of succession were concerned, but it would make his task considerably more difficult in view of the tight hold which the house of Fergus had on the kingship for the past 60 years. The disastrous battle against the Vikings in 839 was not sufficient in itself to explain the sudden eclipse of the house of Fergus son of Eochaid and the morphology of the genealogy argues for Kenneth's status as an outsider of uncertain origin.

While Kenneth may well have been a usurper, he must nevertheless have hailed from a line of kings, however obscure, and he must have had a power base from which to attract *céli* or noble clients who constituted the backbone of his warband. Without such credentials and without a military following, he could never have taken over the kingship of Dál Riata and later that of the Picts. The one thing that we may safely conclude about Kenneth is that he is highly unlikely to have led a Pictish faction. He was remembered in medieval Scottish historiography, rightly, or wrongly, as a member of the Cenél Gabhráin; there are several indications that he violently usurped the Pictish kingship, and his immediate descendants and successors had Gaelic names and imposed Gaelic language and institutions on their Pictish subjects. The *Prophecy of Berchán*, which in its present form is fourteenth-century, but which may have been first compiled in the late twelfth, describes Kenneth as 'the first king who ruled in the east, of the men of Ireland in Alba (*d'fearaibh Eirenn in Albain*)'. Kenneth was not the first Scots king to rule east of the Spine of Britain, but traditions such as this are insistent on his western Gaelic origins.

While Kenneth took over the Scottish kingship in 840, he did not win immediate or automatic recognition as king also of the Picts. Estimates of the time it took for this new king of Dál Riata to extend his sway over the Picts vary from two years in the *Scottish Chronicle* to seven in the *Chronicle of Huntingdon*. In the Pictish king-lists, we find that on the death of Eóganán (Uuen son of Unuist) in the Viking battle of 839, he was succeeded by at least two if not five Pictish leaders, the last of whom would have died any time from 843 to 848. Most of these kings of the Pictish twilight have Pictish rather than Gaelic names, and their presence in the lists confronts us with an alternative tradition which did not accept that Kenneth mac Alpin took over any considerable part of Pictland before 842. Four of the five last Pictish kings who may have ruled in defiance of Kenneth made up a dynasty of a father (Ferat) and three sons, which suggests that before Kenneth could gain recognition among the Picts, he had first to destroy a faction centred on a native Pictish dynasty and one which practised patrilinear succession to boot.

This evidence for the survival of Pictish kings for some years after Kenneth came to power finds some support in traditions from the late eleventh century which held that Kenneth had slaughtered his Pictish rivals. The earliest of these accounts is the *Prophecy of Berchán* which in its cryptic way asserts that the Picts ('fierce men of the east') were tricked and slaughtered by Kenneth 'in the middle of Scone of the high shields'. The poem alludes to digging in the earth as part of Kenneth's feat in disposing of his enemies, and Skene believed that this was the same incident set out in more detail by Giraldus Cambrensis. According to Giraldus, the Scots invited the Pictish aristocracy to a Borgia-type supper, and when their guests were quite drunk the Scots removed the bolts which pegged the benches together. The Picts got somehow jammed in the box-like hollow of the benches and were slaughtered by their hosts. This dubious tale may have cast unnecessary doubt over the basic tradition that Kenneth used treachery against the Picts, or that at the very least he subdued them by force before winning the Pictish kingship. The *Prophecy of Berchán* says that he came to the kingship 'after violent deaths, after violent slaughter'; the *Chronicle of Melrose* refers to his expulsion of the Picts; while the *Chronicle of Huntingdon* claims that Alpín was slain in his efforts to subdue the Picts and that Kenneth eventually overcame them in *c.* 847 after they had been weakened by Danish invasion. The statement in this source that Kenneth subdued the Picts in his seventh year tallies well with those versions of the Pictish king-lists which claim that five Pictish kings succeeded Eóganán in 839, reigning for nine years in all. The most reliable account of Kenneth's reign comes to us in the mid fourteenth-century Poppleton MS of the *Scottish Chronicle* (Version A). This section took its present shape, according to Dr Anderson, in the reign of William (1165-1214) but some of the details offered in this account (such as the date of Kenneth's death) suggest that it may derive from a near-contemporary account. It tells us that Kenneth was two years king of Dál Riata 'before he came to Pictland' (*antequam ueniret Pictauiam*) and tantalizingly it refers back to a lost passage which dealt with Kenneth's destruction of the Picts.

Positive statements to the effect that Kenneth held the Dál Riata kingship for some years prior to his conquest of the Picts, suggests that this conquest was as much territorial as it was political and tells us something of Kenneth's origins. If Kenneth had really belonged to the house of Fergus son of Eochaid or to a near branch of it as the genealogists maintained, and if he had peacefully assumed the kingship of Dál Riata soon after Eóganán's death in 839, then we would have expected him to rule, as his immediate Dál Riata predecessors, if not from Forteviot, then at least from somewhere in Perth or Fife. But the sources do not suggest that this was so. While Eóganán and his Dál Riata predecessors were associated by the sources with Forteviot, Kenneth was clearly seen as coming from the Gaelic west. On the other hand, a note in the Pictish king-lists claims that Drust son of Ferat, the last of the Pictish kings who would have died *c.* 848, was slain at Forteviot. A later gloss on that note changes the place of Drust's end to Scone, perhaps influenced by the *Prophecy of Berchán*. Given that Forteviot was a palace of the kings of Picts and Scots prior to the time of Kenneth, we could interpret this note as referring to Kenneth's destruction of the Pictish power base and to his territorial conquest of the south-east. Such an interpretation fits well with the note in the Latin king-list of Dál Riata (Dr Anderson's List I) which claims that after the reign of Alpín (i.e. in the reign of Kenneth), the *regnum* of the Scots was transferred to the land (*terram*) of the Picts.

This leads us, finally, to the conclusion that medieval Scottish sources were right in seeing Kenneth as a new type of king who hailed from the Gaelic west and who crossed the Spine of Britain to take power in Pictland. The emphasis on his western Gaelic origin is quite marked: In Version D of the *Scottish Chronicle* we are told that Kenneth 'led the Scots from Argyll (*de Ergadia*) into the land of the Picts' which echoes Version A's phrase that Kenneth 'came to Pictland' (*ueniret Pictaviam*), and the *Prophecy of Berchán's* claim that Kenneth was the 'first king that will reign in the east from among the Irish in Scotland'. Kenneth may well have been different, after all, from his Dál Riata predecessors who ruled the Picts and Scots from Forteviot in the east. He could have sprung from a quite separate and even obscure branch of Dál Riata which had always been in the Gaelic west, and as such he was more 'Scottish' or Gaelic than his cousins who had moved east earlier. If this hypothesis is correct, then Kenneth's origins and his achievement can be compared with the career of Brian Boru in late tenth-century Ireland. Brian's dynasty was constantly exposed to Viking attack from the nearby Scandinavian fortress at Limerick, but this frontier relationship with Vikings paved the way for Brian and his dynasty to usurp first the kingship of Munster and later the highkingship of the Uí Néill. If Kenneth mac Alpin had hailed from a western tribe in Argyll as later sources claimed (which would perhaps fit a tradition that Alpín died fighting in Galloway), then he too, was reared to kingship on a turbulent Viking frontier. Argyll in the early ninth century was a battle-ground for Viking marauders who had settled in the Isles and for freebooters coming further afield along the Atlantic route from Norway and even, as we have seen, from Iceland. A dynasty based in this region had every incentive to force its way into the rich lands of the Pictish south-east, and if it managed to survive the Viking onslaught and even to come to terms with the invaders, the military and tactical experience gained by such a warband would give it a formidable political advantage in the crisis of 839 when both the Dál Riata and Pictish houses were slaughtered by the Vikings. We shall explore the relationship of Kenneth mac Alpin's dynasty with Vikings later on, but we must first look briefly at other evidence of an ecclesiastical nature which helps us to understand the profound changes which were at work in Scottish society at this time.

These new eastern developments in Scottish politics were heralded not only by the establishment of a new dynasty under Kenneth in 840, but also by the creation or elevation of new Christian cult centres in the east which quickly replaced Iona and its western Gaelic influence in the life of the new kingdom. We have seen how, after enduring several attacks, Iona was abandoned by its abbot and by most of its monks in 807, but that a token community survived as is clear from Abbot Cellach's retirement back to Iona in 815 and from the account of Blathmac's martyrdom there in 825. Most of Iona's monks migrated to Kells along a line of retreat that seemed natural to a community whose leading members were still largely drawn from Ireland, and who on Iona still continued to live within what was essentially an Irish cultural zone. It was also a decision taken in the context of great demographic upheavals which the Norsemen brought to northern Britain

compared with sporadic Norse raiding and limited attempts at settlement by Vikings in Irela.. d. The decision of the Iona abbots
to retreat to Kells may have been prudent, and their continued
attempts to visit Iona and their Scottish flock in the teeth of the
Viking onslaught may well be viewed as heroic, but their reluctance
to follow their royal Scottish patrons into Perth and Fife must surely
mark one of the major events in the political life of the church in the
British Isles. Since its foundation over two and a half centuries
before, the leaders of the church of Iona had acted as a major prop
to the kings of Cenél Gabhráin, but during the Viking crisis of the
ninth century the leaders of the ecclesiastical and political life of
Dál Riata parted company. This move was in direct contrast to
events in Wessex for instance, where the bishops, and eventually
the metropolitan at Canterbury, moved into a close alliance with
the English kings to repel the Danish menace.

It is no coincidence that the Pictish king-lists note that Constantine son of Fergus who died in AD 820, was the founder of
Dunkeld, which by implication must refer to the church rather than
a fortress. Constantine may have revitalized an older Columban
monastery there, but it is significant that this king, who ruled both
Scots and Picts, founded a major new church on the Tay in the east
sometime between 811 and 820, when Iona's leaders had departed
for Ireland.[1] This founding or refounding of Dunkeld was a major
event: by 865 we hear of an 'archbishop (prim-epscop) of Fortriu'
who died as abbot of Dunkeld and his name, Tuathal son of Artgus,
shows him to have been of Gaelic or Scottish origin. His jurisdiction over Fortriu meant that he controlled the heartlands of the
southern Pictish region stretching from the Tay to the Forth, if
indeed he were not simply the chief bishop of Scotland south of the
Mounth. The seat of this bishopric at Dunkeld had become rich
enough by 903 to have been singled out for attack by a Norse
plundering expedition led by Ivar II from Viking Dublin. King
Constantine, who died in 820 was succeeded by his brother,
Óengus son of Fergus, who was also remembered in the Pictish
king-lists for founding a church – in his case at Kilremonth, later St
Andrews in Fife. This must refer to a re-founding of St Andrews or
to a change in its status because we hear earlier of a Gaelic abbot
of that house called Tuathalán who died back in 747. This led

[1] Constantine became king of Dál Riata in 811, but he had been king of
the Picts since 789.

A.O. Anderson to believe that St Andrews was founded not by the ninth-century Óengus son of Fergus, but by his predecessor of that name who ruled in the eighth century. The note in the king-list, however, refers to the brother of Constantine, and the legend of St Andrew, however far-fetched in its assertion that relics of that saint were carried by Regulus from Constantinople to Fife, firmly associates the founding of St Andrews with the reign of the ninth-century Óengus and his family. Again, it is remarkable that this cult centre whose new and exotic patron would eventually rival Columba in his claim to protect the Scottish church, should have been founded in that period (820-834) in eastern Scotland when the Dál Riata kings were consolidating their grip on this territory. Indeed, the very name *Constantine*, which appears for the first time in the Scots dynasty just now, may have been inspired by the legend of St Andrew's relics, which asserted that they were taken to Constantinople during the joint reigns of Constantine, Constantius and Constans.[2]

It would be wrong to write off the influence of Iona after the departure of its abbots in 807. Its community survived in its new Irish home, and the old centre off Mull would remain forever hallowed ground for Scot and Pict alike, and eventually even for Norsemen. When Ivar II fell in Fortriu while leading his Viking hordes against the fortresses and holy places of Strathearn, he was defeated by a Scottish army which had the crozier or *bachall* of Columba carried before it in battle. If we are to believe the Scottish Chronicle, Iona was chosen for the burial place of the kings, Constantine I (d. 877) and Áed (d. 878) the sons of Kenneth mac Alpin; and for Kenneth's nephew Giric (d. 889) and for his grandson Donald II son of Constantine (d. 900). Yet if Iona persisted as a holy place worthy to receive a king's bones in spite of its remoteness from Fife, there is evidence to show that by 849 a crucial decision had been taken to remove whatever remained of Columba's relics from Iona. In that year, Indrechtach, abbot of the Iona community, carried Columba's *minna* or reliquaries to Ireland, presumably to Kells, while, according to the Poppleton Manuscript of the *Scottish Chronicle*, Kenneth mac Alpin 'transported the relics of Columba to a church that he had built' in the seventh year of his reign (*c.* 848). It appears, therefore, that Columba's relics

[2] There are hagiographical legends of a British saint, Constantine, who may have belonged to the royal house of Strathclyde in the sixth century.

were divided up, and that Kenneth, while willing to lose the chief members of Columba's community to Ireland, saw to it that a share in the all-important relics were saved for his Scottish dynasty and housed in a church which has been assumed by Skene and others to have been Dunkeld.

Alongside the infiltration of the south-east by Dál Riata kings and churchmen there is evidence of a growing intolerance on the part of the new Gaelic rulers of Scotia against the ecclesiastical and secular laws of their Pictish subjects, for although new cult centres sprang up in the east, they were not Pictish in ethos. The *Scottish Chronicle* claims that the Picts deserved the harsh fate meted out to them by Kenneth mac Alpin because not only had they spurned 'the mass and precept' of presumably the Scottish church (as when King Nechtan expelled the Columban clergy back in 717), but more ominously 'they wished to be held equal to others in the law of Justice'.[3] In other words the Picts resented any attempt to turn them into a servile people. The *Scottish Chronicle* informs us that in the reign of Kenneth's brother, Donald I (d. 862), 'The Gaels [i.e. the Scots] with their king made the rights and laws of the kingdom [the laws] of Áed son of Eochaid'. This enactment was proclaimed at Forteviot in Fortriu, and it seems that Scottish law as promulgated in the reign of the Dál Riata king, Áed Find (736-778) was enforced on Pict and Scot alike. Secular law and church organization were being brought under the control of the Scots, although we can only glimpse the stages by which this took place. When Donald I was eventually succeeded by his son Giric, sometime after 878, a note in the Latin king-list says he 'was the first to give liberty to the Scottish church, which was in servitude up to that time after the custom and fashion of the Picts.' It is not clear whether this means that the hereditary rights of Pictish lay proprietors were now abolished, or whether it refers to other disadvantages suffered by Dál Riata clergy within Pictland.

Skene and Anderson compared the passage quoted above relating to friction between Pictish and Dál Riata law and church discipline with a subsequent passage, also in the *Scottish Chronicle*, which seems to mark the final triumph of the Gaelic order over the older Pictish system of the east. This account tells us that in 906,

---

[3] This is M.O. Anderson's reading of the passage. A.O. Anderson and Skene read: 'they refused to be held equal to others in the law of justice.'

Constantine II (900-952) along with his bishop Cellach (of St Andrews)

> pledged themselves upon the hill of Faith near the royal city of Scone, that the laws and disciplines of the Faith, and the rights in churches and gospels, should be kept in conformity with [the customs of] the Scots.

By the opening of the tenth century, the dynasty of Kenneth had established itself at Scone, and its church at St Andrews was confident enough to impose Gaelic ways on the native Picts. It would be wrong to assume, however, that Kenneth's dynasty was imposing an undiluted form of Irish Columban monasticism in the east. Whatever Bishop Cellach's ecclesiastical organization looked like in detail, it seems (unlike its Columban counterpart) to have emphasized episcopal authority, and may not have been predominantly monastic in the rank and file of its clergy. The participation of Constantine's bishop in the proclamation of 906 reminds us of the notice given to an 'archbishop' of Fortriu by the *Annals of Ulster* in 865. Times were changing, too, even for the crucial choice of a 'place of resurrection' for a Dark Age monarch. Constantine II, who was one of the greatest and longest-reigning kings in early medieval Scotland, chose not to follow his ancestors to a grave in Iona. He resigned his throne in 943, and retired as a Céli Dé monk to St Andrews, where he died in 952. For Dark Age kings, the patronage of holy founders and the veneration of their relics and resting places were obsessions surpassed only by their desire to succeed in war. While it is true that Constantine's choice of St Andrews for his monastic retirement did not mark the end of Iona's popularity in this respect, it was nevertheless a sign of the changing times. These brief records of new trends in royal patronage and the emergence of new saints and new cult centres can offer us just as valuable insights into the changes that were taking place in ninth and tenth-century Scotland as the many involved and tortuous discussions of the elusive king-lists.

The shift of the Gaelic power base in Scotland from west to east and the consequent domination of the Picts under a new Scottish dynasty were major developments all accomplished during the period of greatest Viking activity and were undoubtedly related to it. We saw how by 866, Olaf, king of Viking Dublin, had assumed the leadership of the Scottish Vikings on a major expedition against the Picts of Fortriu, and how in 870 he captured the Strathclyde stronghold at Dumbarton with the help of Ivar. Olaf was succeeded in the kingship of Dublin *c.* 871 by his ally Ivar, who united the Norse territories of the Irish Sea zone with Danish conquests in Northumbria. From the death of Ivar in 873 until the fall of Danish York in 954, the frantic efforts of the Dublin and York kings to hold their sprawling realm intact constitute a major theme in the history of the British Isles. It was inevitable that Scottish kings of Kenneth's house would get drawn into the power struggles of their Norse neighbours, and a case can be made to show that Scottish rulers consistently followed a policy over a century which sought to exploit the ambitions of the Norsemen for their own ends. Just as the origins of Kenneth mac Alpin are obscure so, inevitably, are the details of his dealings with the Norsemen. Kenneth grew to manhood in the period prior to 840 when the earliest phase of Norse freebooting was giving way to more stable if no less hostile attempts at settlement. By that time, the *Gall-Gaedhil* were settling down in the Hebrides. The *Four Masters* inform us that in AD 836 a certain Gothfrith Fergusson (Gofraidh mac Ferghusa) 'went to Scotland to strengthen Dál Riata at the request of Kenneth mac Alpin.' In that year Gothfrith is called *toísech* or 'leader' of Airgialla, but a Gothfrith Fergusson died as toísech of the Hebrides or *Innsi Gall* in 853. Gothfrith had a Norse name, but he seems to have had a Gaelic father, claiming descent either from the Irish Airgialla of central Ulster or more likely from that branch of the tribe who lived in the nearby Scottish territory of the Cenél Loairn. He was, then, a leader of the *Gall-Gaedhil*, which fits perfectly with his role as jarl or king of the Hebrides in the mid-ninth century.[4] Of even greater interest is the statement that this Gothfrith had helped Kenneth mac Alpin consolidate his position in Dál Riata in 836. According to the received chronology of the Scottish and Pictish royal succession, Kenneth had not become king of Dál Riata until 839 or 840, and the Picts were being ruled jointly perhaps by Talorgen and by Drust the son of Constantine, while the Scots had Drest's first cousin, Eóganán, as their king. It seems, therefore, that already before Kenneth had ousted the house of Fergus son of Eochaid from power in south-east Scotland, he had enlisted the aid of his Viking neighbours in the west. This ties in with a reference to Kenneth's brother, Donald, in the *Prophecy of Berchán*, as 'the

---

[4] Gothfrith died in the same year as the arrival of Olaf the White and he may have been succeeded in the Hebrides by Ketil Flatnose.

wanton son of a foreign wife (*An mear mhac na Gaillsighthe*)', which if it were correct would imply that Alpín had once taken a Norse queen. Such marriages were often contracted to consolidate political or military alliances between potentially hostile groups, and the Scots were not alone in seeking these unions with Vikings. King Athelstan of England married his sister to Sitric of Dublin in 926, for instance, and numerous Irish and Scottish kings intermarried with that same Dublin house. What is particularly interesting about the oblique reference to Donald's mother is that it affords the earliest evidence for an alliance between a native dynasty and Vikings in the British Isles, which is what we should expect considering the Scottish Norse colonies were founded much earlier than those further south in Ireland or England.

This fragmentary evidence for Kenneth's friendly relations with his Hebridean Viking neighbours is consistent with the statement in the *Chronicle of Huntingdon* that Kenneth overcame the Picts at a time when they had been slaughtered by the Vikings:

> Danish pirates occupied the shores and destroyed the Picts (who were defending themselves) with a great slaughter. He [Kenneth] passed into the remainder of their territories, turned his arms against the Picts, and having slain many compelled them to fly, and he thus gained the monarchy of the whole of Alba, and first reigned in it over the Scots.

The *Chronicle of Huntingdon* is clearly wrong in claiming that Alpín was slain by the Picts in 834 and that his son Kenneth succeeded to the Dál Riata kingship at so early a time. On the other hand, by dating the collapse of the Picts at the hands of the Vikings to the seventh year of Kenneth, the Huntingdon tradition clearly maintained that Kenneth availed himself of the Viking slaughter of the Picto-Scottish house of Fergus son of Eochaid in 839 to seize power among the Picts.

Irish annals present a picture of the Dublin Olaf's campaigns in Scotland during the period 866 to 871 which strongly suggests that either Constantine son of Kenneth allied with the Dublin Norsemen or at the very least that he connived at Norse attacks on his Pictish and British neighbours. In 866 Olaf led a coalition of Hiberno-Norse and Scottish Vikings against Fortriu. Although we are told Olaf led the 'Foreigners' of *Alba*, it was neither 'the men of Alba' (*Fir nAlban*) nor Dál Riata whom he attacked. His target was the 'tribes of the Picts' (*Cruithentuath*) and he took their hostages, and tribute was paid 'for a long time afterwards'. It is impossible to tell whether the Picts plundered by Olaf were nominally under Constantine's rule in the south-east, or whether they lived to the north of the Mounth, a Pictish region then under pressure from Thorstein the Red, son of Olaf of Dublin, who had carved out a kingdom for himself in Caithness and Sutherland. Either way, the continued Norse attacks on the Picts could only have helped Constantine tighten his grip on their territories, particularly if the Pictish king-lists are correct in showing that a native dynasty survived for some years after Kenneth's coming to power in 840. Irish annalists could still recognize the Picts as a people distinct from the Britons and Saxons, when all three groups were ferried back as slaves to Dublin by the victorious Olaf and Ivar in 871. The Scots were conspicuously absent from the list of slaves which the Norsemen carried off from Scotland then, nor is there any record of the Scots being attacked. While the Picts were harried from 866 for several months, if not indeed longer, it was the turn of the Strathclyde Britons in 870-1 when Olaf and Ivar besieged and sacked Dumbarton. If Constantine had not helped them in this, he can only have been pleased by it, for in the following year (872) we know he plotted the death of Artgal, king of Strathclyde. Finally, there is a reference in the Irish *Three Fragments* which claims that Olaf of Dublin was married to 'the daughter of Cináed (Kenneth).' The Cináed in question may have been an Irish petty king of northern Brega who died in 851, but it is more likely that the king of Dublin and the Isles had married a daughter of Kenneth mac Alpin, since the context of the tale of Olaf's marriage to this lady fits in with the Scottish phase of the Dublin leader's career. The prospect of Constantine's sister being married to the king of Norse Dublin would fit in well not only with his apparently friendly relations with the Dublin army, but also with the statement in the *Prophecy of Berchán* regarding Alpín's earlier union with a Viking lady. Later on in the 930s, when we have much clearer evidence for the Dublin–Scottish alliance, Florence of Worcester informs us that Constantine's nephew, Constantine II, had married his daughter off to another Olaf of Dublin, Olaf III Gothfrithsson. The evidence may not be conclusive, but the fragments of information which survive do nonetheless point to the conclusion that the house of Kenneth mac Alpín rose to power in Scotland, if not openly allied with Viking rulers from the Hebrides and Dublin, then certainly profiting from their attacks on the Picts and Britons.

Scotland's relations with the Scandinavian rulers of York and Dublin were complicated by two important factors. In the first place, an outside party such as the Scots had to take account of rival Norse factions within the Scandinavian camp when conducting their delicate alliances, and secondly, the Scottish position itself changed dramatically over the century from 850 to 950. While the Scots entered that century as an insecure and embattled political group caught up in the path of what was virtually a new Viking empire, they emerged at the end to see the York and Dublin alliance prized apart and to find that their own role had evolved from one of passive onlookers to a position where the Scots king was taking the initiative in northern Britain. By 870, it was clear that the map of the British Isles had been violently re-drawn by the Vikings for a century to come. The old patchwork pattern of tribal kingdoms in Britain had been replaced by three major spheres of political influence. The house of Alfred of Wessex dominated southern England, and just as Kenneth mac Alpin had profited from the decimation of his British and Pictish neighbours by Vikings in Scotland, so too Alfred had seen the elimination of his traditional English enemies in Mercia, East Anglia and Northumbria. The Vikings had cleared the boards, and by so doing had strengthened the hand of the West Saxons and the Scots, while the Scandinavians themselves held the middle ground based on a new York–Dublin axis. A three-cornered struggle ensued in which the Scots not only managed to survive but succeeded in establishing themselves and their culture as the dominant political and cultural group in northern Britain.

With the arrival of Danish Vikings in strength in Northumbria the Scots chose to ally with the kings of Norse Dublin who needed Scottish help in furthering their own ambitions in northern England. The Dublin kings for their part were in a position to dominate the waters of the Clyde and of the western firths, and to control unruly Viking marauders of the Hebrides who posed a permanent threat to the Scots in Argyll. By choosing to ally with the Dublin Norsemen, the Scots were vulnerable to being caught up in feuds between Norwegian Dublin and Danish York, and this seems to have been the situation during the period 875 to 920. With the death of Ivar in Dublin in 873, his brother Hálfdan, who had been campaigning against Alfred in southern England, moved his warband to Northumbria to claim Ivar's conquests at York and Dublin. Hálfdan, having secured his position at York, wintered on the Tyne in 874-5. From that base, we know from Anglo-Saxon and Irish sources that he harried the Picts and the Strathclyde Britons, while Irish records show him in Dublin later in 875 where he slew Eystein who had succeeded his father, Olaf, as king of Dublin. Hálfdan was soon driven off from Dublin by the Norwegian faction and we find him back in Northumbria in 876 where he settled his warband as farmers in the Vale of York. In the following year, 877, he made a last desperate bid for the Dublin kingship, when with a greatly reduced following, he was slain by the Dublin fleet in Strangford Lough on the Co. Down coast in northern Ireland. Hálfdan, in his two expeditions to Dublin, seems to have followed the route taken earlier by his brother Ivar in 870-1, by sailing from the Tyne to the Forth, going overland to Dumbarton, and from there sailing to the Irish coast. He was in Strathclyde before sailing to Dublin in 875 and he fought his last battle against the Dubliners off the Down coast within sight of Galloway in 877. The Scottish lowlands played a major geographical role in York–Dublin communications, and it was inevitable that the Scots would either gain or suffer from their key intermediary position.

Hálfdan's massacre of the Picts in 875 may have included Scots. The *Scottish Chronicle* (Version A) notes that Constantine was defeated by the Danes at Dollar two years before the end of his reign (in his fourteenth year) which would fit well with Hálfdan's defeat of the Picts in 875. Several Scottish sources vouch for Constantine's death in battle at the hands of the Danes.[5] The *Annals of Ulster* place his death in AD 876 but Scottish sources assigning him a reign of 15 or 16 years suggest 877-8 as a more appropriate date. According to the Irish saga, *The Wars of the Irish with the Foreigners*, Constantine was slain by the remnants of Hálfdan's army who were returning through Scotland after their defeat at the hands of the Dublin Norsemen at Strangford Lough in 877. It is unlikely that this unusual information was invented by a twelfth-century Munster compiler, and it almost certainly derives from the earlier annalistic material used by him. The incident must have once formed an episode in its own right in the tradition of the Viking wars, as is shown by the brief Irish comment: 'It was on that occasion that the earth burst open under the men of Scotland '.

[5]Version D of the *Scottish Chronicle* claims Constantine was slain by Norwegians.

The idea of the York army returning from Dublin across lowland Scotland in 877 is substantiated by a whole body of evidence from Irish and English sources which suggests that this was the major route between the two Viking cities in the ninth and tenth centuries. It ties in, too, with Scottish accounts of Constantine's earlier defeat at the hands of the Danes (*Danarios* as opposed to Norwegians) at Dollar, some six miles north of the Forth in Clackmannanshire, at precisely the time we know Hálfdan's Danes had moved from the Tyne to attack the Picts, Dumbarton Britons and Dubliners. After the Dollar defeat in 875, Constantine's army appears to have retreated (Version A) up the Tay valley to the highlands in Atholl. In his last battle with the Danes, Constantine fell at *Inverdufatha*, which Skene believed was Inverdovat in north-east Fife. According to the *Scottish Chronicle*, (Version A), the Vikings spent a whole year in Pictland (*Pictavia*) at this time, which is consistent with what we know of the fate of Hálfdan's warband from English and Irish sources in 877-8. The *History of the Church of Durham* claims that Hálfdan was deposed and exiled by his Danish warriors at York and we know that he lost his life in a vain bid to retake Dublin in 877. His defeated warband which followed him to Dublin – only three ships' crews if we are to believe the Durham account – found themselves in Scotland as outlaws without a leader and unable to return to York. A life of piracy and plunder was their only option, but such a depleted and demoralized force cannot have posed a serious threat to the Scottish kingdom.

From the death of Constantine I in 877 up to the death of his son, Donald II, in 900 the Scots had a breathing space from serious Viking attack to take stock of their new situation in relation to their neighbours. The Northumbrian kingdom now reverted to its early seventh-century divisions, with Danes ruling Deira as far north as the Wear, while Bernicia survived under the English rule of the reeve of Bamburgh. This Bernician independence was not won from a position of strength; it was more a matter of the native population being left to its own devices by a Danish army which was not numerous enough to colonize all the lands it had conquered. Inevitably, the Scots, by now settled in the Central Lowlands, were drawn into competition for the domination of this unstable zone between them and the Danes of York. In theory at least, the Firth of Forth had separated the Angles from the Picts since the defeat of Ecgfrith of Northumbria in 685, but

Northumbrian anarchy and political collapse throughout the ninth century, together with the shift in the Scottish power base from Argyll to Perth and Fife, left Lothian once more a prey to Scots expansion. The progress of that expansion south of the Forth is not only poorly documented but due to the strategic importance of this region its history is complicated by recurring involvement of Vikings from York and Dublin. In spite of Bernician weakness, it took the Scots a century and a half after the Danish conquest of Northumbria to complete their annexation of Lothian and Berwick. The *History of the Church of Durham* claims that Egbert, set up as a puppet king by the Danes of York in 867, was given jurisdiction over 'the Northumbrians beyond the Tyne'. Since the Danish warband and its king held York as their permanent headquarters from at least as early as 876, it is clear that Egbert and his English successors were relegated to rule Bernicia, which had not been colonized by Danish invaders. We find that by *c.* 913 a native Anglian dynasty under Ealdred son of Eadwulf ruled from Bamburgh and it claimed responsibility for the defence of church lands of Lindisfarne to the south of the Tyne in the valley of the Wear.

These Bernician rulers had escaped the fate meted out in 867 to the Northumbrian kings in the carnage at York by recognizing the overlordship of the Danes. Bamburgh must have strengthened its position after the collapse of the Danish leadership on the death of Hálfdan in 877. Out of the turmoil which ensued, a Christian Danish king, Guthfrith, emerged in the period 882-4, and his election coincided with the rehousing of the Lindisfarne monks at the safer location of Chester-le-Street. Guthfrith, who was given Christian burial in York Minster in 895, was succeeded by a series of kings with Christian sympathies and it looked for a while as if the new Anglo-Danish realm north of the Humber would be little different from its pre-Viking counterpart. But this peaceful evolution of the Northumbrian kingdom was not to be. From the south, Alfred's son and successor, Edward the Elder, was determined to push his conquests north to the Humber and if possible beyond, while the Viking dream of a united realm based on Dublin and York menaced the security of Wessex and of the Scottish kings. The Anglo-Danish aristocracy at York was massacred by the army of Edward the Elder in a battle at Tettenhall near Wolverhampton in 910, and with the collapse of the Northumbrian Danes, the way was open for the descendants of Ivar at Dublin to regain control of York. The Scandinavian dynasty which was waiting to reassert

York and Dublin power was that of Ivar's grandsons led by Ragnall, who captured York with a large fleet soon after 910 and set about colonizing church land in the Wear valley to the dismay of the monks of Chester-le-Street. Ragnall drove Ealdred of Bamburgh into flight to the court of Constantine II, king of Scots, and there followed a battle at Corbridge on the Tyne in which the pagan Ragnall routed the Bernicians and their Scottish allies, and confirmed his followers in their conquests in Bernicia.

Ragnall spent the next four years until 918 in the Irish Sea zone, where his kinsman, Sitric, had captured Dublin in 917, while Ragnall dominated Munster from Waterford. Ragnall left Waterford in 918, returning to Northumbria by the now established route through lowland Scotland. He was accompanied by his brother or cousin, Gothfrith, who eventually succeeded him at York in 927 and by two Viking allies, Otter and Crowfoot (Krákubeinn). This army sacked Dunblane but was pursued by the Scots and brought to battle yet again at Corbridge, where the Roman Dere Street ran south to York across the Tyne. In this second battle at Corbridge, the Scots were again fighting with the Bernicians of Bamburgh against Ragnall's York army and for the second time Ragnall was victorious. But the Northmen did not have it all their own way. Contemporary Irish accounts show the Scots defeated three of the four Scandinavian divisions, slaying Otter and Crowfoot, while all the Scottish leaders survived. It was only when, towards nightfall, Ragnall managed to ambush the victorious Scots that the tide of battle turned. Indeed, the Scots were so pleased with this encounter that the *Scottish Chronicle* (Version A) not unreasonably claimed it as a Scots victory. The Bernician Angles came worst out of this conflict. According to the *History of St Cuthbert*, they were defeated by Ragnall's army and had to allow the confiscation of Lindisfarne church lands between the Derwent and the Wear.

The second battle of Corbridge was a turning point in Constantine's relations with the Danes of York and Dublin. The Scottish king had every incentive to back the Bernicians against Ragnall and other grandsons of Ivar. That dynasty had been consistently hostile to the Scots ever since Hálfdan had taken up his feud with the Dublin Norsemen back in 875. Hálfdan's army had twice attacked the Scots, and his kinsmen, the grandsons of Ivar, 'plundered Dunkeld and all Scotland' in 903 in a campaign which lasted two years before ending with a Scottish victory in Strathearn. In that encounter, one of the grandsons, Ivar II, lost his life as the

Scots went into battle behind the crozier of Columba. That same saint, according to the *Three Fragments*, had also helped the Scots win 'victory and triumph' over Ragnall on the Tyne in 918. The Scots had every reason to prevent the emergence of a powerful Danish kingdom at York which viewed them as allies of an enemy Viking faction at Dublin. The Bernicians, who initially had been allowed to survive as the satellites of York, viewed the rise of the pagan grandsons of Ivar with dismay and turned for help to the Scots. Constantine, for his part, had much to gain by receiving the beleaguered Bernicians into a client relationship. The fact that Constantine came to the aid of the Bernicians twice (in 914 and 918), and that he fought so far south on the Northumbrian Tyne suggests that he was already acting as overlord of the English of Bamburgh and that the battles at Corbridge may have been seen by the Scots as a border war with the Danes of York. The one certain outcome of the second battle at Corbridge was that it saw the last of hostility between Constantine II and the York Danes, or as the compiler of the *Three Fragments* put it: 'it was long after this before either Danes or Norwegians attacked the Scots, but they enjoyed peace and tranquillity'.

For the rest of his remarkably long reign which still had some 25 years to run, Constantine can be seen not as the enemy, but as the consistent ally of the York dynasty. What had happened at Corbridge to bring about such a change? The Scots may have so weakened Ragnall's warband that he was forced to come to terms. By 918 Ragnall achieved his objective of reuniting the Dublin kingdom with York, and it was vital to win the cooperation of the Scots if lines of communication across lowland Scotland were to be kept open for men and merchandise to pass freely between the Firths of Clyde and Forth. Other more alarming events for Scot and Dane alike were taking shape south of the Humber. Since the death of Alfred of Wessex in 899, his son and successor Edward the Elder, and Alfred's daughter Ethelflaed, Lady of the Mercians, had been working relentlessly to undermine the Danish hold on the Five Boroughs (those Danish territories south of the Humber). Those boroughs had either surrendered or had been seized one by one. By 918, as Ragnall returned from Ireland across Scotland to reclaim his York throne, Edward had finally succeeded in taking Danish Stamford and Nottingham. Lincoln may still have held out or given only nominal submission, but the Anglo-Saxon chronicler could boast that 'all the people who had settled in Mercia, both

Danish and English, submitted to him [i.e. Edward].' The English frontier now stretched from the Wirral to the Humber and Ragnall's hold on York was made even more insecure by news that a York faction was planning to submit to the Lady of the Mercians, a development which was prevented only by her death in June 918. The English king's decision to cross that frontier and put a Mercian garrison in Northumbrian Manchester in 919 showed how seriously Edward viewed the York–Dublin alliance, and indicated a West-Saxon ambition to conquer all the old Anglo-Saxon kingdoms. This West-Saxon advance must have driven Scots and Danes into the same camp. The Danes saw the kings of Wessex as the one real threat to their hold on York, while Constantine must have feared the rising power of Edward, who, if he toppled the kings of York, might well move against the Scots. It was now in Constantine's interest to shore up the Danish hold on York and maintain a convenient buffer between himself and Wessex. For the rest of his reign Constantine can be seen manipulating the York kings and holding the balance of power in the struggle for the domination of England between York and Winchester. As for the Bernicians, they ceased to count in the larger scheme of things after the second battle of Corbridge.

It is in the context of these tangled political alliances and conflicting objectives that we must view the so-called 'submission' to Edward the Elder in 920. According to the *Anglo-Saxon Chronicle*, 'The king of the Scots and all the people of the Scots' together with Ragnall of York, the sons of Eadwulf of Bamburgh, the king of Strathclyde 'and all the Strathclyde Welsh, chose him [Edward] as father and lord'. This is a West-Saxon account and it must be treated with caution, since it was in the interest of Wessex to record what was essentially a treaty between kings as nothing less than a submission to Wessex. It would be nonsense to assume that Edward was strong enough to impose the same conditions on Constantine or Ragnall as he had forced on the men of Bedford or Nottingham. It is unlikely, for instance, that Edward received an undertaking from York and the Scots to respect any novel West Saxon claims to overlordship in Bernicia. What he may have achieved in 920 was a promise from the Scots and Strathclyde Britons not to enter an active alliance with Danish York. But Edward must have conceded something too, and the fact that Ragnall of York was succeeded peacefully as king later in that same year by his kinsman Sitric of Dublin strongly suggests that Edward had no choice but to recognize the continued claims of the house of Ivar to the York kingdom. At best, Edward hoped to establish peace with northern England while gaining time to reinforce his new frontier with York on the Humber. At this point in West-Saxon expansion, there was no possibility of an English king being immediately concerned with, or indeed able to interfere in, the internal affairs of the Scots.

The treaty of 920 was but the first of a series of tenth-century negotiations between the kings of the West-Saxons and the kings of the Scots and all these treaties must be studied in relation to each other if we are to grasp their true significance. Of one thing we can be certain: Wessex entered into negotiations with Scottish rulers solely with a view to securing an English hold, not on Scotland but on Northumbria. We can be certain, too, that Edward's pacification of the north in 920 marked a stage in West-Saxon expansion which showed Wessex now capable of interfering in Northumbrian politics while not yet strong enough to dominate Northumbria by force. This new political strength of Wessex is shown by a whole series of treaties and submissions which the York kings were forced to enter into in their bid to hold on to Northumbria. Thus, we have Sitric's baptism and marriage to King Athelstan's sister at Tamworth in 926; the defeat and (according to William of Malmesbury) the submission of Sitric's brother, Gothfrith, to Athelstan at a feast in 927; the baptism of Olaf Cuaran at the court of King Edmund in 943 and Ragnall Gothfrithsson's confirmation at that court later in the same year. Not all of these treaties show Wessex in full control of the political, much less the military situation. Sitric of York repudiated both his baptism and his West-Saxon queen within a year of his treaty at Tamworth, while his son Olaf Cuaran also apostatized in 944 and was expelled from Northumbria by Edmund. There were times when it was York which had the decided military as well as political advantage over Wessex, as when Olaf Gothfrithsson overran the Five Boroughs in 940 and forced King Edmund to accept terms at Leicester which put the clock back to the earliest years of the Viking Age by recognizing a new Danish frontier along Watling Street. These are factors which must be taken into account when assessing the controversial dealings of Wessex kings with Scotland. We must approach the study of West-Saxon negotiations with the Scots in the knowledge that Wessex desperately needed friends in her long struggle to annex England north of the Humber. Any suggestions from Wessex chroniclers or from later medieval historians such as William of Malmesbury that the Scots – who were holding several trump cards in this contest – submitted unconditionally to the Wessex kings must be totally disregarded.

The key role of the Scottish king in holding the balance of power between York and Wessex can be seen in the struggle for the Northumbrian succession on the death of Sitric of York in 927. Athelstan marched on York but met serious opposition from Gothfrith, Sitric's kinsman who ruled in Dublin. Gothfrith made use of the good offices of Owen, king of Strathclyde and of Constantine, king of Scots, for after he failed to take York in the first round of the contest, he retreated north to lowland Scotland. The northern kings now made the most of their position. Athelstan sent an embassy 'to demand the fugitive under threat of war' and all sides prepared for a border conference at Eamont near Penrith on 12 July 927. The Scottish and Strathclyde kings were faced for the first time with having a West-Saxon permanently ruling on their borders, but they still had a key card to play in undermining Athelstan's hold on Northumbria. Athelstan might well rule York by force, but he could never be certain of it as long as his rival at Dublin remained alive and was confident of Scottish support. And so Gothfrith conveniently escaped from Constantine's and Owen's party before they reached Penrith, and he instantly made a second bid for York with the help of a certain Earl Thurferth who may have come from the Western Isles. With Gothfrith still at large, and with his Dublin army still in the field, Athelstan cannot have been in a position to dictate terms at his border conference. The *Anglo-Saxon Chronicle* states that the leaders present 'established peace with pledge and oaths and renounced all idolatry and afterwards departed in peace'. Malmesbury, with the hindsight of the twelfth century, saw things differently. He had no hesitation in believing that the northern kings 'surrendered themselves and their kingdoms to the king of the English'. This conference was seen at the time as a meeting between equals in status if not in military power.

The *Chronicle's* mention of the renunciation of idolatry underlines the confused religious situation which prevailed in the British Isles during these worst centuries of Viking heathenism. Unlike most of his kinsmen Gothfrith never even experimented with Christianity and one of the major strengths of the Dublin dynasty was its uncompromising heathenism. Constantine of Scotland was an ally of this man, and gave his daughter in marriage to his son,

Olaf, while to the west of the kingdom of Scotia lived the *Gall-Gaedhil* of the Hebrides and Galloway, 'a people who had renounced their baptism', a renegade tribe who behaved even more cruelly to the Christian church than the Northmen proper. Athelstan's concern at Penrith with the renunciation of idolatry meant in effect persuading Constantine and Owen to turn their back on the Dublin alliance; thereby strengthening Athelstan's hold on Northumbria. Malmesbury's statement that Athelstan 'ordered' the son of Constantine to be baptized and that the English king stood sponsor to him at baptism may be suggestive of a half-pagan atmosphere prevailing at the Scottish court due to the strength of the Scandinavian alliance and of the intermarriage which undoubtedly went hand in hand with it. Athelstan's sponsorship of the Scottish prince could have implications of a political as well as spiritual superiority, as in the case of contemporary baptisms of Slavonic leaders in the Byzantine world. On the other hand, Alfred stood sponsor to Guthrum at Aller in 878 without affecting the defeated Dane's unshakeable hold on East Anglia.

If Owen and Constantine were forced into renouncing the Dublin alliance in July 927, it certainly was not in their interest to do so. The fact that Gothfrith was driven back to Dublin 'from the kingdom of the Britons' later in 927 shows that the Dublin king had retreated back to his allies on the Clyde yet again after his second attempt on York failed. Athelstan now ruled Northumbria unchallenged for seven years until events in Ireland suddenly opened up a new prospect for the kings of Scotland. Gothfrith died in 934 and was succeeded by his son Olaf, the son-in-law of Constantine, who speedily set about conquering a rival Norwegian stronghold at Limerick in order to gain tighter control of the Norse colony in Ireland. Olaf's succession to the Dublin throne heralded the hope of a new and major offensive against West-Saxon control of Northumbria which eventually materialized at the battle of Brunanburh in 937 but which must have been in the air as soon as Olaf became king of Dublin. It is no coincidence that the accession of Constantine's son-in-law in Dublin coincided with Athelstan's decision to invade Scotland, an invasion which, according to the Durham *History*, was prompted by the breaking of pledges by Owen of Strathclyde and by Constantine. Clearly, the pledges broken were those taken at Penrith in 927, and Athelstan determined to use force to prevent the Scottish kings intriguing with the new and ambitious king of Dublin. This first West-Saxon invasion of Scotland was an impressive affair and must have convinced the northern rulers that Athelstan's determination to hold Northumbria left little room for Scottish kings to choose their friends, and if unchecked it might see Scotia and Strathclyde dragged into a client relationship with Wessex. Athelstan's army set out from Chester-le-Street in Durham and attacked Scotland south of the Mounth as far as Dunnottar. The English fleet ravaged along the coast as far north as the Norwegian colony in Caithness. The object was neither permanent subjugation nor the establishment of a permanent client relationship. Scotland was too remote geographically and too diverse in its political make-up for a king of York, much less at Winchester, to achieve anything more than a successful raid. The compiler of the *Annals of Clonmacnoise*, who had little reason to take sides in this dispute, state that Athelstan returned home 'without any great victory'. But Constantine was forced to attend his third parley with a West Saxon king, and Florence of Worcester believed he had to hand over his son as a hostage to Athelstan. If that were true, the boy's fate cannot have been pleasant, unless he were released within three years, for by 937 Constantine was fighting at *Brunanburh* alongside Olaf of Dublin and Owen of Strathclyde in a major struggle to drive Athelstan out of Northumbria, if not off his English throne.

The evidence that Athelstan invaded Scotland in 934 in the knowledge that Constantine and Owen had broken their pledges suggests they had reverted to their 'idolatrous' alliance with Dublin, and were plotting to place the young and energetic Olaf Gothfrithsson on the throne of York. It may even have been in this precise year that Constantine cemented the alliance with Olaf by giving him his Christian daughter in marriage. Such a marriage could not have been concealed from Athelstan: its pagan dimension would have been repugnant both to him and to his archbishop of Canterbury, and its political consequences would have been obvious and alarming. Hence the breaking of the pledge against idolatry instantly called forth an expedition from Chester-le-Street. Whatever pledges were renewed or hostages given by Constantine in 934, the die had already been cast. Once Athelstan returned to distant Wessex overtures to Norse Dublin were again renewed. It took Olaf Gothfrithsson until August 937 finally to destroy his Norwegian rivals at Limerick when he broke up their longships on Lough Ree. He had no sooner made himself overlord of all the Scandinavian towns of Ireland than he instantly launched his

invasion of Britain in that same autumn. This was a grandiose
scheme involving armies led by Olaf of Dublin, the Scottish king,
and Owen of Strathclyde, together with leaders from York, the
Southern Danelaw and the Hebrides. We also know that although
the Welsh of Wales did not take part, nevertheless 'valiant long-
haired warriors' from Dublin had been trying to seduce them from
their alliance with Athelstan for some time before 937. Olaf did not
have time to organize and lead a major military coalition across
Britain between August 937 and the onset of winter in that year.
Such elaborate preparations must have been made long before, and
required the cooperation of the Scottish king in particular. A later
medieval Latin poem recalls Constantine's central role in these
military and diplomatic preparations for battle:

> At the will of the king of the Scots, the northern land lends a
> quiet assent to the raving fury [of Olaf's army].

Constantine gave more than quiet assent. He was remembered in
the Anglo-Saxon poem on *Brunanburh* as 'the aged Constantine, the
hoary-haired warrior' whose 'people of the Scots and the pirates fell
doomed' on the field of battle where Athelstan 'won undying glory
by the sword's edge'.

The battle of *Brunanburh*, when viewed from the standpoint of
Scottish history, can be seen to have been as much an attempt by
the Scottish king to curb the expansion of Wessex as it was part of
Olaf's struggle to conquer York. For it is possible that this, the
greatest battle in Anglo-Saxon history, was stage-managed by Constantine of Scotland. It is true that Anglo-Saxon, Irish and Norse
sources all saw Olaf as the prime mover of the war with Athelstan,
and it is equally true that the central issue at stake was the struggle
between the House of Alfred and the House of Ivar for control of
York. But that said, we can be equally certain that Olaf and his successors operated at *Brunanburh* and after in the context of a Scottish
alliance which was absolutely crucial for the Dublin kings to establish
and maintain their position in northern England. Without the cooperation of Strathclyde and Scotia, Dublin would have lost its back-
door to Britain – a door which Wessex kings sought to close again
and again in a succession of treaties and trials of strength with the
kings of Scotland. This back-door had a physical reality in the Firth
of Clyde and its control was vital for whoever wished to rule Northumbria, in so far as the Clyde provided the kings of Dublin and their
armies with the major entry point into northern England.

It was the strategic importance of the Clyde which in turn provided added incentive to the Scottish dynasty of Kenneth mac Alpin to dominate the Britons of Dumbarton whose territory controlled the mouth of that Firth. We have seen how Olaf the White of Dublin and Constantine I, son of Kenneth, each attacked Dumbarton and its king back in the 870s. The Strathclyde kingdom emerged in the 920s acting in permanent unison with the Scots, a change of heart which cannot be explained solely in terms of the common threat posed by Athelstan. By this time, the Scots had taken Strathclyde into a permanent client relationship facilitated first by military victories and also by inter-marriage. Already by the 920s the native British dynasty in Strathclyde had been replaced by rulers from the Scottish house of Kenneth.

This rapid integration of the Strathclyde kingdom into the expanding kingdom of the Scots, together with a Wessex obsession with closing the Clyde to Dublin fleets, is nicely drawn together in the *Anglo-Saxon Chronicle's* account of events in 945. Although Olaf and Constantine had been defeated by Athelstan at *Brunanburh* in 937, that battle was a mere prelude to the most daring achievement of Olaf Gothfrithsson. On Athelstan's death in October 939 he returned to make himself master not only of York but of the Five Boroughs of the southern Danelåw. Athelstan's successor and younger brother, Edmund, gradually recovered his position south of the Humber, and tried in vain to bring Northumbria into a client relationship with Wessex. In 945 he succeeded in driving out two Dublin kings from York, and toyed with a new policy of trying to prize the Scots king from the Dublin alliance by offering the carrot of territorial gain over the Norwegian colonies in north-west England. In return the king of the Scots was to block the path of the Dublin warriors through the Firth of Clyde. The *Anglo-Saxon Chronicle* reported in 945:

> In this year King Edmund ravaged all *Cumbraland*, and granted it all to Malcolm king of the Scots, on condition that he should be his ally both on sea and on land.

Cumbraland included Strathclyde and its recently acquired territories among the Norwegian settlers south of the Solway in north-west England. The English king was recognizing Malcolm's overlordship of the extended British kingdom of Strathclyde-Cumbria on condition that he prevented Dublin longships from using the Firth of Clyde as the back-door to Northumbria – hence the oft-quoted reference to 'on sea and on land'. This Anglo-Saxon initiative was doomed to failure, since the Scots king had by this time become master of the political arena in northern Britain. The Dublin armies were now led by Olaf Cuaran, a much weaker king than his predecessor and cousin, Olaf Gothfrithsson, and the weakness of all other contending parties including York and even Wessex served only to strengthen the hand of the king of Scots.

Before Edmund's new diplomacy could be put to the test, he was assassinated in 946 and in the following year an entirely new situation developed in northern Britain with the arrival in the Orkneys from Norway of the fleet of the exiled Norwegian king, Eirík Bloodaxe. The Scots and the men of York, according to the *Anglo-Saxon Chronicle*, renewed their customary pledges to the new West-Saxon king, Eadred, who travelled north to Tanshelf in 947, but Archbishop Wulfstan and the York witan, despairing of any further help from Dublin and fearing complete loss of autonomy to Wessex, invited the notorious Eirík Bloodaxe to take the York kingship. The Scots king now found himself in a situation which he and his dynasty must have always dreaded. He was encircled by a hostile Norwegian king who controlled the Orkneys and Caithness to the north, and the kingdom of York to the south. The Scottish alliance with York was determined by self-interest, and Eirík's presence there now posed an unacceptable threat to the Scots. Eirík ruled from York as the puppet of Archbishop Wulfstan and in defiance of Dublin, Wessex and the Scots. The details of his turbulent two reigns at York do not concern us, but there is evidence to suggest that the Scots yet again exploited their key geographical and political position by inviting the Dublin king, Olaf Cuaran, to return and make a second and final bid for York. The Scots had everything to gain by destroying the usurper Eirík who menaced them on several fronts and to restore the old Dublin dynasty which as their traditional ally would act as a shield against Wessex. Eadred of Wessex forced the men of York to expel Eirík in 948, and he had earlier persuaded the Scots to give 'oaths to him that they would agree to all that he wanted'. But Olaf Cuaran had already left Dublin in 947 after hearing news of Edmund's assassination and was waiting in the wings – no doubt at Dumbarton or Scone – to seize the York throne for the second time, which he did in 948 or soon after. It was precisely in 948-9 when the Dublin Olaf was poised to seize York, that according to the *Scottish*

Chronicle (Version A), King Malcolm 'plundered the English as far as the river Tees', seizing captives and cattle in an operation which the Scots referred to as the raid of the 'Men of the Isles from beyond the Spine of Britain'. The Scottish chronicler goes on to suggest that Malcolm was incited to this raid by his aged predecessor and cousin, Constantine II, then living in retirement as a monk at St Andrews. There was even a tale that Constantine had come out of retirement to assume the kingship for a week 'in order to visit the English'. Whatever the truth behind these stories, it is reasonable that Constantine would have supported his relative Olaf Cuaran in his struggle for York, and that Malcolm's expedition against the Bernicians was in some way connected with Olaf's second expedition to take Northumbria, which he held from 948-9 until 952. The evidence as we have it suggests that both Malcolm I and Eadred of Wessex preferred to see Olaf Cuaran on the York throne instead of the more dangerous Eirík. Archbishop Wulfstan drove Olaf out of York in 952 and once more installed Eirík Bloodaxe, who had been living in exile on Orkney since 948. Once again, the crisis in the reign of the Dublin king was accompanied by Scottish intervention. We read in Irish annals of a victory gained 'over the men of Alba [the Scots], the Britons [of Strathclyde] and the Saxons [i.e. Bernicians] by the Foreigners.' In this case the Foreigners can only be the Viking followers of Eirík Bloodaxe whom the Scots and Strathclyde Britons tried to prevent returning to York.

The anarchy at York and the frantic efforts of Dublin, Norwegian and York magnates to control the rich city came to an inglorious end with the capture of Archbishop Wulfstan by Eadred of Wessex in 952 and with the assassination of Eirík Bloodaxe on Stainmore in 954. Thereafter northern England was ruled by English kings and was slowly and painfully integrated with the English south over the next century and a half. But the failure of York to maintain its Scandinavian dynasty did not spell ruin for the Scots. On the contrary, a century of Scandinavian rule in Northumbria had seen the transformation of the Scottish house from a remote Gaelic warband, perched on Dunollie and Dunadd, into a self-confident dynasty which controlled the richest land of the conquered Picts from St Andrews and Scone. If Kenneth mac Alpin had achieved the overthrow of the Pictish aristocracy, it was clearly his grandson Constantine II who consolidated the strength of the dynasty at home and who transformed Scottish politics by masterfully manipulating the York Danes and their kinsmen at Dublin, and by playing those factions off against each other and against the rising house of Wessex. We saw how, as a younger man, Constantine had three times opposed Ragnall and the grandsons of Ivar who threatened the Scots from York and from the Tyne, and how with the advance of the West Saxons into Northumbria, Constantine changed his tune and consistently supported Ragnall's successors in order to maintain a weak but cooperative Scandinavian dynasty at York.

The *Anglo-Saxon Chronicle* put quite a different construction on these events offering us a series of 'submissions' made by Constantine, first to Edward and twice later to Athelstan, while on the other hand every crisis in York–Wessex relations seemed to involve the Scots in a military expedition as in 927, 934, 949 and 952. These major political and military upheavals testify to the crucial role which the Scots played in the power struggle for northern England, but they are merely the tip of an iceberg, and beneath the surface of the sparse documentary record must lie the reality of Constantine's central part in the history of Britain from 900 to 950. He not only held the balance of power between the House of Ivar and the House of Alfred, but as the strongest ruler north of Humber he constantly manipulated York politics, and it was during his long reign that Scotia consolidated its hold over the intervening territories of Lothian and Strathclyde. If we are looking for historical milestones in terms of the reigns of particular kings, then we can identify the reign of Constantine II with that period when Dark Age Scotland, to the north of the Forth–Clyde isthmus, made its influence felt throughout the whole of Britain. Not since the Severan age had northern Britain loomed so large in the politics of the whole island, but whereas in the second century the Caledonians were cast in the role of disruptive barbarians, the Scots of the tenth provided a stabilizing influence which went far to prevent the complete Scandinavian conquest of Britain. Constantine had shown there were limits to what the Northmen could achieve even from their surest foothold in the far north, and he set limits, too, to the expansion of Wessex. In short, the medieval kingdom of Scotland had come of age.

Constantine had negotiated for half a century with the kings of Wessex and Dublin and with the archbishops of York, all of whom sought conflicting objectives which might be exploited by the Scots. His power base in the Scottish lowlands assured him supremacy over nearby Strathclyde and over at least the northern part of

Bernicia. To the north, his hold over Moray might be in doubt and his relations with the Norse earls of Orkney cannot always have been cordial, but none of the northern rulers ever made any serious attempt to shake his firm hold on the richest land in Scotland. Constantine gave his daughter in marriage to the heathen Olaf Gothfrithsson, and perhaps his son's baptism was long overdue and had to be forced on him by Athelstan in 927. Yet in spite of his long-standing 'idolatrous' alliance with Dublin, the overall Christian ethos of the man and his court cannot be doubted in the long term. This king, who shared with his uncle and predecessor the name of the first Christian emperor, had made a covenant with his bishop, Cellach, at Scone in 906 to enforce the laws of the Scottish church, and he was remembered in the late tenth-century *Life* of Catroe for befriending that Scottish saint and for personally escorting him from St Brigit's church at Abernethy to the Cumbrian border. At the end of his reign in 943 he chose to retire to St Andrews, by now the new centre of the Scottish church, where, 'enjoying the law of religion', he died in 952.

Constantine had steered his people out of the Viking Age and by skilfully manipulating those treacherous allies he ensured that the heartlands of modern Scotland were never conquered or colonized by Northmen. On the other hand his alliance with Dublin which he inherited from his predecessors had a profound influence on the destiny of Scottish kingship and culture. Not only had the Scandinavians driven a wedge between the House of Kenneth and its Irish homeland, with the Norse occupation of coastal Argyll and the Hebrides, but the Scots chose as their new friends those very Norsemen who were the scourge of Irish life. This meant in effect that the house of Kenneth became permanently separated (though not alienated) by geography and politics from its Gaelic roots. It is surely significant that the first people outside the British Isles who clearly distinguished between the Scots (*Skotar* and *Skozkr*) and the Irish (*Írar* and *Irskr*) as different peoples inhabiting different countries (*Skotland* and *Írland*) were the tenth- and eleventh-century Norse poets. The ancient world of the *Scoti*, which had sprawled along Atlantic Europe from Mizen Head in Cork to far-off Shetland, had now been permanently fragmented into separate cultural zones inhabited by Irish, Northmen and Scots.

The proximity of the Scots to their new northern Germanic neighbours and the common political aims which they shared must have had a marked influence on the Gaelic dynasty of Kenneth and must have served to point that dynasty on a road away from its tribal Gaelic past towards a new self-awareness of its role as leader of a whole confederation of peoples of different ethnic origins. Significantly, Constantine II chose a Scandinavian name for his son and successor, Indulf (Old Norse *Hildulfr*), while Indulf's two sons who both succeeded to the Scottish kingship also had Scandinavian names. The first was Olaf who died in 977, and his brother Culen had the well-attested Scandinavian royal nickname, *Ring* (Old Norse *Hringr*). The tribal bonds within the Scots dynasty must have been severely strained, if not broken, by the convergence of a number of factors – the migration away from older tribal assemblies and cult centres in the west; the advent of Germanic Viking colonists, and the fact that Kenneth's dynasty was trying to establish its position among a Pictish population. Yet Scottish kingship was still essentially Gaelic and among the many qualities which Kenneth's dynasty had inherited from its Gaelic past was the ability to defeat the Northmen in battle. The prowess of Irish and Scottish kings in the Viking wars when set against the disasters in England and Francia proved time and time again that the Gaelic warband was an effective fighting force in the Dark Ages. What did distinguish the new Scottish dynasty from its Irish parent, however, was its ability to adjust to rapidly changing circumstances in a turbulent age and its success in offering cohesion and leadership to a new nation of Scots, Britons, Picts, Angles and Northmen.

The Vikings, too, were greatly influenced by their Scottish neighbours. While paganism and the cult of Odin held out into the eleventh century on Orkney, the more southerly Hebridean Vikings, as we have seen, were quickly influenced by the Christianity and culture of their Dál Riata neighbours, and Iona, which the Norsemen initially tried to destroy, survived the Viking storm to become a shrine for Scottish Vikings of the late tenth and eleventh centuries. It is not always clear from Irish annals whether they refer to abbots of Kells as opposed to abbots *on* Iona when they refer to leaders of the Columban community in the Viking age. Iona reached its lowest ebb when Abbot Indrechtach removed Columba's relics to Ireland in 849. The saint's relics were again taken from Scotland into Ireland in 878. Abbot Feradach who died in 880 had earlier escaped capture from the Dublin leader, Bardur, when his Vikings were raiding across Roscommon in western Ireland in 873. Important Iona clerics were seeking refuge all over the Celtic world and beyond. Feradach's predecessor, Indrechtach 'the wisest of scholars' was slain by the Anglo-Saxons while making his way to Rome in 854, while earlier in the century scholars such as Dicuil had fled to the Carolingian court and to Irish centres such as Kells and Durrow. Columban monks joined forces with other larger Irish houses in their efforts to survive, and we find that in 927 Maelbrigte was head of both the Columban community and of the church of Armagh. We can assume, too, that men such as Abbot Dubthach who died in 938 or Robhartach who died in 954 were heads of the united houses of Kells and Raphoe rather than occupants of Iona. From the middle of the tenth century onwards however there is evidence that Iona, thanks to the bravery of its token community, had made a come-back and was by then occupied by prominent ecclesiastics who may or may not have been subject to Kells. It is possible that Iona's recovery was accompanied by a greater emphasis on episcopal organization in Dál Riata territories, for we read of Fingin, bishop of the community (*muintire*) of Iona who died in 966[6] and even more significantly of Fothad mac Brain 'scribe and bishop of the islands of Scotland' who died in 963.[7] Fothad clearly had episcopal jurisdiction over the *Gall-Gaedhil* of the Hebrides who by now, a century after the days of Ketil Flatnose and his half-Christian kin, had their church restored on an organized footing. We are reminded of the *Landnámabók* tradition of that early tenth-century bishop, Patrick of the Hebrides, who exported Columba's cult to western Iceland.

The church of the *Gall-Gaedhil* with its resurgent centre on Iona was neither Irish in the same sense as the churches of Kells or Armagh, nor Scottish in the sense of the church of Dunkeld or St Andrews. These Irish and Scottish foundations had completely identified with the political fortunes of their particular lay patrons whose interests did not coincide with those of the Gaelic-Norse seafarers of the Isles. Duncan, abbot of Dunkeld, for instance, who was slain in the struggle between the rival contenders (Dub and Culen) for the Scottish crown in 965, was a churchman in the mould of the new Scottish kingdom whose ambitions were interwoven with those of the house of Kenneth mac Alpin. Duncan probably belonged to a dynasty of lay 'royal' abbots, similar to those who flourished in Ireland and Francia at this time. He may have been the father of Crinan, another abbot of Dunkeld and

[6]*Four Masters*, sub anno 964
[7]*Four Masters*, sub anno 961

father in turn of King Duncan I, slain by Macbeth in 1040. Such men had little immediate interest in the affairs of Argyll and the Western Isles, a region which had now become remote from the point of view of those who ruled from Scone. A dramatic illustration of the emergence of south-west Scotland as a new cultural zone in its own right towards the close of the millennium can be found in a series of contrasting events recorded in contemporary annals of the time. Olaf Cuaran, the former ally and kinsman of Constantine II, survived his expulsion from York in 952 to rule at Dublin for another 28 years. His apostasy from his earlier English baptism is confirmed by his looting of the church of Kells, for instance, in 970, a Columban house which was looted yet again by Olaf's son, Sitric Silkenbeard in 1019. Yet when Olaf Cuaran finally decided in old age to resign his Dublin throne, he followed Constantine's example by entering a monastery and chose Iona and not Kells as his monastic home. The battle-weary Viking could never have faced a hostile Irish community, but Iona was acceptable in its new role as head of the Gaelic-Norse Church. The Dublin kings were now turning towards the Christianity of the Isles, while continuing to loot churches on the Irish mainland. The Isles, in contrast, were being attacked by the Irish Uí Néill kings as when Muirchertach of the Leather Cloaks attacked them with his fleet in 941. The strong Scandinavian ethos of Iona and Hebridean Christianity at this time is shown by the presence of a cross-shaft on Iona with a carving of a Viking ship with a legendary Germanic smith accompanied by his array of hammers and tongs. There is evidence, too, that it was Iona and the Isles rather than Ireland proper which first provided the infant Norwegian church in Dublin with its first ministers and bishops. The earliest known Dublin bishops, Dunán and Gillapádraic, in the third quarter of the eleventh century were so hostile to the native Irish clergy that they sought consecration at the hands of Lanfranc at Canterbury. But their names were Gaelic at a time when Dublin was still Norse speaking, and they almost certainly had come from the Christian community of the Hebrides.

In spite of the natural sympathies between Norse Dublin and the Western Isles, it would be clearly wrong to think of south-west Scotland as completely cut off either from Gaelic Ireland or from the Scots at the turn of the millennium. What is true is that the region found a new cultural and political identity in the aftermath of the Viking Age, and Scandinavian dominance had lasted long enough to leave its distinctive mark and to promote, as we have seen, a radical change in direction of Scottish life to the east of the Spine of Britain. But that said, by the turn of the millennium, Gaelic culture was reasserting itself in south-west Scotland and something of the old unity of the Gaelic world was preserved in spite of those Norse longships which still monitored all traffic through western Scottish waters and the Irish sea. It may have been a return to Gaelic Christianity and life, but it took place under new masters of mixed Norse descent. The lords of Cenél Gabhráin and Cenél Loairn had gone forever from the western firths. They had been replaced by a new breed of Gaelicized warlords such as Gothfrith Haroldsson king of the Hebrides (d. 989) and his son Ronald (d. 1005), or by Suibne son of Kenneth who sported the title 'king of the *Gall Gaedhil*' (of the Hebrides or Galleway) before he died in 1034.

In spite of the political and demographic changes we find that Iona, athough caught in the eye of the Viking storm, continued to influence the destinies of Irish, Norse and Scottish rulers, and it provided a fragile unity at a spiritual level in a world otherwise torn apart by warring Scandinavian and Celtic factions. We are told when Iona's abbot died in 989 that Dub-Da-Lethi, abbot of Armagh, assumed the headship of the Columban community 'with the consent of the men of Ireland and Alba'. The Armagh connection with Iona, which was of long standing, continued into the next century. We hear of Muiredach who resigned the abbacy of Iona 'for God' in 1007 and died as a lector in Armagh four years later. In spite of partisan policies followed by the kings of Norse Dublin, Kells and Iona clearly remained in friendly contact with each other, as when the lector of Kells was reported drowned with 30 of his crew in 1034 returning from Scotland to Ireland. The incident was remarkable not only for the loss of life but for the loss of Columba's flabellum, or liturgical fan, and three relics of Patrick. Nor was Olaf of Dublin alone among kings in seeking out Iona as a place of rest. Numerous Scottish rulers continued to be buried here, for in spite of the rise of St Andrews and Dunkeld, Iona still surpassed them all with the untarnished reputation of its founder. Kings such as Malcolm (d. 954) and Indulf (d. 962) were buried on Iona while the body of Dub was carried from the bridge of Kinloss beside the Moray Firth all the way to Columba's monastery in 966 – a hazardous journey of at least some 180 miles. A prophecy recorded by Adomnán, which Columba was believed to have uttered from the little hill above Iona on the last day of his life in June 597, had come true in a special way in the late tenth century:

> On this place, small and mean though it be, not only the kings of the Irish with their peoples, but also the rulers of barbarous and foreign nations, with their subjects, will bestow great and especial honour.

7

'To the Rere-Cross on Stainmore': The Conquest of the Southern Uplands

The downfall of the British dynasty in Strathclyde came in 870 when Ivar, flushed with his victories in Northumbria and East Anglia, joined forces with Olaf, overlord of the Irish and Scottish Vikings, and together they laid siege to Al Cluith, the Strathclyde capital on Dumbarton Rock. A contemporary account in the *Annals of Ulster* shows this was no casual encounter between Northmen and Britons. It was a four-month siege – an unheard of phenomenon in Dark Age Britain – and testifies to the determination of the Norsemen to destroy Strathclyde. A later Irish account tells how the Vikings cut off the water supply to the beleaguered Rock and how 'having wasted the people who were in it by hunger and thirst . . . they carried off all the riches that were within it and afterwards a great host of prisoners were brought into captivity.' Olaf and Ivar led their British, Pictish and English slaves back to Dublin from the Clyde in 871 in 200 longships – a huge fleet even by Viking standards. It is a fair assumption that the flower of the northern British aristocracy was caught in that trap. There can have been little hope of ransom by their Scottish neighbours, since in the following year the Strathclyde king, Artgal son of Dumnagual, who had survived the fall of Dumbarton, 'was slain on the advice (*consilio*) of Constantine son of Kenneth mac Alpin'.

The last we hear of Artgal's dynasty follows close on the catastrophe of 870-2. Áed son of Kenneth, who succeeded his brother Constantine I in the Scottish kingship, was slain in Strathallan in 878 by his first cousin, Giric. On Áed's death, the kingship of the Scots seems to have been shared by the victorious Giric and by Eochaid son of Rhun, king of the Britons, who also happened to be Kenneth mac Alpin's grandson. Eochaid's mother was a daughter of Kenneth, while his father, Rhun, appears in the genealogy of the Strathclyde kings, as the son of that Artgal who had been slain on

Constantine's advice in 872. In spite of the cryptic moaning in the *Prophecy of Berchán* that 'a Briton is placed over the Gaels! The Briton from Clyde will take sovereignty', the evidence does not suggest that Eochaid's reign marks a Strathclyde takeover of the Scots. Common sense would preclude such an idea: the Scots were in the ascendant having recently conquered the Picts, and their dynasty was going from strength to strength, while the Britons had seen the capture of their stronghold and the enslavement of their people only seven years before. Eochaid son of Rhun was the last of his British dynasty to find mention in Scottish historical records and we must seek another explanation for the significance of his reign. The slaying of Áed son of Kenneth by Giric's party in 878 was a family affair whereby the son of Kenneth's brother (Donald I) intervened violently to stake a claim to the kingship in opposition to Kenneth's sons. Giric may have won Eochaid's support with the promise of preserving the remnants of the Strathclyde dynasty against the encroachments of the sons of Kenneth. Eochaid had every reason to support Giric against Áed, since Eochaid's grand-father, Artgal, had been slain by Áed's brother.

The marriage between Rhun and Kenneth's daughter must have taken place long before the collapse of Dumbarton in 870 if a son of that marriage was ruling in Strathclyde by 878. Strangely, histo-rians who have tried to explain the union of Scots and Picts under Kenneth on the basis of a marriage alliance for which there is no good historical evidence, have ignored the much better documenta-tion on this crucial marriage between Kenneth's daughter and Rhun, the last Strathclyde king whose name appears in the Welsh genealogy of the northern Britons. Nor is it generally appreciated that at the time when the Scots were involved in annexing the Picts, they were equally successful in their efforts to conquer the Strathclyde Britons. The notion that this British kingdom survived under a native dynasty down to the early eleventh century is deeply rooted in the accepted view of medieval Scottish history. All the evidence suggests, however, that while Strathclyde preserved its territorial identity until that time, its native British kings died out with Eochaid son of Rhun who, according to the *Scottish Chronicle* (Version A), was expelled along with his ally Giric in 889. Eochaid may have ruled in Strathclyde while Giric held the kingship of the Scots, but from the meagre facts at our disposal it is clear that the kingships of the Scots and northern Britons were merging at this time, and since Eochaid was the last of his line it is equally obvious that Strathclyde kingship passed into Scottish hands. Giric and Eochaid were close kinsmen by Dark Age standards, and Version A of the *Scottish Chronicle* significantly describes Eochaid the Briton as 'a grandson of Kenneth by his daughter' while also asserting that Giric was Eochaïd's foster-father and guardian. It would seem that Eochaid and Giric ruled jointly for 11 or 12 years until their expulsion in 889, when the anti-Strathclyde faction led by Kenneth's sons returned to power in the person of Donald II son of Constantine. Both Eochaid's and Giric's segments of Alpín's dynasty were excluded from the succession after 889 and henceforth the Scottish kingship was shared first by the descendants of Constantine I and of Áed, two sons of Kenneth, and later by new and competing segments of the line of Constantine I alone.

The realization that the native British dynasty in Strathclyde came to an end with the expulsion of Eochaid in 889 has important consequences not only for the history of south-west Scotland but for our understanding of much of early British historiography. Kenneth Jackson had concluded from his study of the *Gododdin* and related northern British texts that these earliest 'Welsh' sources relating to Lothian and Rheged had been transmitted in manuscript form from Strathclyde to Wales sometime 'between the end of the eighth century and the end of the ninth'. Strathclyde has been seen as the obvious kingdom where manuscripts and oral traditions were preserved in the north since Strathclyde alone of all northern British kingdoms had survived the Anglo-Saxon advance of the seventh century. A verse of Strathclyde poetry celebrating the victory of its king Owen, over Domnall Brecc in Strathcarron in 642 lies embedded in the *Gododdin*, a work otherwise devoted to the neighbouring kingdom in Lothian. The presence of that verse would seem to clinch the argument for Strathclyde – and perhaps for Glasgow in particular – as the centre where much of the early history, genealogy, and literature of the northern Britons had been preserved. Jackson even suggested that these northern British sources could have been taken to Wales by a band of Strathclyde exiles who went there in 890. We may now not only fully endorse that conclusion, but offer an explanation as to why the refugees and their manuscripts arrived in Wales at that particular time. The Welsh *Chronicle of the Princes (Brut y Tywyssogion)* informs us that in 890:

The men of Strathclyde, those that refused to unite with the

English, had to depart from their country, and to go to Gwynedd.

The chronicle goes on to say that the northern Welsh king, Anarawd (eldest son and successor of Rhodri Mawr), settled the exiles in the Vale of Clwyd and elsewhere on his frontier with the English, on condition that they cleared those territories of English settlers. The statement that the men of Strathclyde had 'refused to unite with the English' is meaningless in a late ninth-century context, for by then the old Anglian kingdom of Northumbria was no more, and while a Danish king was ruling in York, the English inhabitants on the Cumbrian frontier were fleeing before Norwegian settlers invading from the Irish Sea. We have concluded however, that with the expulsion of Eochaid son of Rhun and his Scots kinsman Giric, in 889, Strathclyde was finally annexed by the new Scottish king, Donald II, and henceforth, as we shall see, Strathclyde was ruled by kings of the house of Kenneth mac Alpin. The lower grades of Strathclyde society would have remained to serve their new Gaelic masters, but the people immediately affected would have been the great landowning magnates, particularly those with royal blood who had a claim on the tribal loyalties of the people. It was these northern British warriors and their learned following, whose entire life-style depended on British rather than Gaelic patronage, who arrived in Gwynedd in 890 – the very year in which Donald II came to power in Scotland. The men of Strathclyde had fled down the Irish Sea not because they refused to unite with the already beleaguered English, but because they refused to be subsumed into the new Scottish realm. There had obviously been continuous and long-standing contact by sea between Strathclyde and North Wales. We know, for instance, that the Welsh historian, Nennius, had contact with Strathclyde scholars at the beginning of the ninth century. What is significant about the migration of 890 is that it marked the end of Strathclyde independence and it is for this obvious reason that the Old Welsh genealogies have no record of any Strathclyde king later than the time of Rhun, the father of that Eochaid who was driven out in 889. It was presumably Eochaid or his kinsmen who took over the defence of Anarawd's frontier with the English in the late ninth century.

An understanding of Scottish alternating succession as practised from the ninth to the eleventh centuries is crucial not only for our knowledge of Scottish kingship but for the history of Strathclyde at this period. Under the alternating system, which may have been borrowed from Ireland, two major rival but related segments (or sub-dynasties) agreed to participate in power-sharing so that a member of each segment held power in alternate reigns. In this way, father might be succeeded by son and grandson but with members of the competing faction reigning in between. Irish custom may have influenced Scottish practice, but whether we opt for independent evolution or not, the alternating system was a marked advance on earlier and more primitive Celtic forms of oscillating succession, which meant that high office was a prey to the most violent claimant, often even regardless of his military or political strength. The Scottish dynasty was in a much more secure position than its Irish counterparts, because Kenneth's dynasty practised the new system of succession with far fewer rivals in the field. Contemporary Irish warlords struggled in vain towards creating a centralized monarchy against a tide of grass-roots tribalism and dynastic feuding which operated to the detriment of ambitious over-kings. Apart from major political divisions north and south of the Mounth and the survival of Strathclyde as a sub-kingdom of the Scots, tribal loyalties do not seem to have dogged the progress of Scottish kingship after the demographic upheavals of the ninth century. The *tuatha* or smaller tribal kingdoms survived the Viking wars and Scottish migration to the east to become administrative areas largely deprived of their autonomous tribal status. So while Atholl, for instance, was ruled by a tribal king under the Pictish system back in 739, we find that its ruler, Dubdond, had been reduced to the status of a *satrapas* or 'governor' by 966. Similarly, in 995, we read of the daughter of Cunthar 'earl or count (*comitis*) of Angus' who plotted the death of Kenneth II.

These Latin titles for the new breed of regional leaders who emerged in tenth-century Scotland translated the Gaelic term *mórmaer* ('Great Steward'), a word now found in Scottish sources for the first time. We first hear of mórmaer in Scotland fighting alongside Constantine II in the battle of Corbridge in 918. We read of a mórmaer of Angus in 938, while the *Annals of Tigernach* name three such Scottish magnates in 976. It is clear from the information surviving on the mórmaer of eleventh-century Moray that the office could be inherited as in the case of the Norse *jarls* ('earls') and that at least some mórmaer, belonged to families of erstwhile kings who had been reduced to the level of the Scottish

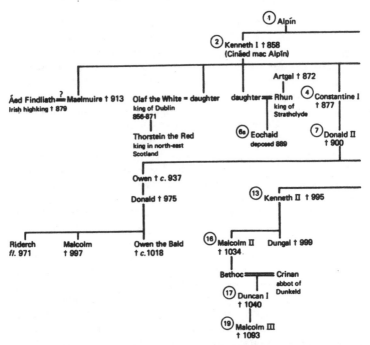

king's representative in the former tribal territory. In the case of Moray, the transition from tribal ruler to king's man had not been fully effected by the eleventh century, and its mórmaer (e.g. Findlaech, 1020) are described as kings in some reliable sources. It was Findlaech's son, Macbeth, who seized the kingship of Scotland in 1040. The Moray dynasty may have descended from the Dál Riata tribe of Cenél Loairn who migrated up the Great Glen in the face of the Viking conquests and established themselves as overlords of the old Pictish kingdoms north of the Mounth. The rivalry between the house of Macbeth and that of Kenneth mac Alpin in the eleventh century may therefore have owed much not only to inherited Dál Riata disputes but to earlier feuds between Pictish overlords north and south of the Mounth.

A major problem for any alternating system of succession was what to do with the heir apparent of the rival segment while he was waiting eagerly to succeed to the kingship of the Scots. The Scots tackled this problem in the period 900 to 1018 by allocating the sub-kingship of Strathclyde to the heir or tanist (tánaise) of the

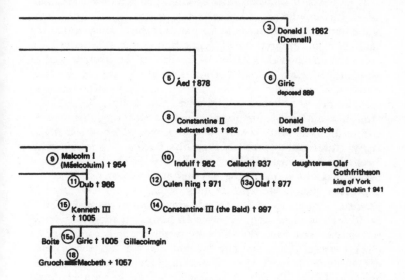

4 Kings of the Scots AD 850–1050

whole kingdom of the Scots. By this means remarkable stability was
maintained within the royal succession as a whole, while at the
same time the conquered Britons of the Clyde Valley were gradually integrated into the Scottish realm. While the Britons still
preserved some semblance of territorial identity, they were nonetheless ruled by Scots. These Scottish sub-kings came from two
different dynastic segments who were thereby discouraged from
establishing new dynasties in what was for them unfamiliar British
territory. Thus Indulf (d. 962) ruled Strathclyde as subking under
Malcolm I king of Scots, while on Malcolm's death his son, Dub,
ruled Strathclyde when Indulf moved up to the kingship of the
Scots (See Table 4). This system continued down to the time of
Malcolm II who is first heard of campaigning in Cumbria before
graduating to the Scottish kingship in 1005. The custom even
continued into the later eleventh century in more restricted form
as when Duncan (d. 1040) held Cumbria under his grandfather
Malcolm II (d. 1034) and Duncan's son, Malcolm III (d. 1093)
held Cumbria under his father.

The system of using Strathclyde-Cumbria as a dower kingdom for the tanist to the Scottish throne may well go back to the collapse of the north British dynasty at the hands of the Vikings and at the hands of Constantine I, son of Kenneth, in 870-2. Alternatively, it could date from the expulsion of Eochaid of Strathclyde and of Giric in 889, while John of Fordun claimed that the Scottish king who first established his heir as king of Cumbria and who intended that the practice should continue was Constantine II *c.* 915-16. Fordun's comment is important in that he attributed this innovation to the early tenth century and to a man whom we otherwise know transformed Scottish kingship during his long reign. Strathclyde was certainly ruled by a Scottish sub-king from at least as early as Constantine's time and continued to be so ruled through the second half of the tenth century. While it may have been in Fordun's interest to tie Strathclyde kingship into the main line of Scottish royal succession, nevertheless his information was almost certainly derived from elsewhere and is substantially confirmed by other sources. It is thanks to Fordun that we can identify one of Constantine's sub-kings in Cumbria as Eugenius or Owen, son and heir of Donald II son of Constantine I. Owen of Strathclyde did not eventually survive his overlord Constantine II and succeed to the Scottish throne because of Constantine's remarkably long reign of about 43 years (900-943). It is probable, as Kirby suggested, that Owen fell in the battle of *Brunanburh* in 937. It was Owen's brother, Malcolm I (954) who eventually succeeded Constantine in the kingship of the Scots, and it was this Malcolm who was confirmed by Edmund of Wessex as ruler of Strathclyde in 945 when the English king ravaged the territory and blinded the sons of *Dunmail* or Donald, convincingly identified by Kirby with the sons of Donald son of Áed son of Kenneth mac Alpin. Their father Donald, the brother of Constantine II, is the 'Donald son of Áed' mentioned as king of the Britons in the *Scottish Chronicle* (Version A) in the context of events of 908-916.

What the sources seem to tell us is that when Edmund visited northern Britain in 945, Malcolm I had succeeded to the kingship of the Scots (after Constantine had retired to St Andrews in 943) while a rival branch of Constantine's segment of the dynasty – the sons of Donald – were holding out in Strathclyde. Edmund had his own reasons for objecting to this, since Olaf Cuaran whom he had driven out of York the year before was still hiding in Strathclyde. Edmund therefore invaded Strathclyde, drove Olaf back to

Dublin, and mutilated the sons of Donald, thereby making them ineligible to reign according to Gaelic law. He gave Malcolm I a free hand in disposing of the sub-kingdom to whichever relative he wished, provided (as Roger Wendover put it) he should 'defend the northern parts of England from incursions of enemy raiders by land and sea' – in other words, provided he kept Olaf out of the Clyde and Solway. Malcolm was careful in disposing of Strathclyde not to alienate the entire segment of his dynastic rivals descended from Áed son of Kenneth, two of whom had just been mutilated. Such an act would have upset the alternating system. According to Fordun, he gave the British kingdom to Indulf (d. 962), the son of his predecessor Constantine II. Constantine was still alive, in retirement at St Andrews. So this latest decision pleased most parties. The alternating system continued to work smoothly in tandem with the sub-kingdom of Strathclyde, for when Indulf graduated to the kingship of the Scots in 954, he appointed his rival and heir, Dub son of Malcolm, to the kingship of Strathclyde. It was towards the end of Dub's reign that two factors combined to undermine the stability of this system of succession. The first was the refusal by one rival segment to await patiently the death of the ruling party in the other, the second was a parallel attempt by a third segment to found a dynasty in Strathclyde.

As the Scots approached the millennium their kingship seemed to revert to that heroic anarchy of the Celtic past when a bewildering succession of kings fell under the hands of assassins. This crisis in the royal succession was but a temporary affair explicable in terms of an upheaval in the alternating system. In the longer term the firm foundations laid by such kings as Constantine II and Malcolm I proved to be the rock on which future kings, such as Malcolm II, could build. The crisis began with the feud between the reigning king, Dub son of Malcolm I and his heir and rival, Culen son of Indulf. It was a disastrous conflict between two alternating segments descended from Constantine I and Áed, two sons of Kenneth mac Alpin, and it marked the end of a century of kingly coexistence. Some time before 966 Dub was challenged by Culen, and was first victorious in a battle in Perthshire, but was soon after driven from his kingdom and was slain in Forres by 'the treacherous nation of Moray'. It may be that Culen's opposition to Dub and his refusal to wait his turn for the kingship of the Scots related not so much to a struggle for ultimate sovereignty as to a struggle for control of Strathclyde. For while Culen's father Indulf had once held Strathclyde before succeeding to the Scottish kingship, we have no indication that Culen himself reigned in Strathclyde at any time. Since Donald son of Owen was king of Strathclyde before he died on pilgrimage in Rome in 975, there is reason to suppose that he had ruled Strathclyde ever since Dub vacated that kingdom to take up the kingship of the Scots in 962. Donald is usually equated with Dufnal, one of the sub-kings who rowed Edgar on the Dee in 973. This Donald upset the smooth working of the alternating system, and the related pecking order between Strathclyde and Scotia whereby Culen and not he ought to have held Strathclyde. He had in effect established a new dynastic segment in a tribal area reserved hitherto for heirs to the Scottish throne. This threatened to undermine the entire succession system. If the reigning king, Dub, had connived at keeping his heir, Culen, out of Strathclyde, then the feud between Dub and Culen is explained.

There is further evidence not only for the violent exclusion of the descendants of Áed from the Scots kingship, by their cousins descended from Constantine I, but also for the rise of a new dynastic segment within Strathclyde. Thus Culen, who seized power in 966, was struck down in 971, not by the Scots, but by Rhiderch son of that king, Donald of Strathclyde, who almost certainly once excluded Culen from the Strathclyde kingship. On Culen's death the kingship of the Scots swung back to the segment descended from Constantine I, in the person of Kenneth II, who kept up the feud with his rivals by slaying Olaf the brother of Culen in 977. The last of Áed's segment to hold the Scots kingship was Constantine III (the Bald) who succeeded on the death of Kenneth II in 995 and who we learn from Fordun had been plotting against Kenneth during his life – a credible enough statement considering that Constantine's father and uncle had been slain in the power struggles against Kenneth's family.

With the knowledge that Constantine III was the last of his line, we ought to take Fordun seriously when he claims that Kenneth II won a section of the Scottish magnates over to accepting new rules in the succession system, whereby in effect the alternating system was abandoned in favour of confining the kingship within Kenneth's immediate family and their descendants. The details of Fordun's tale of how this decision led to the elaborate plotting of Kenneth's death with a mechanical contraption of James Bond proportions are entirely fabulous. But Fordun's basic point is consistent with other earlier sources, namely that Kenneth tried to

engineer new succession laws which would exclude all rival segments from the kingship and secure it for his son Malcolm II.
Kenneth was opposed in this not only by the future Constantine III
son of Culen but also by a branch of his own house descended from
his brother, Dub. Fordun names the malcontents within Kenneth's
own ranks as rallying round Giric son of Kenneth III son of Dub.
There is some confusion as to who held the kingship after Constantine III. The majority of Scottish king-lists supported by the
Annals of Ulster and *Chronicon Scotorum* favour Kenneth III, while the
Scottish Chronicle (Version F) followed by the *Chronicle of Melrose* and
Fordun favour Giric. But Giric like his father Kenneth III is
assigned an eight-year reign and like his father too, he was slain by
Malcolm II. So, the discrepancies are not serious: Constantine III
was succeeded by either Kenneth III or by Kenneth's son, Giric, or
perhaps father and son ruled jointly. They were defeated and slain
in 1005 by Malcolm II who at last realized his father's ambition
triumphing over the house of Dub and the house of Culen.
Malcolm's long reign, lasting until 1034, saw the end of the
alternating system and the evolution of a new and more tightly
organized succession which he was to pass on to his grandson
Duncan. Malcolm's long reign was to prove that the apparent
anarchy of the late tenth century had prepared the way for a more
advanced and centralized form of kingship which would sustain the
Scottish monarchy into the high Middle Ages.

These dynastic struggles which led to the triumph of Kenneth II
and his son Malcolm II over their rivals were intimately connected
with the full integration of Strathclyde into the Scottish realm.
It was inevitable that as soon as the Scottish alternating system
came under strain and finally collapsed, Strathclyde would play a
central role in those events, since whoever held Strathclyde had
traditionally been recognized as tanist or heir designate to the overkingship of the Scots. Any attempt to change the system of succession had immediate repercussions within Strathclyde. We have
seen that, while Malcolm I was not prepared to accept the sons of
Donald in Strathclyde in 945, he was nevertheless happy to appoint
Donald's nephew Indulf to that kingdom, and Indulf eventually
became king of Scots in 954. But as Malcolm's son, Kenneth II,
strove to exclude other families from the kingship of the Scots, he
also had to keep his rivals out of Strathclyde. Kenneth's party
appears to have backed a new dynasty of Scottish sub-kings in
Strathclyde which was willing to support Kenneth II's bid for

power in Scotland. This accounts for the slaying of Culen in 971 by Riderch son of Donald, king of Strathclyde, and I have suggested how Donald had previously been allowed by Dub to exclude Culen from the Strathclyde kingship. Apart from a garbled record of an attack by Kenneth II on 'part' of the Strathclyde kingdom in 971 there is otherwise a consistent record of friendship between him and the sub-kings of Strathclyde. Fordun informs us that when Constantine III (the Bald) and Giric son of Kenneth III held power in the period 995 to 1005, their enemy, the future Malcolm II (son of Kenneth II) retired to Cumbria from where he emerged to do battle with them and gain victory in 1005. Earlier, according to Fordun, this same Malcolm mac Kenneth had defended Cumbria from the invasion of Æthelred II in AD 1000, – an invasion otherwise vouched for in the *Anglo-Saxon Chronicle*. So, however much Constantine III and Giric may have wished to support their own puppets in Strathclyde–Cumbria, clearly, the future Malcolm II had also established himself in Cumbria as heir apparent to the Scots throne.

This feud between the descendants of Dub and his son Kenneth III on the one hand, and the descendants of Kenneth II on the other, may have persisted into the eleventh century and it was against this background that Macbeth came to power in 1040. In 999, for instance, we read how Dungal the son of one Kenneth [?II] was slain by Gillacoimgin the son of the other Kenneth [?III]. In 1033 the grandson of Boite son of Kenneth [?III] was slain by Malcolm II. Gruoch, the daughter of that same Boite, married Macbeth who slew Malcolm II's grandson and heir, Duncan, in 1040. This eleventh-century feud between Macbeth's dynasty in Moray and the house of Kenneth mac Alpin may have had its origins in the remote Pictish past, but it was clearly intensified when Macbeth married into the house of Kenneth III which was so bitterly opposed to that of Kenneth II.

Florence of Worcester presents us with a list of kings who attended on Edgar soon after his coronation at Bath in 973, when the English king assembled his fleet at Chester. According to Florence, Edgar was ceremoniously rowed on the Dee by those kings who, in Florence's view at least, had come to do homage. Among these were Kenneth [II] king of Scots and Malcolm king of the Cumbrians. This must have been Malcolm son of Donald who died in 997. His father Donald, who died in Rome two years after the rowing on the Dee, had presumably already abdicated his kingship in favour of his son, but Donald may also have been present at Chester in 973 if we choose to identify him with *Dufnal* in Florence's list. Fordun appears to have confused Malcolm son of Donald with a fictitious Malcolm son of Dub, supposedly king of Strathclyde in the last quarter of the tenth century. But the evidence, confused as it is, points to Strathclyde being ruled by a line of kinglets descended (in spite of the British names of some) from Donald II son of Constantine I, who were promoted in Strathclyde by Kenneth II and his son Malcolm II in an effort to exclude the houses of Dub and Culen from the kingship of the Scots. We have already met with the pilgrim Donald, and his sons Malcolm and Riderch. According to the *Historia Regum*, Owen the Bald, yet another son of Donald, was king of Strathclyde in 1018 when he fought alongside Malcolm II in the battle of Carham.

The question as to whether we recognize a logical dynastic succession to the kingship of Strathclyde or whether we allow for a multiplicity of rulers such as Malcolm son of Dub and Malcolm son of Donald who would have ruled jointly, has an important bearing on the territorial extent of the kingdom in the period AD 900-1000. Kirby was undoubtedly correct in accepting that already by 927, the frontier of Strathclyde–Cumbria reached south to Eamont near Penrith where King Athelstan met the Scots and Strathclyde rulers in that year. Just as the Scots were moving south across Lothian in the tenth century so, too, the Scottish sub-kings of Strathclyde were moving south of the Solway into a region which had become a no-man's-land following the collapse of Anglian power in 867. Cumbria had been left to its own devices in the decades following the Danish capture of York. Anglian settlers in southern Galloway must have passed very quickly under the control of Norsemen and *Gall-Gaedhil* in the late ninth century, but the Eden valley may have remained undisturbed until the crisis in the York kingdom after the defeat at Tettenhall in 910 which brought the grandsons of Ivạr back into Northumbria. This event coincided with intense Norse colonization in Lancashire, the Eden valley and coastal Cumbria. Echoes of the chaos in north-west England in the early tenth century appear in the Durham *History of St Cuthbert* which provides glimpses of English lay and ecclesiastical magnates fleeing east across the Pennines into the Tyne valley and to the relative safety of the old Bernician homelands. In spite of the Norse colonization of Cumbria, however, it was the Scottish rulers of Strathclyde who effectively filled the vacuum created by the collapse of Anglian York. By 927 the Strathclyde border may well have reached Penrith, for Athelstan's parley with the kings of the Scots and Britons is likely to have taken place on their frontier if the remote location at Penrith was to have any meaning, particularly for the Scottish king. Some 45 years later we find Kenneth II plundering England (*Saxoniam*) as far as Stainmore soon after the beginning of his reign in 971, which suggests that the Scots were pushing Strathclyde rule southwards along the old Roman road from Carlisle to York, and up the Eden valley to Stainmore. Eirík Bloodaxe, the last Danish king of York, met his death on Stainmore while fleeing from York. Possibly, he was struck down on the frontier between his kingdom and that of Strathclyde. By 1069 the border between the Anglo-Normans and the Scots ran from the river Duddon eastward to the Rere-cross on Stainmore, a boundary which Kirby rightly saw as being of tenth-century origin.

If Kenneth II were establishing his claim to Cumbria as far as Stainmore at the beginning of his reign, then his rowing of Edgar on the Dee, perhaps in the following year, makes some sense. Kenneth's presence at Chester, whatever exotic form it took, must have been voluntary. Edgar was not attended by the northern kings at his coronation at Bath. The parley at Chester took place on middle ground at the most important port on the Irish Sea, and there is no reason to believe that this meeting of kings was any different from similar northern treaties convened by Edward or Athelstan earlier in the century. To describe events at Chester as a 'submission' is to follow the prejudice of Anglo-Norman chroniclers and to imply claims of Anglo-Saxon suzerainty which are not only anachronistic but which go far beyond the wishful thinking of even contemporary Anglo-Saxon writers. These meetings between tenth-century kings in Britain were no different from those gatherings in Ireland known as *ríg-dál*, a term best translated as 'royal conference' or 'parliament of kings'. The conference in 973-4 must have had something to offer Kenneth, and in view of his hurrying to Stainmore, it seems reasonable that he obtained recognition of his hold on his English territories south of the Solway and in Lothian, and his under-king, Malcolm son of Donald of Strathclyde was present as the under-king of Kenneth in charge of Strathclyde. As for the 'pledges' given to Edgar, these must surely have related to the safety and protection of vulnerable English border-lands in Northumbria.

Even if we were to ignore all the evidence for the role of

Strathclyde as a pawn in internal Scottish dynastic politics from 872 until 1018, we would still be left with impressive evidence which points to Strathclyde's essentially satellite status vis-à-vis its Scottish overlords. We find that throughout the tenth century, as Wessex tried to coax or bully the kingdoms of northern Britain into cooperation, the kings of Strathclyde never acted on their own initiative but always in tandem with the kings of the Scots. Scots kings on the other hand, acted on their own or with other satellites, as when Constantine II supported the Bernicians against Ragnall on the Tyne in 914 and 918. But Athelstan met the king of the Scots and the Strathclyde king together near Penrith in 927 and we gather from the *History of the Church of Durham* that when Athelstan attacked the Scots in 934, the Strathclyde king had joined the Scots and broken faith with the English. According to Symeon of Durham, Owen of Strathclyde fought alongside Constantine II in the battle of *Brunanburh* against Athelstan in 937. Here we have a case of Owen and Constantine consistently acting in unison over a 10-year period. Owen was clearly the weaker partner in military terms and this record amounts to proof of his tributary position to the Scots. Similarly, we hear of Britons on the side of the Scots in battle against the York Danes of Eirík Bloodaxe in 952, while the last we hear of Strathclyde in its rôle as a satellite kingdom is the news that its sub-king, Owen the Bald, followed Malcolm II to the battle of Carham in 1018. These records, in spite of the unsatisfactory way they have sometimes been copied by later medieval chroniclers, present us with a strong case for the subject status of the kings of Strathclyde, a status which in the Celtic world placed an obligation on the under-king to join the hosting of his overlord in expeditions into enemy territory.

The recognition that the Strathclyde Britons went the way of the Picts in the period 870-890 deprives the debate as to whether English Cumbria was or was not a separate kingdom from Strathclyde of much of its relevance. If we accept that all of Strathclyde–Cumbria was ultimately controlled by the king of Scots, then whether or not this satellite territory was sub-divided is of little importance. It seems clear that the region of modern Cumbria, separated as it is from Galloway on the one hand by the Solway Firth, and from Bernicia by the Pennines, must have had its own distinct personality throughout the early Middle Ages. The dominant character of the region during the tenth century was Norse rather than Celtic or Anglian, for the place-name evidence suggests a thorough-going colonization by Scandinavian settlers all over coastal Cumbria. The culture of these Norsemen shows strong *Gall-Gaedhil* influence from nearby Galloway and the Western Isles, but equally, their Christianity as exemplified in their sculptured crosses shows strong native Anglian influence.

The stone crosses at Gosforth, Aspatria and Cross Canonby, together with more explicitly pagan hog-back Viking tombs, show that in the period when this region was falling under the control of Strathclyde it was enjoying something of an economic boom. Cumbria was isolated from northern and midland England, which was virtually a battleground between Wessex and York in the tenth century. Its sheltered position, together with its easy access to Viking trade and piracy in the Irish Sea combined to promote prosperity in the region. This prosperity drew the attention of Scottish kings and their Strathclyde satellites who were in any event preoccupied with Northumbrian politics. As the tenth century progressed, and as the tottering Danish kingdom of York relied more and more on the support of Scottish kings, the Scots tightened their grip on the Eden Valley, moving up on to Stainmore and thereby consolidating their hold on the northern Pennines. History was now repeating itself in a remarkable way with the dramatic highland landscape of northern Britain once more asserting itself as a key factor in the politics of the region. For just as the legionary commander at Roman York encountered the Caledonian problem in effect at a frontier which came south to Catterick, so now the kings of Danish York and their English successors were faced with a resurgent Scottish nation whose frontier on the Stainmore Pass brought it within striking distance of the Vale of York.

It was not until William Rufus built his castle at Carlisle in 1092 that the Scots were forced to cede their territories south of the Solway to the Anglo-Norman power, and henceforth the border in the west ran up the Esk to the Liddel Water and up Liddesdale along the Kershope Burn to the Cheviots. Scottish influence in Cumbria, however, died hard and control of Cumbria was contested into the middle of the twelfth century. The bishops of Glasgow claimed ecclesiastical jurisdiction over Cumbria to the old boundary of the Rere-Cross on Stainmore not just until 1133, when the new English diocese of Carlisle deprived them of lands east and south of Annandale, but even as late as the 1260s. In 1136 King David I of Scotland seized Carlisle, which remained in Scottish hands for another 21 years. But while twelfth-century Scottish kings regarded Cumbria as an integral part of their territory, the region was in reality a no-man's land of divided loyalties inhabited mostly by Britons and Norsemen all of whom had been overtaken by events of the eleventh century. It mattered little to such people whether they were ruled from Scone or Westminster, and life in the fells went on regardless of who held the castle at Carlisle. Ekwall noted numerous Brythonic compound place-names in north-east Cumberland and the Eden Valley, and in particular the occurrence of old Anglian place-names which had later been taken over as hybrid forms by a British population. From this he suggested that Strathclyde ascendancy in this area from the end of the ninth century may have restored Brythonic as the dominant speech of the region; but alongside these British speakers, we must allow for Gaelicized Norse settlers whose language survived in the Lake District into the twelfth century.

Scottish expansion southwards in the tenth century was not an exclusively 'highland' phenomenon, although control of the Cheviots and the northern Pennines inevitably led to Scottish domination of the coastal strip from the Forth to the Tees. Scottish control of this Bernician territory could be either direct in the form of conquest and settlement, or indirect involving overlordship of the earldom of Bamburgh. Clearly, overlordship and settlement were related phenomena, since one might lead to the other, nevertheless, a confusion of these two distinct forms of expansion has led to much misunderstanding and unnecessary argument relating to Scottish control of Lothian and Bernicia in the tenth and eleventh centuries. We have seen how Stirling and West Lothian may have reverted to Pictish hands after the defeat and death of Ecgfrith of Northumbria in the battle of Dunnichen Moss back in 685, while Bede rather vaguely set the Forth as the boundary between Picts and Angles in the early eighth century. Anglian gains in the plain of Kyle in south-west Scotland in 752 were short lived, because the Northumbrian kings had expanded too far and too fast in the seventh century, lacking both man-power and resources to annex the northern British highlands south of the Forth–Clyde isthmus. This was a region whose conquest had eluded the Romans, and which was very definitely beyond the grasp of the faction-ridden Northumbrians in the eighth and ninth centuries. The house of Kenneth mac Alpin had annexed Stirling and Pictish Fife at the very time when the Northumbrian kings were conquered by the Danes, and this Danish conquest in turn provided a breathing space for the

Scots to consolidate their position north of the Forth, and to move south and east over Lothian. The Danes had concentrated all their efforts on the conquest and settlement of Deira, relegating control of Bernicia north of the Tees to a dynasty of client rulers, styled 'kings' immediately after the Danish conquest in 867 but later appearing as 'high reeves' of Bamburgh in the early tenth century. These north-eastern rulers had by tradition and from their Anglian origin looked south to York as the centre of their world. The thorough-going nature of the Scandinavian settlement of York must have not only increased the sense of Bernician alienation from its Danish neighbours but also (as in the time of Ragnall, 910-920) have produced conflicting interests between the two communities. This was a situation which the new Scottish dynasty north of the Forth could and did exploit. The Bernicians found themselves caught between two powerful and expanding peoples, and inevitably they had to choose the overlordship of one or the other, changing sides from time to time when necessary, in order to survive. Scottish interference in Bernicia must therefore be studied at two levels – direct Scottish annexation and settlement of lands in Lothian which lay immediately within the grasp of the expanding Scots kingdom, and more ill-defined Scottish ambitions for the overlordship of Bernicia as a whole.

We are told in the *Scottish Chronicle* (Version A) that 'in Indulf's time [954-962] the fortress of Edinburgh (*oppidum Eden*) was evacuated and abandoned to the Scots until the present day.' This reference to evacuation and abandonment (*vacuatum est ac relictum*) relates to Scottish conquest as opposed to overlordship in Lothian in the period after 954 – a period which significantly coincided with the aftermath of the final collapse of Danish rule at York, when the English kings Eadwig and Edgar were too busy trying to win acceptance in Deira to have time or resources to care about distant Lothian. A Durham tract, *De Primo Saxonum Adventu*, claims that Edgar of Wessex received the homage of Kenneth II king of Scots, who was granted Lothian in return. This refers to Edgar's meeting with Kenneth at Chester in *c.* 973 when, as we have already concluded, Kenneth probably won recognition of his Cumbrian territories as far as the Rere-Cross on Stainmore. This Durham record of *c.* 1100 relating to the ceding of Lothian to Kenneth at the same meeting at Chester makes much sense when shorn of its feudal accretions and later English claims. There is no reason to reject the *Scottish Chronicle's* record of the Scottish occupation of Edinburgh some time

after 954, and that being so, the meeting at Chester involved not
the formal granting of Lothian to the Scots, but the English king's
recognition of Scottish *de facto* rule there for some time before. For
his part, Kenneth most likely recognized Edgar's overlordship
over the remainder of the Bernician earldom to the south. It was
this more contentious struggle between West-Saxons and Scots for
the overlordship of all Bernicia which seems to lie behind the record
of Scottish interference there in the reigns of Giric, Constantine II
and Malcolm I. Malcolm's raiding of the English 'as far as the
Tees' in 949 sheds no light on the location of the frontier between
Scot and Angle in Lothian, but it is part of a lengthy record of
consistent Scottish efforts to dominate the earls of Bamburgh
throughout the tenth century. This separate issue of the overlordship of Bernicia continued long after the Scots had annexed
Lothian, and surfaced in a dramatic way in the reign of Malcolm II
during the first two decades of the eleventh century.

The *Scottish Chronicle* (Version E) informs us that Malcolm II
'fought a great battle at Carham' just south of the Tweed where it
flows between Berwickshire and Northumberland. This Scottish
victory is dated to 1018 by the *History of the Church of Durham*, where
it is said the Bernicians between the Tees and Tweed suffered heavy
losses at the hands of a huge Scottish army. The *Historia Regum*
claims that Malcolm was assisted at Carham by 'Owen the Bald,
king of the men of Clyde' (*Eugenius Calvus rex Clutinensium*) and the
defeated Northumbrians were led by their earl, Uhtred. Few things
appear simple in early Scottish history, and the battle of Carham is
no exception. Some historians, e.g. B. Meehan, believed that
Carham 'had [no] more than local importance', while A.A.M.
Duncan argued forcibly that 'it is not possible to cause the battle of
Carham as a Scottish victory to evaporate.' Central to the whole
tangled issue of Carham is the statement in the late eleventh-
century tract on *The Siege of Durham (De obsessione Dunelmi)* that after
the Bernician defeat at Carham, Earl Uhtred's successor in North-
umbria ceded Lothian to the Scots. This statement cannot be easily
reconciled with much firmer evidence for the Scottish conquest of
Lothian sometime after 954 and for the formal recognition of the
Scottish occupation there by Edgar in *c.* 973. The question of
Carham, then, relates not only to a single battle between Malcolm
II and his English neighbours but to the much wider issue of
Scottish annexation of Lothian. Since, however, a case can be
made for Scottish interference in the affairs of Bernicia generally

from the late ninth century onwards, it is important that problems relating to documentation on Carham are neither allowed to obscure the wider issue of Bernician overlordship nor allowed to restrict our conception of Scottish influence in Lothian to an exclusively eleventh-century context. Too much emphasis on the importance of Carham can cause yet another of the many distortions in Scottish historiography whereby the expansion of the Scottish realm south of the Forth–Clyde isthmus is wrongly attributed to the eleventh century rather than to the early tenth.

Even the date of the battle of Carham is in doubt, although 1018 is the more probable in spite of the fact that the *Anglo-Saxon Chronicle* records the killing of Earl Uhtred on Cnut's orders in 1016. Either the English chronicle is in error, or Uhtred could not have defended Bernicia in 1018. The problem of precise dating is not so serious as Mr Meehan's scepticism regarding the claim in the *History of the Church of Durham* that Carham resulted in a resounding Scottish victory. Not only is this point conceded in a Durham source, but Meehan did not appreciate the importance of the statement in the *Scottish Chronicle* that Malcolm 'distributed many offerings, both to the clergy. and to the churches, on that day'. There is the clear implication here of a Scottish victory and of much more besides. Royal gifts to the church were commonplace in the Dark Ages, but it was rare to record such gifts in chronicles unless they were endowed with important political significance. Thus Roger Wendover tells us that in 947 Eadred of Wessex presented two large bells to York Minster, while in 1004 we read in the *Annals of Ulster* how the Irish highking, Brian Boru, placed 22 ounces of gold as an offering on the altar of the church of Armagh. These two incidents had one important feature in common, for while Eadred had only a tenuous claim and hold on Danish York, so too the southern Irish king, Brian, was looked upon as a usurper at Armagh. These royal gifts then, were symbolic of the overlordship claimed by ambitious kings over both their tributary territories and their principal churches. It is in this context of the ritual gift made by an aspiring overlord to the chief church of a client territory, that the gifts of Athelstan to Chester-le-Street in 934 may take on added meaning. Athelstan's gifts to the church of St Cuthbert (the patron of Bernicia), immediately prior to his invasion of Scotland, can be seen not only as an assertion of his overlordship in Bernicia, but as a challenge to the claims of Constantine II of Scotland over that same territory. Athelstan's West-Saxon claim to Bernicia cannot have been any more credible than those of the Munster Brian over Armagh, and on Athelstan's death in 940, West-Saxon influence north even of the Humber, not to mention the Tees, vanished overnight. Athelstan's largesse at Chester-le-Street, then, was as much a witness to the reality of Constantine's influence in this region as it was to West-Saxon efforts to buy the loyalties of the clergy and rulers of a distant territory.

The claims of both Athelstan and Constantine II to overlordship in Bernicia were based on the realities of contemporary politics rather than on any appeal to history. Athelstan's earliest opportunity to interfere in Bernician affairs came with the death of Sitric king of York in 927, but the West-Saxon hold on the north-east must have been tenuous and intermittent even in Athelstan's reign. We cannot accept the unsubstantiated claim of the *Anglo-Saxon Chronicle* that Bernicia formally acknowledged the overlordship of Edward the Elder in 920. The claim that all the peoples of northern Britain – Scots, Britons, Danes and Angles – 'chose [Edward] as father and lord' is an oversimplified piece of West-Saxon propaganda, particularly in view of the turmoil which ensued in Northumbria into the middle of the tenth century. It is, for instance, very likely that if Constantine had agreed with Edward in 920 not to join any Scandinavian alliance against the English of Mercia, Edward in turn confirmed Constantine's overlordship in Bernicia, since Constantine was already exercising precisely that role *de facto*. We find when Ragnall, king of York, attacked the Bernicians back in 914, their high reeve, Ealdred of Bamburgh, fled (according to the *History of St Cuthbert*) to seek help from Constantine of Scotland. Constantine responded by leading his armies to assist the Bernicians at Corbridge. Five years later, we find Constantine once more defending Bernicia against this same Ragnall in a great battle on the Tyne. By the standards of any Dark Age society we have here convincing evidence to show that the ruler of Bamburgh regarded himself as the tributary of the king of the Scots in the early tenth century. In this connection, it is significant that Bernician rulers had abandoned the title of 'king' which they had enjoyed as client rulers under Danish York in the ninth century, in favour of the more modest *heah-gerefa* ('high reeve') in the tenth. This English title is an exact translation of the Scottish *mórmaer* ('great steward'), which is precisely what the ruler of Bamburgh had become in relation to his Scottish overlord. Constantine's predecessor and kinsman, Giric (878-889), who ruled the Scots at a time when the

kingship of their Danish neighbours at York had temporarily collapsed after the expulsion of Hálfdan, is said in Version I of the
Scottish Chronicle to have 'subdued to himself Bernicia and nearly all
England'. When we allow for obvious exaggeration, we are still left
with a new and consistent record in Scottish ninth- and tenth-
century sources relating to sustained and successful warfare against
the Bernician Angles. Not only Giric, but also Malcolm I and
Indulf were credited with successful English campaigns, while the
case for Constantine's overlordship in Bernicia seems unassailable.

It is in the light of this evidence for Scottish overlordship
in tenth-century Bernicia that we may interpret the record of
Athelstan's gifts to the church of St Cuthbert in 934 and the distribution of gifts by Malcolm II on the same day (*ea die*) as his victory
over the Bernicians at Carham. The record of Malcolm's gifts,
doled out not as booty to his warriors, but to churchmen, suggests
that his gifts were made to Cuthbert's clergy and their new church,
founded at Durham in 995, and they symbolized the Scottish victor's role as overlord of Bernicia. The importance of the role of
Durham, not only as the new centre for Cuthbert's relics but for the
custody of Cuthbert's treasure – the visible sign of royal patronage
and overlordship in Bernicia – places the account of an earlier
abortive siege of Durham by Malcolm II in a new and more credible light. Mr Meehan rejected the account of Malcolm's siege (in
the tract on *The Siege of Durham*) either in 969 (the date given in the
tract) or in 1006 (as suggested by the *Annals of Ulster*) on the grounds
that the earlier siege was a garbled tradition which originally
referred to Malcolm's victory at Carham in 1018 or to some other
encounter between English and Scots. But Carham was remembered as a resounding Scottish victory, even by the Bernicians,
while the tale of the siege of Durham, and the battle recorded in the
Annals of Ulster were both registered as Scottish defeats. The
'slaughter of the good men (i.e. the nobles) of Scotland' at the
hands of the English as recorded by the *Annals of Ulster* in 1006, is a
contemporary account of a battle which can neither be ignored nor
consigned, against all the evidence, to the wilderness of Cumbria.
Such a battle was most likely to have taken place somewhere along
that great stretch of coastal lowland which ran from Lothian to
Durham. In view of Durham's new-found position in the early
eleventh century, together with a tradition there of Malcolm's
unsuccessful siege, it is reasonable to follow Skene in equating the
battle of 1006 with the tale of the siege of Durham. 1006 was the

first year of Malcolm's reign and an attack by him on Bernicia at that time would make it a *crech ríg* or 'inaugural raid' launched by a Gaelic king against his neighbouring tributaries.

Some of the problems relating to Carham and the siege of Durham are not quite so important as they may seem. It does not radically affect our view of Anglo-Scottish relations if we deny that Earl Uhtred was present at the battle; or whether we believe that Carham was fought in 1016 or 1018; or whether we accept the account of an unsuccessful siege of Durham by Malcolm some time earlier in his reign. It is important however, that we accept that Malcolm tried unsuccessfully to impose his overlordship on Bernicia in 1006, and that he later regained the military initiative at Carham in either 1018 or 1016. Malcolm's victory at Carham can have had little bearing on the Scottish occupation of Lothian, which had been an accomplished fact for half a century, but it could have had everything to do with more ambitious Scottish claims on the overlordship of Bernicia. If we seek a reason for the slaying of Uhtred after his visit to Cnut's court, it must surely be in part at least for his apparent disloyalty in recognizing Malcolm (after Carham) as his overlord in Bernicia. And so Cnut's invasion of Scotland in 1031 and Duncan's raid on Durham in 1039, far from being isolated cross-border skirmishes, were part of a continuous struggle between the kings of the Scots and the English for control of the earldom of Northumbria between the Tees and the Tweed. It was a struggle which would continue to exercise the minds of Scottish kings in the twelfth century and its roots lay deep in the Viking past when Bernicia as an English territory found itself iso-lated and alone, sandwiched between the Danes of York and the king of the Scots.

When we look at the decline of Anglo-Saxon monarchy in the late tenth and early eleventh centuries, or at the demise of Scandina-vian York, we are struck by the security and vitality of Scottish kingship in this same period. The comparison is important, because from the twelfth-century onwards Anglo-Norman histo-rians had a vested interest in rewriting Anglo-Scottish history in a way that showed the Dark Age Scottish realm as a client kingdom of Wessex. Their task was made easier because the *Anglo-Saxon Chroni-cle* on which they relied so heavily for information, provided a West-Saxon account of events which lent itself easily to a more developed feudal interpretation. And so any meetings between Scot and Saxon where oaths were sworn and alliances formed were later easily transformed into accounts of the English suzerain receiving the homage of subservient northern kings. Sadly, the views of chroniclers such as Roger Wendover, Florence of Worcester, and several other uncritical compilers of Dark Age material, have coloured the whole of medieval Scottish historiography with the shadow of Anglo-Norman claims on Scottish sovereignty. An undue emphasis, too, by modern scholars on the value of West-Saxon sources has until recently failed to produce a balanced reconstruction of events in the ninth and tenth centuries. A remarkable conclusion then, emerges from a study of northern Britain in the Dark Ages. Although the king of the Scots undoubtedly did not command resources comparable with those of his English counterpart, and while written government had clearly not developed in Scotland to the extent that it had done in the Anglo-Saxon south, nevertheless the Scots had established the most stable and successful monarchy in Britain prior to the Norman Invasion. It was a dynasty that would survive and rule Scotland for centuries to come.

A Note on Further Reading

General

A.A.M. Duncan, *Scotland: the Making of the Kingdom* (Edinburgh, 1975), is an authoritative survey of this period which follows the fortunes of Scottish history into the central Middle Ages, and provides extensive bibliography which is especially valuable on settlement studies. W.F. Skene's *Celtic Scotland: A History of Ancient Alban* (3 vols. Edinburgh, 1886–90) is a landmark in Scottish historiography and its author's breadth of vision and powers of historical perception have still much to teach today's student. H.M. Chadwick's *Early Scotland: the Picts, the Scots and the Welsh of Southern Scotland* (Cambridge, 1949) although conceived on a much more modest scale than Skene's work brought more rigorous scholarly techniques to the subject. The 1950s and 60s saw a series of remarkable *Studies* devoted to aspects of northern British history. Pride of place among these must go to *The Problem of the Picts*, ed. F.T. Wainwright (Edinburgh, 1955). Other volumes of almost equal importance were *Studies in Early British History*, ed. H.M. Chadwick, *et al*. (Cambridge, 1954); *Studies in the Early British Church*, ed. N.K. Chadwick *et al*., (Cambridge, 1958); and *Celt and Saxon: Studies in the Early British Border*, ed. K. Jackson, *et al*. (Cambridge, 1964). M.O. Anderson, *Kings and Kingship in Early Scotland* (Edinburgh, 1973) is the most definitive work on Scottish and Pictish dynastic history and includes a most valuable synthesis on the research of an entire generation. It is important for the student to keep constantly in touch with original sources and to gain some knowledge of the spirit of early Scottish records. *Early Sources of Scottish History AD 500 to 1286*, ed. A.O. Anderson (2 vols, Edinburgh, 1922) provides a magnificent corpus of sources in translation as well as an extensive discussion and description of sources (arranged in alphabetical order). *Chronicles of the Picts: Chronicles of the Scots and other early memorials of Scottish History*, ed. W.F. Skene (Edinburgh, 1867) provides texts and translations which although in much need of revision are still valuable. J.F. Kenney, *The Sources for the Early History of Ireland* (Dublin, 1979, reprint) contains an enormous amount of information on early Scottish sources and the introduction has not been surpassed for its treatment of early Gaelic Christianity. Other useful works of reference are: I.B. Cowan and D.E. Easson, *Medieval Religious Houses: Scotland* (London, 1976) and B. Webster, *Scotland from the Eleventh Century to 1603* (Sources of History, 1975). J. Romilly Allen, *The Early Christian Monuments of Scotland: a classified, illustrated, descriptive list of the monuments, with an analysis of their symbolism and ornamentation*, introduction, J. Anderson (Edinburgh, 1903) with over a thousand pages of painstaking scholarship and recording is unlikely to be surpassed by any individual scholar of a future generation. Scottish prehistory is covered by more general books such as V.G. Childe, *The Prehistory of Scotland* (London, 1935); R.W. Feachem, *Guide to Prehistoric Scotland* (London, 2nd edn, 1977); *The Prehistoric Peoples of Scotland*, ed. S. Piggott (London, 1962). R. Munro, *Ancient Scottish Lake-Dwellings or Crannogs* (Edinburgh, 1882) is an old classic which is still valuable. More recent general works include S.H. Cruden, *The Early Christian and Pictish Monuments of Scotland* (Edinburgh, 1964); G. Ritchie and A. Ritchie, *Scotland: Archaeology and Early History* (London, 1981); and L. Laing, *The Archaeology of Late Celtic Britain and Ireland c. 400–1200 AD* (London, 1975). L. Alcock, 'Early historic fortifications in Scotland', in *Hill-fort Studies: Essays for A.H.A. Hogg*, ed. G. Guilbert (Leicester, 1981), provides a gazeteer of historical sites and an excellent bibliography on forts and settlements for Scotland as a whole. A review of the sculpture will be found in R.B.K. Stevenson, 'Sculpture in Scotland in the 6th-9th Centuries AD' in *Kolloquium über spätantike und frühmittelalterliche Skulptur, Heidelberg 1970* (Mainz, 1970), pp. 65–74. *An Historical Atlas of Scotland c. 400–c. 1600*, ed. P. McNeill and R. Nicholson (St Andrews, 1975) may be recommended as the student's constant guide for this and later periods of Scottish history. Other important historical and archaeological map sources are: *Map of Roman Britain* (Ordnance Survey, Southampton, 4th edn, 1978); *Map of Britain in the Dark Ages* (Ordnance Survey, Chessington, 1966); *Britain before the Norman Conquest* (Ordnance Survey, Southampton, 1973); *Hadrian's Wall* (Ordnance Survey, Southampton, 2nd edn, 1975); and *The Antonine Wall* (Ordnance Survey, Southampton, 1969). Inventories of archaeological monuments have been prepared according to counties (some are still in preparation) and published by *The Royal Commission on the Ancient and Historical Monuments of Scotland* (HMSO). A number of very important works cover the subject of Scottish placenames: A. MacBain, *Place Names: Highlands and Islands of Scotland* (Stirling, 1922); W.J. Watson, *The History of the Celtic Place-Names of Scotland*

(Edinburgh, 1926); and W.F.H. Nicolaisen, *Scottish Place-Names: their Study and Significance* (London, 1976). This last includes an excellent bibliography on early Scottish history. Cf. G. Whittington, 'Placenames and the Settlement Pattern of Dark Age Scotland', *Proc. Soc. Antiq. Scotland*, cvi (1977), 99–100.

The Romano-Britons

General and introductory works are: S. Frere, *Britannia: A History of Roman Britain* (London, 1974); R.G. Collingwood and I. Richmond, *The Archaeology of Roman Britain* (London, 2nd edn, 1969); M. Todd, *Roman Britain 55 BC – AD 400: the Province Beyond the Ocean* (Brighton, 1981); I.A. Richmond, *Roman Britain* (Pelican History of England, I, Harmondsworth, 1973, reprint of 2nd edn). P. Salway, *Roman Britain* (Oxford, 1981) supplants the older classic by R.G. Collingwood and J.N.L. Myres, *Roman Britain and the English Settlements* (Oxford, 1st edn, 1936) and provides a definitive bibliography which includes the works of Ammianus Marcellinus, Dio Cassius and panegyrists who wrote on Roman Britain. P. Salway, *The Frontier People of Roman Britain* (Cambridge, reprint, 1967) in addition to its discussion on civil and military settlements also includes a corpus of inscriptions and sculptures relating to civilians on the frontier. *Roman and Native in Northern Britain*, ed. I.A. Richmond (Edinburgh, 1958) contains among other papers a contribution from the editor on *Ancient Geographical Sources for Britain North of Cheviot* (pp. 131–55), which includes a discussion on Ptolemy's Geography of Scotland. The text and commentary on Tacitus's *Agricola* will be found in *Cornelii Taciti: De Vita Agricolae*, ed. R.M. Ogilvie and I.A. Richmond (Oxford, 1967), with a translation in *Tacitus on Britain and Germany*, transl., H. Mattingly, revised S.A. Handford (Penguin Classics, 1970). C. Fox, *The Personality of Britain: its Influence on Inhabitant and Invader in Prehistoric and Roman Times* (Cardiff, 4th edn, 1943) still exerts a dominant influence on settlement theory with one unfortunate result that virtually everything Scottish is relegated to the status of a peripheral wilderness. Other works on settlement include: *The Effect of Man on the Landscape: The Highland Zone*, ed. J.G. Evans, S. Limbrey and H. Cleere (CBA Research Report No. 11, 1975); O.G.S. Crawford, *The Topography of Roman Scotland North of the Antonine Wall* (Cambridge, 1949); G. Jobey, 'Early Settlement and Topography in the Border Counties', *Scottish Archaeological Forum*, ii (1970), 73–84; *The Iron Age in Northern Britain*, ed. A.L.F. Rivet (Edinburgh,

1966); J.G. Scott, 'The Roman Occupation of South-West Scotland from the recall of Agricola to the withdrawal under Trajan', *Glasgow Archaeological Journal*, iv (1976), 29–44; A.S. Robertson, 'Roman Finds from Non-Roman Sites in Scotland', *Britannia*, i (1970), 198–226; ibid., 'Agricola's Campaigns in Scotland and their Aftermath', *Scottish Archaeological Forum*, vii (1975), 1–12. Roman frontier fortifications are dealt with in: J. Collingwood Bruce, *Handbook to the Roman Wall with the Cumbrian Coast and Outpost Forts*, ed. C.M. Daniel (Newcastle upon Tyne, 1978); D.J. Breeze and B. Dobson, *Hadrian's Wall* (Harmondsworth, 1978); A.S. Robertson, *The Antonine Wall: A Handbook to the Roman Wall between Forth and Clyde and a Guide to its Surviving Remains* (Glasgow, 3rd edn, 1979); J.C. Mann, 'The Frontiers of the Principate' in *Aufstieg und Niedergang der römischen Welt*, ed. H. Temporini, II, i (Berlin and New York, 1974) 508–33; ibid., 'The Northern Frontier after AD 369', *Glasgow Archaeological Journal*, iii (1974), 34–42; and J.P. Gillam, 'The Frontier after Hadrian – a History of the Problem', *Archaeologia Aeliana*, 5th Ser., ii (1974), 1–15. Pottery and coinage are covered by: J.P. Gillam, 'Types of Roman Coarse Pottery Vessels in Northern Britain', *Archaeologia Aeliana*, 4th Ser. XXXV (1957), pp. 180–251; *Current Research in Romano-British Coarse Pottery*, ed. A. Detsicas (CBA Research Report No. 10, 1973); B.R. Hartley, 'The Roman Occupation of Scotland: the evidence of Samian Ware', *Britannia*, iii (1972), 1–55; *Roman Pottery Studies in Britain and Beyond: papers presented to John Gillam, July, 1977* ed. J. Dore and K. Greene; C.H.V. Sutherland, *Coinage and Currency in Roman Britain* (Oxford, 1937); and A.S. Robertson, 'Roman Coins Found in Scotland', *Proc. Soc. Antiq. Scotland*, lxxxiv (1949–50), 137–69.

The Northern Britons
The general background to early Celtic Britain is scarcely an historical subject due to the nature of the evidence that survives. L. Alcock, *Arthur's Britain: History and Archaeology AD 367–634* (London, 1971); N.K. Chadwick, *Celtic Britain* (London, 1963); and J. Morris, *The Age of Arthur* (London, 1973) will all help to introduce the reader to the documentary chaos of sub-Roman Britain. W. Davies, *Wales in the Early Middle Ages* (Leicester, 1982) avoids the Arthurian debate and provides an excellent background for the historical Welsh dimension. N. Chadwick, *The British Heroic Age: the*

Welsh and the Men of the North (Cardiff, 1976) deals in some detail with the northern Britons. For the art history of the Britons, E.T. Leeds, *Celtic Ornament in the British Isles down to AD 700* (Oxford, 1933) is still a classic. K.H. Jackson, *Language and History in Early Britain* (Edinburgh, reprint 1963) is a work of great scholarship not suited to the needs of the novice, but is an essential reference book for anyone studying Celtic Britain. The best place to begin for more specialized study is with K.H. Jackson, 'The Britons in Southern Scotland', *Antiquity*, xxix (1955), 77–88, which adds to an equally useful paper by I. Williams, 'Wales and the North', *Trans. Cumberland and Westmorland Antiq. and Archaeolog. Soc.*, n.s. li (1951), 73–88. D.P. Kirby, 'Strathclyde and Cumbria', *loc. cit.*, lxii (1962), 77–94 is a courageous attempt to survey the genealogical and dynastic problems in the poorly recorded history of the Strathclyde Britons. P.A. Wilson, 'On the Use of the Terms "Strathclyde" and "Cumbria" ', *loc. cit.* lxvi, (1966), 57–92, reviewed Kirby's ideas on the extent and location of Cumbria. K.H. Jackson, *The Gododdin: the Oldest Scottish Poem* (Edinburgh, 1969), provides the definitive text and translation of the Old Welsh poem of Aneirin. Other papers on Gododdin archaeology include A.W. Hogg, 'The Votadini', in *Aspects of Archaeology in Britain and Beyond: Essays Presented to O.G.S. Crawford*, ed. W.F. Grimes (London, 1951), pp. 200–20; A.O. Curle, *Treasure of Traprain* (Glasgow, 1923); R.W. Feachem, 'The Fortifications on Traprain Law', *Proc. Soc. Antiq. Scotland*, lxxxiv (1958), 284–9 (including a detailed map); and E. Burley, 'A Catalogue and Survey of the Metal-Work from Traprain Law', *loc. cit.*, pp. 118–226. K.H. Jackson, 'On the Northern British Section in Nennius' in *Celt and Saxon* ed. K.H. Jackson *et al.*, pp. 20–62; D.N. Dumville, 'On the Northern British Section of the *Historia Brittonum*', *Welsh Historical Review*, viii (1977), 345–54; *ibid.*, 'Sub-Roman Britain: History and Legend', *History*, lxii (1977) pp. 173–92; J. MacQueen, 'Yvain, Ewen, and Owein ap Urien', *Trans. Dumfries. and Galloway Nat. Hist. and Antiq. Soc.*, xxxiii (1955), 107–31; are important studies on fragmentary northern British sources relating to Rheged, Gododdin and Strathclyde. C. Thomas, *The Early Christian Archaeology of North Britain* (London and Glasgow, 1971) is the most comprehensive survey on this difficult subject with a full bibliography. More detailed studies on northern British Christianity and its archaeology include: K.H. Jackson, 'The Sources for the Life of St Kentigern', in *Studies in the Early British Church*, ed. N.K. Chadwick *et al.*, pp. 273–357; A.C.

Thomas, 'The Evidence from North Britain' in *Christianity in Britain, 300–700*, ed. M.W. Barley and R.P.C. Hanson (Leicester, 1968), pp. 93–121; A.S. Henshall, 'A Long Cist Cemetery at Parkburn Sand Pit, Lasswade, Midlothian', *Proc. Soc. Antiq. Scotland*, lxxxix (1958), 252–83; G.A.F. Knight, *Archaeological Light on the Early Christianizing of Scotland* (2 vols, London, 1933); J. MacQueen, *St Nynia: a Study of Literary and Linguistic Evidence* (Edinburgh, 1961); *ibid.*, 'History and Miracle Stories in the Biography of Nynia', *Innes Review*, xiii (1962), 115–29; C.A.R. Radford, 'Excavations at Whithorn (Final Report)', *Trans. Dumfries. and Galloway Nat. Hist. and Antiq. Soc.*, xxxiv (1957), 131–94; C. Thomas, 'An Early Christian Cemetery and Chapel on Ardwall Isle, Kirkcudbright,' *Medieval Archaeology*, xi (1967), 127–88; E.A. Thompson, 'The Origin of Christianity in Scotland', *Scottish Historical Review*, xxxvii (1958), 17–22; P.A. Wilson, 'St Ninian and Candida Casa: Literary Evidence from Ireland', *Trans. Dumfries. and Galloway Nat. Hist. and Antiq. Soc.*, xli (1964), 156–85; and L. Laing, 'The Mote of Mark and the Origins of Celtic Interlace', *Antiquity*, xlix (1975), 98–108. Cf. the reply to this last paper by J. Graham-Campbell and J. Close-Brooks, 'The Mote of Mark and Celtic Interlace', *loc cit*, l (1976), 48–53.

The Picts

Pictish regnal lists and some related texts are edited in M.O. Anderson, *Kings and Kingship*, and an extensive range of sources are edited or translated in A.O. Anderson, *Early Sources of Scottish History*, i, and in Skene's *Chronicles of the Picts*. I. Henderson, *The Picts* (London, 1967) is primarily concerned with Pictish art and provides an excellent discussion on this and includes a splendid collection of photographic plates. The starting point for historical studies on the Picts must be with F.T. Wainwright's *Problem of the Picts* and with that editor's, 'The Picts and the Problem', *op. cit.*, pp. 1–53; S. Piggott, 'The Archaeological Background', *op. cit.*, pp. 54–65; R.W. Feachem, 'Fortifications', *op. cit.*, pp. 66–86; R.B.K. Stevenson, 'Pictish Art', *op. cit.* pp. 97–128; and finally with the masterly paper by K.H. Jackson, 'The Pictish Language', *op. cit.*, pp. 129–66.

Other detailed studies include: D.P. Kirby, '. . . *per universas Pictorum provincias*', in *Famulus Christi: Essays in commemoration of the thirteenth centenary of the Birth of the Venerable Bede*, ed. G. Bonner (London, 1976), pp. 286–324; M. Miller, 'The Disputed Historical

Horizon of the Pictish King Lists', *Scottish Historical Review*, lviii (1979), 7-34; and K. Hughes, *Early Christianity in Pictland* (Jarrow Lecture, 1970). A.A.M. Duncan, 'Bede, Iona, and the Picts', in *The Writing of History in the Middle Ages: Essays Presented to Richard William Southern*, ed. R.H.C. Davis and J.M. Wallace-Hadrill (Oxford, 1981), 1-42, deals not only with aspects of Northumbrian, Scottish and Pictish history, but also offers new and challenging ideas on Ninian's mission to the northern Britons. A. Boyle, 'Matrilineal Succession in the Pictish Monarchy', *Scottish Historical Review*, lvi (1977), 1-10, accepts the matrilinear hypothesis as fact.

Important papers on Pictish archaeology include L. Alcock, '*Populi bestiales Pictorum feroci animo*: A Survey of Pictish Settlement Archaeology', in *Roman Frontier Studies 1979: Papers Presented to the 12th International Congress of Roman Frontier Studies*, ed. W.S. Hanson and L.J.F. Keppie (BAR International Ser., 71, 1980), pp. 61-95. Cf. L. Alcock, 'Forteviot: A Pictish and Scottish Royal Church and Palace', in *The Early Church in Western Britain and Ireland: Studies presented to C.A. Ralegh Radford*, ed. S.M. Pearce (BAR British Ser. 102, 1982), pp. 211-39. M. Cottam and A. Small, 'The Distribution of Settlement in Southern Pictland', *Medieval Archaeology*, xviii (1974), 43-65, provides a geographical analysis of the distribution of symbol stones and *pit* placenames in relation to forts and the better agricultural land. G. Whittington and J.A. Soulsby, 'A Preliminary Report on an Investigation into *Pit* Place-Names', *Scottish Geographical Magazine*, lxxxiv (1968), 117-25, should be read alongside Nicolaisen's *Scottish Place-Names*. I.A. Crawford, and R. Switsur, 'Sandscaping and C14: the Udal, N. Uist', *Antiquity*, li (1977), 124-36, examines the prehistoric and medieval ecology of a coastal site in north-west Pictland. Other important works on Pictish art and archaeology include: I.M. Henderson, 'The Origin Centre of the Pictish Symbol Stones', *Proc. Soc. Antiq. Scotland*, xci (1957-8), 44-60; ibid., 'North Pictland' in *The Dark Ages in the Highlands* (Inverness Field Club, 1971), pp. 37-52; ibid., 'The Meaning of the Pictish Symbol Stones', *op. cit.*, pp. 53-67; A. Jackson, 'Pictish Social Structure and Symbol-Stones', *Scottish Studies*, xv (1971), 121-40; A.C. Thomas, 'The Animal Art of the Scottish Iron Age and its Origins', *Archaeological Journal*, cxviii (1961), 14-64; ibid., 'The Interpretation of the Pictish Symbol Stones', *op. cit.*, cxx (1963), 31-97; A. Small, 'Burghead', *Scottish Archaeological Forum*, i (1969), 31-40; A. Small and M.B. Cottam, *Craig Phadrig: interim report on the 1971 Excavation* (Dundee

University, 1972); R.B.K. Stevenson, 'The Earlier Metalwork of Pictland' in *To Illustrate the Monuments; Essays on Archaeology Presented to Stuart Piggott*, ed. J.V.S. Megaw (London, 1976), pp. 245–51; F.T. Wainwright, *The Souterrains of Southern Pictland*, (London, 1963); and D.M. Wilson, *Reflections on the St Ninian's Isle Treasure* (Jarrow Lecture, 1969). Cf. A.C. O'Dell *et al.*, 'The St Ninian's Isle Silver Hoard', *Antiquity*, xxxiii (1959), 241–268; K. Jackson, 'The St Ninian's Isle Inscription: a Re-appraisal', *Antiquity*, xxxix (1960), 38–42; and A. Small, A.C. Thomas, and D. Wilson, *St Ninian's Isle and its Treasure*, (Aberdeen, 1970).

The Scots of Dál Riata

J. Bannerman, *Studies in the History of Dalriada* (Edinburgh, 1974), conveniently offers a most important collection of papers on early Scottish dynastic history and includes a text, translation, and commentary on the *Senchus Fer nAlban*, as well as a seminal paper on Scottish entries in Irish annals. On this last topic cf. A.P. Smyth, 'The Earliest Irish Annals: their first contemporary entries, and the earliest centres of recording', *Proc. Royal Irish Academy*, lxxii, C(1972), 1–48. Full editions and commentaries on Scottish regnal lists are found in M.O. Anderson, *Kings and Kingship* as well as Scottish material from the Poppleton Manuscript including the *Scottish Chronicle*. This Chronicle was edited by Skene as *The Pictish Chronicle* in his *Chronicles of the Picts* and translated by A.O. Anderson as the *Chronicle of the Kings of Scotland* (Version A.) in his *Early Sources of Scottish History*, i. The commentaries in all these editions need to be studied with care to disentangle the complexity of manuscript and textual problems. Cf. M.O. Anderson, 'The Lists of the Kings [i. Kings of the Scots: ii. Kings of the Picts]', *Scottish Historical Review*, xxviii (1949), 108–18; xxix (1950), 13–22; and E.J. Cowan, 'The Scottish Chronicle in the Poppleton Manuscript', *Innes Review*, xxxii (1981), 3–21. *Adomnán's Life of Columba*, ed. A.O. Anderson and M.O. Anderson (Edinburgh, 1961) offers the finest edition, translation and commentary on one of the most important texts from the early Middle Ages in these islands. *The Life of St Columba founder of Hy written by Adamnan*, ed. W. Reeves (Dublin, 1857) is still a mine of information not only on Columba but on a host of topics relating to early Scotland. Adomnán's work *On the Holy Places* is edited in *Adomnán's De Locis Sanctis*, ed. and transl. D. Meehan (*Scriptores Latini Hiberniae*, iii, Dublin Institute for Advanced Studies, 1958); an earlier translation of this (and of related early medieval works on the Holy Land) will be found in *Palestine Pilgrims' Texts Society*, iii (London, Committee of Palestine Exploration Fund, 1897), transl. J.R. MacPherson, pp. 1–64. Other more detailed studies on the Scots and their church include: D.A. Bullough, 'Columba, Adomnán, and the Achievement of Iona', *Scottish Historical Review* xliii (1964), 111–30; *ibid.*, xliv (1965), 17–33; W. Reeves, 'Saint Maelrubha: His History and Churches', *Proc. Soc. Antiq. Scotland*, iii (1857–60), 258–96; W.D. Simpson, 'Eileach an Naoimh Reconsidered', *Scottish Gaelic Studies*, viii, pt.2 (1958), 117–29. W.D.H. Sellar, 'Family Origins in Cowal and Knapdale' *Scottish Studies*, xv (1971), 21–37, examines the pedigrees of Highland clans in the light of the tenth- and eleventh-century historical background. K. Hughes, *Celtic Britain in the Early Middle Ages*, ed. D. [M.] Dumville (Woodbridge, 1980) contains three papers – on early Scottish writings, on the Book of Deer, and on Christianity in Pictland. While all three are important, I dissent from them in detail.

The Irish background to Dál Riata politics will be found in F.J. Byrne, *Irish Kings and High-Kings* (London, 1973) and in more detail in the same author's 'The Ireland of St Columba', *Historical Studies*, V, (London, 1965). G. Mac Niocaill, *Ireland Before the Vikings* (Dublin, 1972), and D. Ó Corrain, *Ireland Before the Normans* (Dublin, 1972) provide a narrative history of Irish events up to the twelfth century. A.P. Smyth, *Celtic Leinster: Towards an Historical Geography of Early Irish Civilization* (Dublin, 1982) examines the Irish monastic environment including the connection between Durrow and Iona. The relationships between Irish and Scottish metalwork, manuscripts, and sculpture are covered by F. Henry, *Irish Art in the Early Christian Period to 800 AD* (London, revised edn., 1965); *ibid.*, *Irish Art During the Viking Invasions, 800–1020 AD* (London, 1967). *The Book of Kells* is reproduced in full facsimile in *Evangeliorum Quattuor Codex Cenannensis* (Berne, 1950–51): 3 vols: I and II facsimile; III commentary by E.H. Alton, P. Meyer, and G.O. Simms. See also, E. Sullivan, *The Book of Kells* (London, 1914) and F. Henry, *The Book of Kells* (London, 1974).

A full description of remains on Iona will be found in The Royal Commission on the Ancient and Historical Monuments of Scotland, *Argyll: an Inventory of the Monuments*, iv, *Iona* (HMSO, 1982). Cf. R. Reece, 'Recent Work on Iona', *Scottish Archaeological Forum*, v (1973), 36–46. For Dunadd, see J.H. Craw, 'Excavations at Dunadd and at other sites on the Poltalloch Estates, Argyll', *Proc.*

Soc. Antiq. Scotland, lxiv (1930), 111–46; and F.W.L. Thomas, 'Dunadd, Glassary, Argyllshire; the place of inauguration of the Dalriadic kings', *loc. cit.*, xiii (1879), 28–47; The metalwork is studied from a Scottish point of view in R.B.K. Stevenson's papers for the *Heidelberg Kolloquium* (see under *General* above); in the *Problems of the Picts*, pp. 97–128; and in 'The Hunterston Brooch and its Significance', *Medieval Archaeology*, xviii (1974), 16–42. H.E. Kilbride-Jones, 'Scots Zoomorphic Penannular Brooches', *Proc. Soc. Antiq. Scot.* lxx (1935–36), 124–38, established a basic typology for this Scottish series of brooches.

The Northumbrians

A useful introduction to Anglo-Saxon history will be found in J. Campbell, E. John, and P. Wormald, *The Anglo-Saxons* (Oxford; Phaidon, 1982). The complexities of early Northumbrian history are outlined in F.M. Stenton, *Anglo-Saxon England* (Oxford, 2nd edn, 1947) and ecclesiastical matters are dealt with in H. Mayr-Harting, *The Coming of Christianity to Anglo-Saxon England* (London, 1972). K. Harrison, *The Framework of Anglo-Saxon History to 900* (Cambridge, 1976) is central for understanding chronological data. Northumbrian source material which is both extensive and accessible includes *Bede's Ecclesiastical History of the English People*, ed., and transl. B. Colgrave and R.A.B. Mynors (Oxford, 1969); *The Life of Bishop Wilfrid by Eddius Stephanus*, ed. and transl. B. Colgrave (Cambridge, 1927); and *Two Lives of Saint Cuthbert*, ed. and transl. B. Colgrave (New York, reprint, 1969). *The Anglo-Saxon Chronicle* is edited as *Two of the Saxon Chronicles Parallel* ed. C. Plummer and J. Earle. Introd. D. Whitelock (Oxford, 1965, reprint of 1892–9 edn). The best translation is *The Anglo-Saxon Chronicle*, ed. D. Whitelock, with D.C. Douglas and S.I. Tucker (London, 1961). More detailed papers of relevance to Scottish studies include: P. Hunter Blair, 'The Origins of Northumbria', *Archaeologia Aeliana*, 4th Ser., xxv (1947), 1–51; L. Alcock, 'Quantity or Quality: the Anglian Graves of Bernicia', in *Angles, Saxons and Jutes: Essays presented to J.N.L. Myres* ed. V.A. Evison (Oxford, 1981), pp. 168–86; P. Hunter Blair. 'The Bernicians and their Northern Frontier', in *Studies in Early British History*, ed. H.M. Jackson et al., pp. 137–72; D.P. Kirby, 'Bede and Northumbrian Chronology', *English Historical Review*, lxxviii (1963), 514–27; K.H. Jackson, 'Edinburgh and the Anglian occupation of Lothian', in *The Anglo-Saxons: studies in some aspects of their history and culture presented to Bruce Dickins*, ed. P.

Clemoes (London 1959), pp. 35–42; J. Campbell, 'Bede', in *Latin Historians*, ed. T.A. Dorey (London, 1968 reprint), pp. 159–90; D.P. Kirby, 'Bede's native sources for the *Historia Ecclesiastica*', *Bulletin of the John Rylands Library*, 48 (1966), 341–71; *ibid.*, 'Bede, Eddius Stephanus and 'the Life of Wilfrid', *English Historical Review*, xcviii (1983), 101–114; N.K. Chadwick, 'The Conversion of Northumbria: A Comparison of Sources', in *Celt and Saxon*, ed. K. ʊckson *et al.*, pp. 138–66; E. John, 'The Social and Political Problems of the Early English Church', in *Land, Church and People: Essays Presented to Professor H.P.R. Finberg*, ed. J. Thirsk (Reading, 1970), pp. 39–63; K. Cameron, 'Eccles in English Place-Names', in *Christianity in Britain, 300–700*, ed. Barley and Hanson, pp. 87–92.

Early Christian art in Northumbria is a huge subject and the following works provide a mere sample of what is available: G. Baldwin Brown, *The Arts in Early England* (6 vols., London, 1903–37); W.G. Collingwood, *Northumbrian Crosses in the Pre-Norman Age* (London, 1927); T.D. Kendrick, *Anglo-Saxon Art to AD 900* (London, 1938); R.A. Smith, [*British Museum*] *Guide to Anglo-Saxon Antiquities* (London, 1923); C.R. Peers, 'The Inscribed and Sculptured Stones of Lindisfarne', *Archaeologia*, lxxiv (1925), 255–70; F. Saxl, 'The Ruthwell Cross', *Journal of the Warburg and Courtauld Institutes*, vi (1943), 1–19; E. Mercer, 'The Ruthwell and Bewcastle Crosses', *Antiquity*, xxxviii (1964), 268–76; R. Cramp, *Early Northumbrian Sculpture*, (Jarrow Lecture, 1965); A.W. Clapham, 'Notes on the Origins of Hiberno-Saxon Art', *Antiquity*, viii (1934), 43–57; R.J. Cramp, *The Monastic Arts of Northumbria* (Arts Council Pamphlet, 1967). The Book of Lindisfarne is reproduced in facsimile in *Evangeliorum Quattuor Codex Lindisfarnensis* (Olten, Lausanne, Fribourg, 2 vols, 1956, 1960); I facsimile, II commentary by T.D. Kendrick, T.J. Brown, R.S.L. Bruce-Mitford, H. Rosen-Runge, A.S.C. Ross, E.G. Stanley and A.E.A. Werner. Cf. C.F. Burkitt, 'Kells, Durrow and Lindisfarne', *Antiquity*, ix (1935), 33–7; F. Henry, 'The Lindisfarne Gospels', *loc. cit.*, xxxvii (1963), 100–10.

The Vikings and after

Good general surveys of the period include P.H. Sawyer, *Kings and Vikings: Scandinavia and Europe AD 700–1100* (London, 1982); H.R. Loyn, *The Vikings in Britain* (London, 1977); and G. Jones, *A History of the Vikings* (Oxford, 1968). Archaeological material is covered by

P. Foote and D.M. Wilson, *The Viking Achievement* (London, 1970); J. Graham-Campbell, *Viking Artefacts: a Select Catalogue* (London, 1980); and *Viking Antiquities in Great Britain and Ireland* I-VI ed. H. Shetelig (Oslo, 1940–54) – Scotland is covered in vol. III (1940) by S. Grieg. Viking Scotland is dealt with in some detail in A.P. Smyth, *Scandinavian Kings in the British Isles 850–880* (Oxford, 1977) while tenth-century Scottish affairs are covered by the same author in *Scandinavian York and Dublin: the History and Archaeology of Two Related Viking Kingdoms* (2 vols, Dublin and New Jersey, 1975 and 1979). Other useful works are: G. Henderson, *The Norse Influence on Celtic Scotland* (Glasgow, 1910) and A.W. Brøgger, *Ancient Emigrants: A History of the Norse Settlements of Scotland* (Oxford, 1929). W.D.H. Sellar, 'The Origins and ancestry of Somerled', *Scottish Historical Review*, xlv (1966), 123–42 is an important study of the genealogy of a Scottish-Norse dynasty of the Hebrides. *The Northern Isles*, ed. F.T. Wainwright (London, 1962) deals in some depth with Viking Orkney and Shetland.

Norse sources on Viking Scotland include *Orkneyinga Saga*, ed. F. Gudmundsson (*Íslenzk fornrit*, xxxiv, Reykjavík, 1965). An excellent translation is found in H. Pálsson and P. Edwards, *Orkneyinga Saga: the History of the Earls of Orkney* (London, 1978). Much of our knowledge of Viking Scotland derives from Snorri's *Heimskringla* (or *Sagas of the Kings of Norway*) which is edited as *Snorri Sturluson: Heimskringla*, ed. B. Adalbjarnarson, (*Íslenzk fornrit*, xxvi-xxviii, 3 vols, Reykjavík, 1941–51), and is translated by S. Laing, *Snorri Sturluson, Heimskringla*, Pt. 1, *The Olaf Sagas* (in 2 vols.) revised J. Simpson (Everyman, London, 1964); Pt. 2, *Sagas of the Norse Kings*, revised P. Foote (Everyman, London, 1961). *The Book of the Icelanders* and the Icelandic *Book of Settlements* are edited in *Íslendingabók: Landnámabók* ed. J. Benediktsson (*Íslenzk fornrit* I, 2 vols, Reykjavík, 1968), with a translation by H. Pálsson and P. Edwards, *The Book of Settlements: Landnámabók* (University of Manitoba, 1972). A vast storehouse of information in texts, translations and notes on Old Norse poets, from the Viking Age to the thirteenth century (with much relevance for medieval Scotland), will be found in *Corpus Poeticum Boreale*, ed. G. Vigfusson and F. York Powell (2 vols., New York, 1965, reprint of 1883 edn). Other Icelandic sagas which contain material of Scottish interest are: *Egils Saga*, transl., C. Fell and J. Lucas (London, 1975): *Laxdoela Saga*, transl. M. Press, introd. P. Foote (Everyman, London, reprint 1965); *Eyrbyggja Saga*, transl. H. Pálsson and P. Edwards (Toronto,

1973); *Njals Saga*, transl. M. Magnusson and H. Pálsson (Harmondsworth, reprint 1974); *Hakonar Saga* ed. G. Vigfusson in *Icelandic Sagas*, ii (London, Rolls Series, 1887), transl. by G.W. Dasent, *The Saga of Hacon and a Fragment of the Saga of Magnus*, in *Icelandic Sagas*, iv (London, Rolls Series, 1894); and *The Vinland Sagas: Graenlendinga Saga and Eirik's Saga*, transl. M. Magnusson and H. Pálsson (Penguin Classics, Harmondsworth, 1965). Not all translations include the original genealogical details of the sagas. The twelfth-century Danish historian, Saxo Grammaticus, offers interesting traditions on the Viking invasions of Scotland in *Book Nine* of his *Gesta* which is edited in *Saxonis Gesta Danorum*, ed. J. Olrik and H. Raeder (Copenhagen, 1931), i; and translated by O. Elton (introd. F. York Powell), *The First Nine Books of the Danish History of Saxo Grammaticus* (London, 1894). The remaining books of Saxo's *Gesta* have been translated by E. Christiansen, *Saxo Grammaticus. . . . Books x-xvi . . . with translation and commentary* (BAR Reports, International Ser. 84, 1980). More detailed studies mainly from an archaeological point of view include: L. Alcock, 'The supposed Viking Burials on the Islands of Canna and Sanday', in *From the Stone Age to the Forty Five: Studies presented to R.B.K. Stevenson*, ed. A. O'Connor and D.V. Clarke, (Edinburgh, 1983); L. Alcock and E. Alcock, 'Scandinavian Settlement in the Inner Hebrides: Research on Place-Names and in the Field', in *Settlement in Scotland 1000 BC - AD 1000*, ed. L.M. Thomas (Scottish Archaeological Forum, x, Edinburgh, 1980), pp. 61-73; I.A. Crawford, *Scot (?), Norseman and Gael* (Scottish Archaeological Forum,vi, 1974), pp. 1-16; S. Cruden, 'Excavations at Birsay, Orkney' in *The Fourth Viking Congress, York, 1961*, ed. A. Small (Edinburgh, 1965); J. Graham-Campbell, 'A Fragmentary Bronze Strap-end of the Viking Period from the Udal, North Uist, Inverness-shire', *Medieval Archaeology*, xvii (1973), 128-31; *ibid.*, Bossed Penannular Brooches: a review of recent research', *loc. cit.* xix (1975), 33-47; *ibid*, 'Two Scandinavian Brooch-fragments of Viking Age date from the Outer Hebrides', *Proc. Soc. Antiq. Scotland* cvi (1975-76), 212-14; J.R.C. Hamilton, *Jarlshof, Shetland* (Edinburgh, 1953). J. Lang, 'Hogback Monuments in Scotland', *Proc. Soc. Antiq. Scotland*, cv (1972-4), 206-35, is the first comprehensive study of Norse hogback gravestones in Scotland. A. Maclaren, 'A Norse house on Drinmore machair, South Uist', *Glasgow Archaeol. Journal*, iii (1974) 9-18; C.D. Morris, 'Birsay, Excavation and Survey' in *University of Durham Archaeological Report for 1977*, ed. A.F. Harding (Durham, 1978), pp. 22–25; ibid, 'The Vikings and Irish Monasteries', *Durham University Journal*, lxxi (1979), 175–85; C.A.R. Radford, *The Early Christian and Norse Settlements, Birsay* (HMSO Guide, Edinburgh, 1959); L. Scott, 'The Norse in the Hebrides', in *The Viking Congress, Lerwick, July, 1950*, ed. W.D. Simpson (Edinburgh, 1954); D.M. Wilson, *Scandinavian Settlement in the North and West of the British Isles: an Archaeological point of view* (*Trans. Roy. Historical Soc.*, 5th Ser. xxvi (1976), pp. 95–113; A. Ritchie, 'Picts and Norsemen in Northern Scotland', (*Scottish Archaeological Forum*, vi, 1974), pp. 23–36; *ibid.*, 'Excavation of Pictish and Viking Age Farmsteads at Buckquoy, Orkney', *Proc. Soc. Antiquar. Scot.*, cviii (1976-7), 174–227; For bibliography on Scottish relations with Northumbria and Wessex in the Viking period, see Smyth, *Scandinavian York and Dublin*. The Scottish conquest of Lothian is dealt with in G.W.S. Barrow, *The Kingdom of the Scots* (London, 1973); M.O. Anderson, 'Lothian and the Early Scottish Kings', *Scottish Historical Review*, xxxix (1960), 98–112; A.A.M. Duncan, 'The Battle of Carham, 1018', *loc. cit*, lv (1976), 20–8; B. Meehan, 'The Siege of Durham, the Battle of Carham and the Cession of Lothian', *loc. cit.*, lv (1976), 1–19. For later Cumbria see F.M. Stenton, 'Pre-Conquest Westmorland' in *Preparatory to Anglo-Saxon England*, ed. D.M. Stenton, (Oxford, 1970), pp 214–23; G.W.S. Barrow, 'The Pattern of Lordship and Feudal Settlement in Cumbria', *Journal of Medieval History*, i (1975), 117–38; and the papers by D.P. Kirby and P.A. Wilson under *The Northern Britons* above.

The following societies or their periodicals offer a regular forum for information, bibliography, and discussion on early Scottish archaeology and history: The Council for British Archaeology (CBA) issued the *Archaeological Bulletin for the British Isles, 1940–1946* from 1949, the title changing from 1954 onwards to *Archaeological Bibliography for Great Britain and Ireland*. Other CBA publications include annual *Reports*, and *Discovery and Excavation in Scotland*. Periodicals and occasional papers which cover early Scotland directly or indirectly include: *Antiquity, Archaeologia, Archaeologia Aeliana, The Archaeological Journal, Britannia, Bulletin of the Board of Celtic Studies, Glasgow Archaeological Journal, Innes Review, Inverness Field Club, Journal of Roman Studies, Medieval Archaeology, Northern Scotland, Orkney Miscellany, Proceedings of the International Congresses of Roman Frontier Studies, Proceedings of the Society of Antiquaries of Scotland, Saga-Book of the Viking Society for Northern Research, Scottish Archaeological*

Forum, Scottish Gaelic Studies, Scottish Historical Review, Scottish Studies, Transactions of the Cumberland and Westmorland Antiquarian and Archaeological Society, Transactions of the Dumfriesshire and Galloway Natural History and Antiquarian Soceity, University of Durham Archaeological Reports.

Appendix: Chronology

First century:

43	Emperor Claudius invades Britain;
c. 74	Rebellion of Brigantes led by Venutius;
81	Agricola invades Caledonia;
83	Agricola defeats Caledonians at *Mons Graupius;*
c. 85	Legionary fortress at Inchtuthil abandoned;
90	Evacuation of all Roman positions north of Forth.

Second century:

c. 108	Rebellion in northern Britain: Roman positions north of Tyne-Solway line in ruins;
122–136	Building of Hadrian's Wall on Tyne-Solway line;
c. 143	Building of wall by Antoninus Pius across Forth-Clyde isthmus;
c. 150	Ptolemy's *Geography* compiled in Greek;
c. 150–154	Revolt of Brigantes;
c. 154	Antonine Wall abandoned;
c. 160–200	Second occupation of Antonine frontier;
c. 180–185	Hadrian's Wall overrun by barbarian army.

Third century:

c. 197–211	Severan recovery of Britain: Caledonians and Maeatae actively hostile towards Roman province;
c. 200	Recovery of townships serving forts along Hadrian's Wall;
c. 208	Septimius Severus invades Caledonia;
210	Roman slaughter of the Maeatae;
211	Death of Severus. Withdrawal of Roman frontier to Hadrianic line;
c. 215	Legionary fortress at Carpow abandoned;
297	First mention of Picts by Eumenius.

Fourth century:

306	Constantine proclaimed emperor at York. Frontier consolidated on Hadrianic line;

310	Mention of 'Caledonians and other Picts';
337	Death of Constantine;
367	'Barbarian Conspiracy': Picts and Scots overrun frontier;
368	Ammianus Marcellinus confirms that Picts are divided into two peoples – *Dicalydones* and *Verturiones*;
c. 370	Military recovery completed in northern Britain under Theodosius;
c. 387	Withdrawal of Roman garrisons from Pennines.

Fifth century:

c. 400	Treasure of Roman silver deposited at Traprain Law;
c. 400–550	Germanic mercenaries and settlers gradually organized into later Northumbrian kingdoms of Deira and Bernicia;
c. 407	Withdrawal of Roman army from Britain;
409	Zosimus reports Britons to have expelled Roman officials and to have organized their own defences;
c. 450	Alleged migration of Cuneda and his sons from Manaw to north Wales;
c. 450–500	Earliest Christian cemeteries at Whithorn and Kirkmadrine;
c. 460	Coroticus (Ceretic) of Strathclyde recipient of letter from St Patrick.

Sixth century:

c. 500	*Floruit* of St Ninian; death of Fergus Mór mac Eirc, ancestor of kings of Scots Dál Riata;
c. 500–550	Earliest long-cist Christian cemeteries of Lothian, Fife, and Angus;
c. 525–550	Angles establish coastal territory of Bernicia centred on Bamburgh;
561	Battle of Cúl Drebene in Ireland. Columba in some way implicated;
563	Arrival of Columba in Scotland;
563–583	Exploration in North Atlantic by Cormac Ua Liatháin and Brendan of Clonfert from base in Western Isles;
570	Death of Gildas, British historian;

c. 570	*Floruit* of Riderch Hen, king of the Strathclyde Britons;
c. 570–590	Urien rules kingdom of Rheged;
c. 570–600	*Floruit* of Kentigern;
574	Columba ordains Áedhán mac Gabhráin king of Scots Dál Riata;
575	Convention of Druim Ceat;
c. 575	Beginnings of contemporary annals on Iona;
c. 585	Death of Bridei mac Mailchon, king of Picts;
c. 585–589	Columba founds Durrow;
c. 590	Urien of Rheged slain at Lindisfarne;
593–617	Ethelfrith king of Northumbria;
597	Death of Columba.

Seventh century:

c. 600	Northern Britons led by Gododdin slaughtered at Catterick;
603	Áedán mac Gabhráin defeated by Ethelfrith at *Degsastan*;
c. 608	Death of Áedhán mac Gabhráin;
617	Martyrdom of Donnán on Eigg;
617–633	Edwin king of Northumbria. Eanfrith, Oswald, and Oswiu in exile among Scots and Picts.
c. 625	Alleged foundation of Abernethy by Kildare nuns;
c. 627	Roman mission of Paulinus to Northumbrian Angles;
629–642	Domnall Brecc king of Scots;
634–641	Oswald king of Northumbria;
634–651	Bishop Aidan rules Northumbrian Church;
637	Battle of Mag Rath. Scottish Dál Riata loses control of Irish homeland;
638	Northumbrian assault on Edinburgh;
642	Domnall Brecc slain by Strathclyde Britons in battle of Strathcarron;
641–670	Reign of Oswiu in Bernicia and (from 655) over all Northumbria;
c. 651	Cuthbert enters Melrose;
651–660	Bishop Finán rules Northumbrian Church;
653–657	Talorgen son of Eanfrith king of Picts;
660–664	Bishop Colmán rules Northumbrian Church;

660–680	Anglian conquest of Rheged;
664	Synod of Whitby;
669	Death of Abbot Cummêne of Iona;
670	Death of Oswiu of Northumbria;
670–685	Ecgfrith king of Northumbria;
672	Picts depose Drest from kingship. Pictish army massacred by Ecgfrith;
672–693	Bridei son of Bili king of Picts;
673	Maelrubai founds Applecross;
679	Adomnán ninth abbot of Iona;
679–686	Adomnán writes his work on *The Holy Places*;
c. 681	Northumbrians establish Anglian bishopric at Abercorn;
682–709	British warbands active in northern and eastern Ireland;
685	Picts under Bridei mac Bili defeat and slay Ecgfrith of Northumbria in battle of Dunnichen Moss;
685–705	Aldfrith king of Northumbria;
686	Adomnán's first visit to court of Aldfrith;
687	Death of Cuthbert;
688	Adomnán's second visit to court of Aldfrith;
688–692	Adomnán writing *Life of Columba*;
c. 695–704	Adomnán tries to persuade Picts to adopt Roman usage;
697	Adomnán promulgates his *Law of Innocents*.

Eighth century:

c. 700	Bewcastle Cross erected near Anglian frontier with Britons of south-west Scotland;
c. 700–750	Recovery of Christian mission on Eigg;
704	Death of Adomnán;
c. 706–724	Nechtan son of Derile king of Picts;
711	Picts slaughtered by Northumbrians in plain of Manaw;
c. 712	Egbert arrives at Iona and persuades Columban clergy to accept Roman usage;
717	Nechtan expels Columban clergy;
722	Death of Maelrubai of Applecross;
c. 725	Irish monks (as reported later by Dicuil) now visiting the Faroes from Northern Isles of Scotland;

729–761	Óengus I, son of Fergus, king of Picts;
c. 731	Pehthelm appointed to see of Whithorn;
735	Death of Bede;
747	Death of Cú-Chuimne the Wise of Iona;
750	Conquest of Kyle by Eadberht of Northumbria;
750–752	Teudubr son of Bili, king of Strathclyde Britons, overlord of Picts;
756	Death of Bealdhere (Baldred) of Tyninghame;
c. 780–806	*Book of Kells* begun on Iona;
793	First Viking raid on Lindisfarne;
794	First Viking raid on Scottish Isles;
795	Viking devastation on Isle of Skye and on Iona;
c. 795	Irish monks (as later reported by Dicuil) visiting Iceland from February to August.

Ninth century:

802	Vikings return to burn Iona;
803	Last mention of Northumbrian bishop of Whithorn;
806	Vikings attack Iona for third time and butcher 68 of the *familia*;
807–814	Abbot Cellach of Iona builds new church for his community at Kells;
c. 811–820	Constantine, son of Fergus, king of Dál Riata and of Picts. Major new ecclesiastical foundation at Dunkeld;
820–834	Óengus II, son of Fergus, king of Dál Riata and of Picts. Major new ecclesiastical foundation at St Andrews;
825	Torture and martyrdom of Blathmac on Iona;
839	Major Viking victory over Picts;
c. 840	Kenneth mac Alpin king of Dál Riata;
c. 847	Kenneth mac Alpin king of Scots and Picts;
849	Division of relics of Saint Columba between Kells and church of Kenneth mac Alpin (? at Dunkeld);
c. 850	Danes attack Norwegian colonists in the Isles;
c. 850–857	*Floruit* of Ketil Flatnose in the Hebrides;
853–871	Olaf the White, Norwegian king of Dublin;
858–862	Donald I king of Scots: laws of Dál Riata promulgated at Forteviot;

865	Death of Tuathal, archbishop of Fortriu and abbot of Dunkeld;
866–867	Danish conquest of Northumbria;
866–869	Olaf the White campaigns against Picts;
870–871	Olaf the White and Ivar sack Dumbarton;
870–890	Migration of Hebridean and Caithness Norsemen to Iceland;
874–875	Hálfdan attacks Picts and Strathclyde Britons;
889	Expulsion of Giric, king of Scots, and of Eochaid son of Rhun, king of Strathyclyde Britons;
c. 895	*Floruit* of Turf Einarr, first historical Viking earl of Orkney.

Tenth century:

900	Scots annexe Strathclyde: migration of Strathclyde aristocracy to North Wales;
900–943	Constantine II king of Scots;
903	Grandsons of Ivar plunder Dunkeld 'and all Scotland';
904	Ivar grandson of Ivar slain by Scots in Strathearn;
906	Constantine II and Bishop Cellach of St Andrews enter into agreement at Scone;
914	First battle of Corbridge: Ragnall victorious over Scots and Bernicians;
918	Second battle of Corbridge between Ragnall and Constantine II;
920	Constantine II of Scotland enters into treaty with Edward the Elder;
927	Treaty at Penrith between Athelstan and Scottish rulers;
934	Athelstan invades Scotland;
937	Battle of Brunanburh: Constantine II of Scotland, Olaf Gothfrithsson and Owen of Strathclyde, defeated by Athelstan;
939	Death of Athelstan;
941	Olaf Gothfrithsson sacks St Bealdhere's at Tyninghame in (Bernician) Lothian.
943–952	Constantine II in retirement at St Andrews;
943–954	Malcolm I king of Scots;
945	Edmund invades Cumbria and grants it to Malcolm king of Scots;

948	Malcolm I of Scotland plunders 'the English as far as the Tees';
954	Slaying of Eirík Bloodaxe on Stainmore: Wessex kings rule to Scottish border;
954–962	Indulf king of Scots: Edinburgh occupied and Scots annexe Lothian;
966	Death of Fingin, bishop of Iona;
966–1005	Successful attempt by descendants of Constantine I to exclude descendants of his brother Áed from the kingship;
971	Kenneth II plunders England as far as Stainmore;
973	Kenneth II enters into treaty with Edgar at Chester;
980	Olaf Cuaran resigns Dublin kingship and becomes monk at Iona;
c. 985	Sons of Njál join in Norse raid on Hebrides (as described in *Njáls Saga*);
986	Danish marauders attack Hebrides;
989	Gothfrith Haroldsson, king of Hebrides, slain by men of Dál Riata;
c. 995	Leif Eriksson (later explorer of North America) visiting in Hebrides.

Eleventh century:

1005	Malcolm II king of Scots;
1006	Unsuccessful raid by Malcolm II on Durham;
1014	Earl Sigurd the Stout of Orkney defeated and slain at Clontarf. Decline of Viking paganism in Northern Isles;
1018	Battle of Carham: Malcolm II victorious over English of Bernicia.

Index